FAITH OF OUR FOREMOTHERS

FAITH OF OUR FOREMOTHERS

Women Changing Religious Education

*Carol —
In celebration of mothers
and daughters! Blessings,
Barbara Anne*

Edited by

Barbara Anne Keely

Westminster John Knox Press
Louisville, Kentucky

Book and cover design by Jennifer K. Cox

First Edition
Published by Westminster John Knox Press
Louisville, Kentucky

This book is printed on acid-free paper that meets the
American National Standards Institute Z39.48 standard. ∞

PRINTED IN THE UNITED STATES OF AMERICA
97 98 99 00 01 02 03 04 05 06 — 10 9 8 7 6 5 4 3 2 1

Library of Congress Cataloging-in-Publication Data

Faith of our foremothers : women changing religious education /
Barbara Anne Keely, editor. — 1st ed.
p.   cm.
Includes bibliographical references.
ISBN 0-664-25721-6
1. Women Christian educators—United States—Biography.
I. Keely, Barbara Anne, date.
BV1470.2.F35   1997
268'.082—dc21   97-17077

To my mother, Sara Elizabeth Rowlands Keely,
and her namesake, my niece Sara Elizabeth Hanson

CONTENTS

ACKNOWLEDGMENTS

This is a book about foremothers. Each author wishes to acknowledge some of the women who have shaped her life:

Sherry H. Blumberg's life and faith have been influenced by Phyllis Mintzer, who encouraged her to explore the limits of Jewish education; Helen Meret, a wise congregant who taught her politics and to be a mensch; and Gloria Durka, Maria Harris, and Mary Elizabeth Moore—first through their writings and then later in person.

Elizabeth Francis Caldwell gives thanks for the presence in her life of faithful women who loved and nurtured her: grandmothers, Fannie Glenn Francis and Gladys Pitts Caldwell; aunts, Maureen Harp Pitts and Jane Milner Caldwell; sister, Cathy Lynn Caldwell Hoop; and most especially her mother, Mabel Elizabeth Francis Caldwell.

Judith A. Dorney is grateful for her foremothers, especially her teachers, Maria Harris and Carol Gilligan, and her mother, Elizabeth Sheehan Anderson.

M. Susan Harlow thanks the foremothers in her life, especially her mother, Margaret Anna Thompson Harlow, and her mentor, the later Dr. Jane Cary Peck, professor of social ethics at Andover Newton Theological School.

Carol Lakey Hess thanks Freda Gardner, not only for being mentor but also for providing the subject matter for one of the most enjoyable and personally meaningful articles she has ever researched.

Laura Brooking Lewis thanks the foremothers in her life, especially her mother, Gladys Trull Brooking, and her teacher and *doctormutter,* Sara Little.

Estelle Rountree McCarthy honors her fifth grade teacher, Faye Kirtland, for opening up possibilities and helping her find voice.

ACKNOWLEDGMENTS

Joyce Ann Mercer thanks her foremothers, fourth grade teacher Barbara Powell, Dr. Letty Russell, and the Reverend Elizabeth Downing Heller.

Mary Elizabeth Mullino Moore is thankful to her mother, Elizabeth Heaton Mullino; maternal grandmother, Inez Baker Heaton; maternal great-grandmother, Virginia Adelaid Phillips; paternal grandmother, Ola Olge Mullino; paternal step-grandmother, Angie Mullino; and mothers-in-law, Emily Johnson Mathews and Blanche Crider Moore.

Yolanda Y. Smith thanks Willie E. Jones Smith, paternal grandmother; Angilee Streeter Hearns, maternal grandmother; Vera G. Hearns Smith, mother; Angela G. Smith, sister; and Valencia M. Ward, sister, for touching her life and for giving her the inspiration to be all that God has called her to be.

Linda J. Vogel remembers with gratitude her foremothers and mentors: Gladys Baker Hutson, her mother and friend, who faces life and death with faith and hope; Ellen Oliver, who modeled what it means to be professor, wife, and mother in the 1960s and beyond; and Nelle Slater, who treated her as a colleague and friend from the beginning and continues to care and share.

This book took shape as colleagues responded to the opportunity to tell the stories of foremothers in religious education. These same women, through their encouragement and suggestions, were mentors to me as the project editor. My special thanks to Elizabeth Francis Caldwell, Carol Lakey Hess, and William Myers, who encouraged this project from its inception. Lib Caldwell also made several constructive suggestions throughout the process, for which I am grateful.

I have been blessed to be surrounded by people who encourage, challenge, and help me to see in new ways. Teachers Jody Deering Nyquist, Mae Arnold Bell, Freda Gardner, Maria Harris, and Estelle Rountree McCarthy model and mentor my calling to the educational ministry of the church. Letty M. Russell gives me ideas and words by which to shape my ministry, and Elizabeth Downing Heller gives it shape by living a life worthy of the calling. My colleagues and students at United Theological Seminary of the Twin Cities encourage my teaching and learning. Westminster John Knox Press managing editor Stephanie Egnotovich is a partner in this project with whom I enjoy working; the book is better because of her attention. Special thanks to Robert Pierson, O.S.B., who is a good friend.

Barbara Anne Keely

CONTRIBUTORS

Sherry H. Blumberg is associate professor of Jewish education on the Rabbinic Faculty of Hebrew Union College-Jewish Institute of Religion in New York City.

Elizabeth Francis Caldwell is the Harold Blake Walker Professor of Pastoral Theology at McCormick Theological Seminary in Chicago.

Judith A. Dorney is an assistant professor in the Department of Educational Studies at the State University of New York at New Paltz.

M. Susan Harlow is assistant professor of religious education and director of the Sophia Lyon Fahs Center for Religious Education at Meadville/Lombard Theological School, Chicago, Illinois.

Carol Lakey Hess is assistant professor of Christian education at Princeton Theological Seminary, New Jersey.

Barbara Anne Keely is associate professor of Christian education and director of continuing education at United Theological Seminary of the Twin Cities, Minnesota.

Laura Brooking Lewis is associate professor of Christian education at Austin Presbyterian Theological Seminary, Texas.

Estelle Rountree McCarthy is professor emerita at the Presbyterian School of Christian Education in Richmond, Virginia.

Joyce Ann Mercer is a Ph.D. candidate at Emory University, Atlanta, Georgia.

Mary Elizabeth Mullino Moore is professor of theology and Christian education at Claremont School of Theology in California.

Yolanda Y. Smith is a Ph.D. candidate at Claremont School of Theology in California.

Linda J. Vogel is professor of Christian education at Garrett-Evangelical Theological Seminary in Evanston, Illinois.

INTRODUCTION:
FOREMOTHERS AND MENTORS

Barbara Anne Keely

As part of the process toward ordination to ministry, I completed a form identifying my gifts in ministry. I highlighted Christian education as one of my strengths. A member of the committee looked at me and said, "Christian education. Well, that's a typical thing for a woman to want to do." Then and there I realized the challenge I faced not to box myself into "typical women's work" in the church. There was a tension in this decision, because I also understood clearly that my calling is rooted in the educational ministry of the church.

As my concern with feminist approaches to theology and hermeneutics has grown, I have perceived that my passion, Christian education, has not gained a recognized voice in feminist circles. I worry that the attitude has been "Why bother to develop feminist approaches to education in the church? After all, it's been the place women always have been 'expected' to work." I am struck by the number of conferences I attend where women want to discuss feminist approaches and women's voices in every aspect of ministry except education. Is it too painful to invest energy in reshaping that which has already been labeled "women's work"? Where is the liberation?

My years in congregational ministry and teaching in theological schools have convinced me that this process we call "education" has to be integral to feminist work in the church. How people teach and learn, what is taught, who is encouraged to be a learner—all are explicit in the educational ministry of the church. All are central to feminist approaches to religious education.

Fortunately, feminist voices are growing stronger in the field of religious education; committed women and men are ensuring that annual gatherings of professors of religious education engage in feminist conversations.[1] But unless we are to be without a history, we must go back and claim the voices of those women who led the way, who spoke and taught and reimagined the educational ministry of the church before the idea of a feminist approach even had been named.[2] It is the purpose of this book to name a few of our foremothers, lift their voices, and describe their legacies to the field

1

INTRODUCTION

of religious education that weave part of the fabric that we, the feminist educators of younger generations, claim as ours.

Women have been such a part of religious education that it long has been considered a "women's profession."[3] Historically this was not always the case, but as religion became more privatized in the twentieth century, the religious education of children became the work of the home, that is, the responsibility of women.[4] Because the work of women has traditionally been valued less highly than men's work, religious education has been viewed as less important than those disciplines that were considered to belong in the realm of men.

Moreover, the work of women in religious education has been poorly documented, partly because of the perception of it as "women's work" and partly because religious education developed as a discipline only during the twentieth century.[5] The founding of the Religious Education Association (REA) in 1903 named the emerging field, and its development has continued through the century. More recently, its identity was marked by the founding of the Association of Professors and Researchers in Religious Education (APRRE) in 1970.

Although there were few women in the leadership of REA during its formative years, several women have served in a variety of leadership roles in both REA and APRRE in the last few decades. One of these shaping leaders was Sara Little, the only woman to lead APRRE's predecessor, the National Conference on Christian Education of the National Council of Churches.[6] In 1989 the women's luncheon at the APPRE annual meeting honored Sara Little at her retirement. Yet her story and influence, as well as those of countless other women, will be lost unless their journeys and legacies are documented.

Women's ways of doing religious education permeate our discipline. The purpose of this book is to gather some of the stories, accounts of the scholarship, the mentoring, and the shaping of our discipline by some of the more influential female religious educators of this century. From this history, we are able to identify some of the influences these women have had on the field of religious education, as well as on women currently shaping religious education within feminist frameworks.

This book is primarily a history of women educators. But it is also important to explore the background and development of feminist approaches to religious education, so that the rich history and process of its development will not be lost. The women whose stories and scholarship are discussed in this volume have been both scholars and teachers of other professional educators. They are, however, but exemplars of the women who have led the way; there are many more. This book does not tell the stories of the thousands of women who have served as directors of Christian education or religious education. Instead, we have focused on those women who helped shape the discipline of religious education.

Perhaps the most important legacy of these women, at least as I have experienced it in the shaping of this book and in the story told about each foremother, is the responsibility to mentor. Pamela Holliman, describes mentoring as providing "a relationship in which a woman can experience support, affirmation, and challenge about her uniqueness and gifts. Mentoring is a relational space in which a woman can critically examine her assumptions and those of the culture, and evaluate her choices, opportunities, and realistic limits."[7] These foremothers have understood education as mentoring, a gift offered from one more experienced to one eager to grow. Where eagerness was not at the surface, they have searched, empowered, equipped, and (perhaps most powerfully) named what the benefit to the learner might be to accept the gift offered—not just for oneself but for God's world.

This text honors my experiences of mentoring. Some of the women in this book have shaped my work, from teaching my first graduate course in Christian adult education, to encouraging my journey of doctoral work, to being the topic of my dissertation. Others have been known to me best through their writings, and now through the following chapters. Iris Cully stands out as a woman I never had the privilege of working with, but years into retirement she still faithfully participates in our professional meetings as role model and mentor of those of us who look to her as foremother. I am struck by the blessings that these women have been in my life and the lives of so many others.

This book emerged out of several conversations with women religious educators of my generation. As we talked about our work and about those who have influenced us, the names of certain women educators kept emerging. In 1983 the book *Modern Masters of Religious Education* described the work of "twelve persons who have decisively influenced the texture and direction of religious education in the second half of the twentieth century."[8] All twelve were men. Lost were Rachel Henderlite, Nelle Morton, Iris Cully, Sara Little—all the women. This volume is a tribute to these women who, like many others, have been unnamed in the teaching of the development of religious education.[9]

Although these women are described as foremothers to currently developing feminist approaches to religious education, it is not accurate to assume all would describe themselves as feminist. I invite you to read the story of each woman and hear how she has made current feminist work richer.

The most difficult part of editing this book was deciding whom to include; a more comprehensive volume could have included almost two dozen women religious educators. In the end, however, the primary criteria were historical influence as well as current activity. The women chosen represent different times in the world of religious education, different historical and social contexts of teaching, different interests in scholarship, different approaches to the discipline, and different denominations.

Recent developments in religious education have incorporated ecumenical approaches. Both the Religious Education Association and the

Association of Professors and Researchers in Religious Education are ecumenical and interfaith in membership. My choice of women religious educators also is ecumenical, although predominantly Christian. The chapter on the foremother included for her leadership in ecumenical religious education, Norma Thompson, is written by Sherry Blumberg, a leader in Jewish religious education. Drawing on Thompson's work, women now are actively working to cross interfaith lines and are leading us into more ecumenical ways of framing feminist approaches to religious education.[10] This book is, however, limited to American women; there are others who extend the discipline beyond the United States.[11]

The stories of these twelve foremothers are told with the hope that we can learn from their legacies and identify some of the threads that are being drawn upon as the next generation of religious educators weaves feminist work into a new century.

The Fabric of Feminist Approaches to Religious Education

There is no single definition of feminism, and the purpose of this volume is not to give a monolithic view of feminist approaches to religious education. My basic definition of *feminist* includes a commitment to the equality of women and men and an understanding of all creation as sacred. I identify in this book eight threads that, woven together, are an example of the fabric of feminist work. They are not threads unique to the work of women; but I believe all (or at least most) must be evident for religious education to be "feminist" in its approach.. Although there may be other threads that are equally important, these eight provide our organizing pattern as we explore the emerging fabric of women's work in religious education and the threads evident in these foremothers' lives. In the following chapters, you will discover the threads in these women's lives in varying numbers. Together, they weave a tapestry that has been slowly developing for generations.

1. One thread is the integration of life and experience into the educational event. As The Cornwall Collective reminds us, "Basic to a feminist approach . . . is the understanding of education as a wholistic process."[12] Religious education is not just about cognitive understanding but also about incorporating the whole person. Religious knowing, like other ways of knowing, is grounded and shaped by the lives we live. "All knowledge is constructed, and the knower is an intimate part of the known."[13]

2. Feminist religious education happens in community. Part of the process is hearing the voices of others and allowing others to "hear us into speech."[14] In the educational context, "women are finding that they are not willing to give up the connections between their lives and the lives of other women nor their ways of communication. That cultural connection has

made them who they are. Sharing of time and empowerment and close relationships make women affirm their distinctiveness as women."[15]

3. Feminist religious education is liberating. Reflecting on her own development as a feminist educator, Letty Russell writes, "Since the publication of *Human Liberation in a Feminist Perspective—A Theology,* I have constantly returned to a description of education as liberation: a process of action-reflection on . . . the meaning of oppression in the light of our participation in God's creation of a fully human society."[16] But liberation implies action, and religious education that is liberating is also political.[17] Rachel Henderlite and Nelle Morton, for example, were both deeply involved in the racial justice movement in the South.[18]

4. The fourth thread is attention to power within the church and the emphasis on the collegiality of laity and clergy. For too long the ministry of the laity has been seen as secondary to the ministry of those "ordained" by the church. This is a power issue, and feminists recognize that power must be mutual and should be shared. This allows the gifts of all members of the church to be important to the life of the church. Feminist approaches to religious education include the understanding that the church is the people and that all the people of the church are called to God's ministry.

5. The contextual grounding of religious education extends beyond the immediate community of learning. Because who we are is grounded in our experience, the historical and social contexts of women shape us even as we attempt to impact on those contexts. Related to this is the commitment to do religious education for the sake of all of God's creation.

6. In feminist scholarship, theory and practice are integrated. For education to take seriously the whole person, *why* we do what we do must be woven into *how* we do what we do. Feminist educator Mary Elizabeth Mullino Moore insists that "passion for educational theory and practice [must] stand in relationship."[19] Feminist approaches to religious education take care to be whole in their attention to the educational endeavor.

7. Language shapes religious knowing. As Maria Harris notes, "My first awareness of the impact of contemporary feminism came when I awoke to the issue of inclusive language." We began to understand that "not only were we, as humans, creating language—language was at the same time creating us."[20] Feminist educators have attended to the female and male language we use and to other forms of exclusivity.[21] Most important, in the life of the church feminists understand that "the symbol of God functions as the primary symbol of the whole religious system, the ultimate point of reference for understanding experience, life, and the world. Hence the way in which a faith community shapes language about God implicitly represents what it takes to be the highest good, the profoundest truth, the most appealing beauty."[22] Feminist approaches to religious education understand the power of language to shape our imagination and our images of God. God is not "he," God is "God," and the language we use to talk about

God shapes our understanding of God and of what it means for us—female and male—to be made in the image of God.

8. Religious education is grounded in the partnering of teacher and learner. Letty Russell suggests "Partnership is an idea whose fulfillment is long overdue. . . . For Christians, partnership is to be understood as a relationship of mutuality and trust based on the gift of God's partnership with us in our lives."[23] The teacher is also a learner and the learner also teaches; there is mutuality of respect and openness. Concerns around power and empowerment are important to feminist educators. According to bell hooks, "To make a revolutionary feminist pedagogy, we must relinquish our ties to traditional ways of teaching that reinforce domination. . . . To have a revolutionary feminist pedagogy we must first focus on the student-teacher relationship and the issue of power."[24] Nelle Morton notes, in her article on the feminist movement, "One change in method is the recognition of the power of presence. Abstract teaching is giving way to learning to be present to one another; telling one's own story with its hurts, disappointments, good feelings, and joys. . . . Telling one's own story leads from my story to your story, and in time to feeling 'we are all part of a long, long story.'"[25]

Those involved in weaving the patterns of feminist approaches to feminist religious education are passionate people. We hear the stories of our foremothers and know our passions are well founded. Much has been done, yet still much remains. Judith Dorney challenges us to consider, "The process of including women's voices and experiences in our teaching does not simply mean adding materials to traditional religious education materials. It means rethinking how much of how religious education is done."[26]

The field of feminist religious education is taking shape. Colleagues such as Gloria Durka, Mary Elizabeth Mullino Moore, and Carol Lakey Hess currently are helping us name and understand how feminist epistemology, ways of teaching and learning, and ways of women's knowing are essential to the religious education of women and men in our churches and theological schools.[27] This book is designed to be part of the process. I asked colleagues of my generation to reflect upon some of the women who have come before us. That these women—and more—shaped our field is exciting! One book cannot tell the whole story. Please consider this volume of women as our "for example" list.

Twelve Foremothers

Although I understand myself as a Christian educator, for this book I use the broader term *religious education*. The professional organizations that many of the women discussed herein have led chose the ecumenical term *religious*.[28] Also, some of these women have intentionally chosen to identify themselves as "religious" educators,[29] while others use "Christian" educators. "Religious" provides the more inclusive rubric for these women's stories.

All biographies employ a similar format. Each author begins by introducing her foremother, placing her in her historical and social contexts. The chapter highlights the woman's scholarship and teaching, discusses her impact on the field of religious education, and identifies the threads that she brings to the fabric of feminist education. Finally, her legacy is explored. The twelve women are an impressive group.

Sophia Lyon Fahs (1876–1978) helped shape the liberal religious education movement.[30] She completed her bachelor of divinity degree at Union Theological Seminary in New York in 1926 and was one of the first two women appointed to the faculty there. In addition to her work as principal of the Union School of Religion, she became well known for her progressive work in children's religious education. At age sixty-one, she became editor of children's materials for the American Unitarian Association; she was ordained a Unitarian minister at age eighty-two.

Hulda Niebuhr (1889–1959) was a creative Christian educator, respected in the area of teaching methodologies.[31] After doing doctoral work at Union Theological Seminary and at Columbia University's Teachers College, she served Madison Avenue Presbyterian Church. She also taught at Boston University and New York University. Not so well known as her brothers, Reinhold and H. Richard, Hulda is an important foremother in Christian education. During her thirteen years on the faculties of the Presbyterian College of Christian Education and McCormick Theological Seminary in Chicago, she made an indelible mark on the field of Christian education as teacher and integrator of theory and practice.

Nelle Morton (1905–1987), a lifelong Christian educator who became well known for her work in human rights and feminist theology,[32] earned a master of arts degree at the Biblical Seminary in New York (now New York Theological Seminary). She served as a church educator before joining the Board of Christian Education of the former Presbyterian Church in the United States. Her work for racial justice included serving as general secretary of the Fellowship of Southern Churchmen in the late 1940s. In 1956 she joined the faculty of the School of Theology at Drew University in Madison, New Jersey, where she remained until her retirement in 1971. In active retirement, Morton became a leader in feminist theology and education.

Rachel Henderlite (1905–1991) was highly influential in the educational work of the Presbyterian Church U.S.[33] Earning a master of arts degree at the Biblical Seminary in New York (now New York Theological Seminary) and a doctorate at Yale University, she returned to the South to teach. She joined the faculty of the Presbyterian Church, U.S., General Assembly Training School for Lay Workers (now the Presbyterian School of Christian Education) in 1944 and remained there until she was called as director of curriculum development for the Board of Christian Education of the former

INTRODUCTION

Presbyterian Church U.S. In 1965, Henderlite became the first woman ordained as minister of Word and sacrament in the Presbyterian Church U.S. and the first full-time woman faculty member of a Presbyterian Church, U.S. seminary. She also served as the first woman president of the Consultation on Church Union (COCU).

Iris Cully (b. 1914) is one of the most influential women educators in recent generations. An Episcopalian, she has spent her life committed to the educational work of the church. Having earned her doctorate in the joint program at Garrett Theological Seminary and Northwestern University in Evanston, Illinois, she was the first woman appointed to the faculties of Yale Divinity School in Connecticut and Lexington Theological Seminary in Kentucky. Her work encompasses religious education of children, curriculum development, spiritual growth, worship, and biblical foundations of religious education. In 1974, Cully became the first woman president of APRRE.

Norma Thompson (b. 1915) was president of the APRRE in 1977 and taught on the faculty of New York University until her recent retirement. Known for her commitment to pluralism, Thompson encouraged interreligious dialogue within the profession of religious educators. She also helped shape the relationship of theology and religious education through her own scholarship and teaching.

Olivia Pearl Stokes (b. 1916) was the first African-American woman to receive a doctorate in religious education, from the joint program at Union Theological Seminary and Columbia University's Teachers College in New York.[34] She served on the Massachusetts Council of Churches and as an "urban consultant" on the National Council of Churches. Stokes "has referred to herself as an 'ecumaniac,' taking the best liberal insights from all of the denominations."[35] She served as an adjunct professor of religious education at New York University for several years and now is in retirement.

Sara Little (b. 1919) has helped shape both the teaching of Christian education and the integration of theology and Christian education. She earned the master of religious education degree at the Presbyterian Church, U.S., General Assembly Training School for Lay Workers (now the Presbyterian School of Christian Education [PSCE]) in Richmond, Virginia, and a doctorate at Yale Divinity School. She joined the faculty of PSCE in 1951 and began teaching at Union Theological Seminary in Richmond in 1973. She left the faculty of PSCE in 1976 and retired from Union in 1989, although her affiliation with PSCE continued until 1995.

Dorothy Jean Furnish (b. 1921) earned her master of arts and doctor of philosophy degrees from Garrett-Evangelical Theological Seminary and Northwestern University in Evanston, Illinois. A Methodist, she has been influential in the uses of the Bible in religious education of children. Furnish has also documented histories of women in religious education. She was professor of Christian education at Garrett-Evangelical until her retirement in 1988.

Foremothers and Mentors

Freda Gardner (b. 1929) has shaped generations of religious educators and pastors committed to the teaching ministry of the church. After her completion of a master of arts degree at the Presbyterian School of Christian Education, she became a local church educator. In 1961 she was invited to join the faculty of Princeton Theological Seminary in New Jersey. She was professor of Christian education and director of the School of Christian Education at Princeton until her retirement in 1992.

Letty Russell (b. 1929) began her work as a Christian educator in 1952 in the East Harlem Protestant Parish in New York. After the completion of her masters of divinity degree at Harvard University, Russell was one of the first women ordained in the former United Presbyterian Church U.S.A. She returned to Harlem as a pastor and also became active in the World Council of Churches. She completed master of sacred theology and doctor of theology degrees at Union Theological Seminary and, in 1974, joined the faculty of Yale Divinity School.

Maria Harris (b. 1934) has had widespread influence as a religious educator. A Roman Catholic, she earned a master of arts degree from Manhattan College and a doctorate in education from Union Theological Seminary and Columbia University's Teachers College. From 1967 to 1973, she served on the diocesan religious education staff of the Rockville Center in New York. She has taught at Fordham University in the Bronx and at Drew University and Princeton Theological Seminary in New Jersey and was on the faculty for several years at Andover Newton Theological School in Newton Center, Massachusetts. Harris has been influential in the areas of teaching and religious imagination, interreligious education, youth ministry, and women and teaching. She is active in teaching, providing retreat leadership, and writing on women's spirituality and aging.

One of the important aspects of feminist work is collaboration, the recognition that relationships and experience are valid ways of grounding scholarship. The authors of these chapters were chosen because of their present-day contributions to religious education but also for their relationships with the women they portray. These writers tell us about those women who have mentored them, either personally or through their writings. We are offered glimpses into the lives of these teachers and scholars. As feminists, we recognize that these are not "objective" biographies; they are women telling important stories of other women, weaving together the objective information and the subjective knowing to create the underpinnings for our discipline.[36] As historian Rosemary Skinner Keller reminds us, "The Christian faith becomes transformative only as we are moved by the *presence* of living ordinary saints, not just by their words."[37]

I invite you to read these biographies, stories of gifted and influential women of the church. Discover and reclaim more of the history of religious education. Begin, as we did, to identify the emerging patterns of feminist approaches woven into religious education.

INTRODUCTION

NOTES

1. The Gender and Education Task Force was added in recent years to the annual meeting of the Association of Professors and Researchers in Religious Education.
2. Adrienne Rich notes it is important for feminists to question and reexplore our past. See her "Toward a Woman-Centered University (1973–1974)," in *Women, Culture and Society: A Reader,* ed. Barbara Balliet and Debra Humphreys (Dubuque, Iowa: Kendall/Hunt Publishing Co., 1992), 134.
3. Dorothy Jean Furnish, "Women in Religious Education: Pioneers for Women in Professional Ministry," in *Women and Religion in America,* vol. 3: *1900–1968,* ed. Rosemary Radford Ruether and Rosemary Skinner Keller (San Francisco: Harper & Row, 1986), 310. As Fern Giltner writes, "Religious education has notoriously been the responsibility of women and most professional religious educators are women." See Fern M. Giltner, "Preface" in *Women's Issues in Religious Education,* ed. Fern M. Giltner (Birmingham, Ala.: Religious Education Press, 1985), 1.
4. Susan Thistlethwaite, "The Feminization of American Religious Education," *Religious Education* 76 (July–August 1981):391. Dorothy Jean Furnish notes that the early development of the "profession of director of religious education (DRE) attracted both laymen and laywomen, as well as some ordained men who found a special ministry in the work of religious education. . . . In 1929 there were an almost equal number of men and women in this field." This changed during the depression, and "by 1938 only 26 percent of the directors were men. Women were willing to work for less money, and thus began the myth that it was inherently a women's profession." See Furnish, "Women in Religious Education," 312.
5. Furnish, "Women in Religious Education," 310.
6. Iris Cully, "Women in Religious Education: An Overview," *The Living Light: An Interdisciplinary Review of Christian Education* 12 (spring 1975): 14. This was Dr. Cully's Presidential Address to the Association of Professors and Researchers in Religious Education (APRRE) in 1974; she was this organization's first woman president.
7. Pamela Holliman, "Mentoring as an Art of Intentional Thriving Together," in *The Arts of Ministry: Feminist-Womanist Approaches,* ed. Christie C. Neuger (Louisville, Ky.: Westminster John Knox Press, 1996), 166.
8. Marlene Mayr, *Modern Masters of Religious Education* (Birmingham, Ala.: Religious Education Press, 1983), cover.
9. In their recent text, *A History of Christian Education,* (Nashville, Tn.: Broadman Holman Publishers, 1993), James E. Reed and Ronnie Prevost intentionally address women and education. They include in the list of twenty Christian educators in the twentieth century Edna Baxter, Rachel Henderlite, and Sara Little. It was noted in the March 1996 newsletter of APRRE that "since 1992 . . . Will Kennedy has been collecting oral histories with significant educators of the twentieth century." Fifteen interviews were done; Maria Harris, Sylvia Ettenberg, and Sara Little are the only women included.
10. Among these ecumenical leaders are Sara Lee and Mary Boys, who are guest editors of a 1996 issue of *Religious Education* (vol. 91, no. 4 [Fall 1996]) on the theme of "Religious Traditions in Conversation." This issue includes a report on their two-year colloquium for Catholic and Jewish educators in interreligious learning.
11. If the list expanded beyond the United States, Margaret Webster would have been considered. A Canadian, Margaret Webster was president of APRRE in 1981.

12. Cornwall Collective, *Your Daughters Shall Prophesy: Feminist Alternatives in Theological Education* (New York: Pilgrim Press, 1980), 6.

13. Mary Field Belenky, Blythe McVicker, Nancy Rule Goldberger, and Jill Mattuck Tarule, *Women's Ways of Knowing: The Development of Self, Voice and Mind* (New York: Basic Books, 1986), 137. Gloria Durka has suggested an approach to "research in which methods of inquiry have taken feminists outside of traditional scholarly canons to study women's own religious lives. In this stage, while women's studies has a limited view, i.e. the recovery of women's religious experience, it has a larger view: how one's approach to knowledge and learning is shaped by one's self image." See Gloria Durka, "The Religious Journey of Women: The Educational Task," *Religious Education* 77 (March–April 1982): 164.

14. Nelle Morton, ed. "Hearing to Speech," in *The Journey Is Home*, Nelle Morton (Boston: Beacon Press, 1985), 202–11.

15. Fern M. Giltner, "Structure and Process," in Giltner, ed., *Women's Issues in Religious Education*, 132.

16. Letty M. Russell, "Changing My Mind about Religious Education," *Religious Education* 79 (winter 1984):7; Russell cites her text *Human Liberation in a Feminist Perspective—A Theology* (Philadelphia: Westminster Press, 1974), 20.

17. Maria Harris, *Women and Teaching: Themes for a Spirituality of Pedagogy* (New York: Paulist Press, 1988), 6.

18. Betty A. Thompson, "Nelle Morton: Journeying Home," *Christian Century* 104 (August 26–September 2, 1987): 711.

19. Mary Elizabeth Mullino Moore, *Teaching from the Heart: Theology and Educational Method* (Minneapolis: Fortress Press, 1991), 4. See also Margaret Webster, "Imperative for Religious Education: The Integration of Theory and Practice," *Religious Education* 77 (March–April 1982): 123–31.

20. Maria Harris, "Weaving the Fabric: How My Mind Has Changed," *Religious Education* 79 (winter 1984): 19.

21. A recent translation of scripture notes, "This version has undertaken the effort to *replace or rephrase all gender-specific language not referring to particular historical individuals, all pejorative references to race, color, or religion, and all identifications of persons by their physical disability alone, by means of paraphrase, alternative renderings, and other acceptable means of conforming the language of the work to an inclusive idea."* See Victor Roland Gold, Thomas L. Hoyt, Jr., Sharon H. Ringe, Susan Brooks Thistlethwaite, Burton H. Throckmorton, Jr., and Barbara A. Withers, *The New Testament and Psalms: An Inclusive Version* (New York: Oxford University Press), viii–ix.

22. Elizabeth A. Johnson, *She Who Is: The Mystery of God in Feminist Theological Discourse* (New York: Crossroad, 1992), 4.

23. Letty M. Russell, "Partnership in Educational Ministry," *Religious Education* 74 (March–April 1979):143; idem, *Future of Partnership* (Philadelphia: Westminster Press, 1979). "Partnership" is an image that permeates the work of Letty M. Russell; see Barbara Anne Keely, "Partnership and Christian Education in the Work of Letty M. Russell" (Ed.D. diss., Presbyterian School of Christian Education, 1991).

24. bell hooks, *Talking Back: Thinking Feminist, Thinking Black* (Boston: South End Press, 1989), 52.

25. Nelle Morton, "Feminist Movement," in *Harper's Encyclopedia of Religious Education,* ed. Iris V. Cully and Kendig Brubaker Cully (San Francisco: HarperCollins, 1990), 258.

26. Judith Dorney, "Religious Education and the Development of Young Women," in Giltner, ed., *Women's Issues in Religious Education,* 62–63.

INTRODUCTION

27. For example, see Durka, "Religious Journey of Women," 163–78; Moore, *Teaching from the Heart*; and Carol Lakey Hess, "Getting Dirty with Dignity: A Feminist Approach to Christian Education," in Neuger, ed., *The Arts of Ministry*, 60–87. Thomas H. Groome, in a paper presented at the 1995 APRRE meeting in Chicago, draws on feminist epistemology to develop his thesis; see his "Religious Knowing in an Age of Disbelief" (unpublished paper presented at APRRE meeting, October 15, 1995).
28. For example, the Religious Education Association and the Association of Professors and Researchers in Religious Education.
29. For example, see Harris, "Weaving the Fabric." Sophia Fahs, although raised Presbyterian, became Unitarian in her later years and considered herself a religious educator.
30. Historical information on Fahs is drawn from Edith F. Hunter, "Sophia Lyon Fahs: Educator of Questioning Minds," *Religious Education* 73 (September–October 1978): S126–S138; and Helen Archibald, "Sophia Lyon Fahs," in Cully and Cully, eds., *Harper's Encyclopedia of Religious Education*, 245.
31. Historical information on Niebuhr is drawn from Elizabeth Caldwell, *A Mysterious Mantle: The Biography of Hulda Niebuhr* (Cleveland: Pilgrim Press, 1994).
32. Historical information on Morton is drawn from Thompson, "Nelle Morton," 711–12.
33. Historical information on Henderlite is drawn from Carol Lakey Hess and Estelle Rountree McCarthy, "A Life Lived in Response: Rachel Henderlite," *American Presbyterians* 69 (summer 1991): 133–143.
34. Historical information on Stokes is drawn from Furnish, "Women in Religious Education," 314.
35. Ibid.
36. Mary Field Belenky et al., *Women's Ways of Knowing*. When I chose to spend time with Letty Russell, who was the topic of my doctoral dissertation, I was fortunate to have a committee which agreed that a feminist process of "knowing the subject" was appropriate for the development of scholarship on a feminist theologian and Christian educator.
37. Rosemary Skinner Keller, "Introduction," in Caldwell, *A Mysterious Mantle*, ix.

Sophia Lyon Fahs

RELIGIOUS MODERNIST AND PROGRESSIVE EDUCATOR

M. Susan Harlow

Sophia Blanche Lyon Fahs was born in 1876 in Hangchow, China, the fourth child of Presbyterian missionaries David Nelson Lyon and Mandana Doolittle Lyon. She died in 1978 at the age of 102. Her life spanned a century and her ministry touched thousands. Sophia Fahs was a pioneering force in liberal religious education, emphasizing the innate creativity and curiosity of children.

In 1879, when Sophia was three and a half years old, her parents returned to the United States and settled in Wooster, Ohio. Here she grew up, graduating as valedictorian of her high school class in 1893 and receiving her bachelor's degree, cum laude, in 1897 from the Presbyterian University of Wooster (now the College of Wooster).[1]

Like many young Christian women of her generation, Sophia hoped to serve God through her life's work and planned to become a missionary. During her college years she joined the Student Volunteer Movement, whose goal was the "evangelization of the world in this generation."[2] She was also active in the Young Women's Christian Association (YWCA). In the summer of 1896, after her junior year at Wooster, she attended a YWCA conference at Lake Geneva, Wisconsin, where she met Charles Harvey Fahs, her future husband.

Harvey also was active in the Student Volunteer Movement and, like Sophia, had signed the pledge to the movement to become a foreign missionary. The son of a Methodist minister, he attended Northwestern University in Evanston, Illinois, prior to entering Drew University in Madison, New Jersey, for his bachelor of divinity degree. Harvey and Sophia met while he was a college junior.

13

SOPHIA LYON FAHS

The two were engaged for four years, and during their engagement, Sophia was employed in a variety of jobs. She taught Latin and English in the Wooster High School. She also served for two years as a traveling secretary for the Student Volunteer Movement, visiting colleges in the Midwest and South to encourage students to join the mission field. In 1901, Sophia took a part-time job at the University of Chicago as YWCA secretary to the women students.

While in Chicago, Sophia was greatly influenced by the Higher Criticism, a scholarly approach to studying biblical texts that sought to apply a scientific method to re-creating the historical and cultural contexts present when the Bible was written. Much of Sophia's exposure to Higher Criticism came from her brother-in-law, Henry Burton Sharmon, who was working on his doctorate in biblical studies at the University of Chicago, but she also took an Old Testament course from William Rainey Harper, president of the university and a major advocate of Higher Criticism. These experiences caused her "to rethink ideas that she had taken over uncritically from her Presbyterian parents,"[3] and she began to reshape her own beliefs.

Harvey and Sophia married in 1902. Theirs was a marriage of personal affection and professional inspiration. The couple moved to New York when Harvey was appointed editor of the Methodist Church's monthly mission magazine, *World Wide Missions,* and general editor of all Methodist missionary literature. While in New York, Harvey also served as special assistant to John R. Mott, secretary of student work for the international Young Men's Christian Association (YMCA). As Mott's assistant, Harvey traveled throughout the world to promote mission efforts. In 1910 both Sophia and Harvey attended the historic World Missionary Conference in Edinburgh, where a number of denominational foreign mission boards came together and founded the Missionary Research Library. Harvey became the library's director and curator, collecting over seventy thousand books and pamphlets. In 1929 the library moved from its own building in New York City to the recently constructed Brown Tower at Union Theological Seminary and Harvey became a member of the seminary's faculty.[4] He served as library director until his death in 1948 at the age of seventy-six.

After moving to New York, Sophia began work on a master's degree at Columbia University Teachers College. She studied with Edward L. Thorndike, professor of educational psychology, who pioneered quantitative research methods to study learning in individuals and who wrote extensively on how such psychological data influenced instruction. Thorndike's work highlighted such topics as student interest, attention, reasoning, feeling, and moral training.[5] Sophia also took philosophy of education courses from Nicholas Murray Butler, chair of Columbia's Department of Philosophy, Ethics, and Psychology; founding member (in 1903) and vice-president of the Religious Education Association; and, later, president of Columbia University.[6]

Religious Modernist and Progressive Educator

The most important professor for Sophia, however, was Frank McMurry, chair of the Department of Elementary Education at Teachers College, whose pioneering work in curricula was grounded in functional psychology.[7] McMurry, founder with Nicholas Butler of the Religious Education Association, helped organize the experimental Sunday school of Teachers College in 1903. Under McMurry's leadership, Sophia taught the fourth- and fifth-grade class in the Sunday school, using missionary biography to stimulate children's interest in the Bible, rather than simply teaching Bible stories as did most other Sunday schools. She recalled that this was "a year's revolutionizing experience for me" as she discovered a new and exciting way to teach.[8] Her master's thesis, based on her teaching experience, was titled "Missionary Biography as Supplementary to Biblical Material for the Sunday School Curriculum."

Sophia received her M.A. from Columbia University in 1904. Her first two books were missionary biographies: *Uganda's White Man of Work: A Story of Alexander M. MacKay*, published in 1907 by the Interchurch Press, and *Red, Yellow and Black,* published in 1918 by the Methodist Book Concern.

The Fahses had five children: Dorothy Irene, born in 1905; Ruth Miriam, 1907; Charles Burton, 1908; Gertrude Helen, 1913; and Lois Sophia, 1914. During these years, much of Sophia's time and energy was devoted to raising her children; but her observations of her children's natural curiosities, questions, and growth shaped and sharpened her thinking about religious education. She wrote down many of her conversations with her children and used these experiences to illustrate her educational insights and teachings in later writings. One of these conversations that is often recounted is one she had with her daughter Ruth, who, at age seven and a half, queried, "Mother, where is the *me*? Where is the *me*? It seems to be always my *hand*, my *foot*, my *head* or my *skin*, but where is the *me*?"[9]

Two of the Fahses' children did not live to adulthood. Gertrude Helen died of pneumonia at five months of age in 1913, and Ruth died of infantile paralysis at age thirteen in 1920. Sensitized by her own loss, Sophia observed that most children by age five had experienced the death of someone in either their immediate or their extended family. As a result, children had the capacity to ask serious and probing questions about death. She wrote, "What kinds of thoughts of death do we most care to have our children hold? Shall we create a sympathetic atmosphere . . . and encourage the children to question, or shall we shun the subject to the greatest possible degree?"[10] Sophia hoped that parents would choose the former approach, and she helped create resources to assist in this process. Her most notable writing on this subject is the 1938 children's book *Beginnings of Life and Death*, a collection of stories addressing the issues of why people die and what happens at death.

In 1923, after guiding Dorothy, Charles Burton, and Lois safely into adulthood, Sophia began studies for the bachelor of divinity degree at

Union Theological Seminary in New York. She was forty-seven years old, and she explained her plans to her mother:

> My purpose in doing this is to get a thoroughgoing training for work in religious education. If I work as a director, I need to have the advantage of an equal standing with the pastor in the church. If I should take a little community church someday myself, then I could organize the church on a democratic basis and we could together work out an entirely new program of church activities in which preaching would be merely an occasional feature of the program. At any rate, I am starting out on the adventure at the age of forty-seven.[11]

This marked another stage in Sophia's life, the beginning of a very productive and influential professional career.

In 1923, Union Theological Seminary was an exciting environment for the new field of religious education. George Albert Coe's educational philosophy had shaped the seminary's Department of Religious Education. Coe came to New York in 1909, when Union created the first full-time professorship in religious education at a U.S. theological school.[12] In 1910 the Union School of Religion was founded as the successor to the Sunday school at Columbia's Teachers College, where Sophia had taught. Her connection with the Union School had a major impact on Fahs's understanding of religious education.

Sophia Fahs began fieldwork on the staff of the Union School of Religion during her second year at Union Seminary. The Union School of Religion was described as "an experimental center for religious education, a setting where the best in educational technique would characterize the Sunday sessions of study and worship."[13] Organized and administered by Union's Department of Religious Education, the school gave Sophia and other seminary students a laboratory experience in which to learn progressive teaching methods and to test new educational approaches and curricular content.[14] In 1925 she became elementary supervisor at the Union School of Religion and had primary responsibility for curriculum development for the elementary school age group. She began to write articles related to this work, which were published in the journal of the Religious Education Association. This experience also served as the basis for her bachelor of divinity degree thesis, "Certain Problems Involved in Building a Curriculum in Religious Education."

Scholarship and Teaching

Sophia Fahs's Union Seminary training, her educational studies at Columbia University Teachers College, and her involvement in the Union School of Religion all played a significant role in shaping her theological perspectives and her educational philosophy and practice.

Religious Modernism

Fahs's work embodied the modernist concepts prevalent in liberal religious circles at the turn of the twentieth century, the beliefs that (1) religion must adapt itself to the best of scientific findings and cultural evolution; (2) God is immanent and can be discerned in the development of human culture; and (3) human society is progressive and moving toward the realization of the "kingdom of God."[15]

Her acceptance of the importance of science and evolution is demonstrated in her book *Today's Children and Yesterday's Heritage,* in which she contrasts the "old cosmology" of the salvation story with the modern scientific cosmology. She advocated that children be given a scientifically accurate picture of the universe early in their learning. For Sophia, this scientific viewpoint, taught at an early age, would assist children later, when they were developmentally able to engage in understanding religious myth.[16] The children would be able to analyze critically the "old story of salvation," growing to become "integrated and whole persons with their religion and science harmonized." She believed that children exposed to the newest of the scientific findings of the day would grow with the ability to adapt religious ideas and practices to the advances of modern culture. Without this ability, she feared, the children would "be crippled with a kind of religious infantile paralysis."[17]

Sophia's understanding of religion points to her affinity with the second modernist notion, divine immanence. In several of her writings, *The Old Story of Salvation* and *Today's Children and Yesterday's Heritage* in particular, she reveals her lack of tolerance for what she calls the Christian "old story of salvation" and its need for a supernatural deity to intervene in human history. Instead, she was drawn to psychological interpretations of human nature, to anthropology, and to the stories and experiences of persons from other cultures as means of understanding "universal truth and universal human need."[18] In 1926 she wrote:

> Religion . . . is really a process of learning how to live, and a seeking for an understanding of God and life. We are all searching and hungering for righteousness. Let us go on the quest together, American, East Indian, Chinese and African. Let us share our experiences. . . . Perhaps together, we may develop a better religion than any of us have yet known.[19]

Fahs's reliance on psychological understandings of children's development, rather than on theological language pointing to God's transcendence, led her to understand the role of religious education as that of helping children nurture their own inherent religious sensibilities. Religious education's role, she believed, was to help them draw from "their own direct relations with the universe, their own lessons and patterns for living."[20] If God was immanent, Sophia believed, there should be no struggle between developing one's inner self, one's patterns for life, and "an emphasis on keeping in harmony with God's ways."[21]

The third concept of religious modernism is that human society is moving toward the realization of the kingdom of God. Sophia Fahs moved away from use of Christian language to express her religious insights. Accepting that society moves progressively toward ultimate realization, she and other modernistic liberals described this idea in evolutionary language, rather than in Christian language. She clearly demonstrated this characteristic when she wrote:

> The psychological scientist conceives of living, spiritually, emotionally and ethically, as an evolutionary process, rather than as a continuing battle between good and evil, controlled by God and Satan. Living is growing, learning, experimenting and discovering. How to become a real person of integrity, usefulness, tenderness and breadth of sympathy is not primarily a matter of obedience to principles . . . ; it is rather a way of life that develops through a growing understanding of our own basic needs and deepest yearnings, and the needs and yearnings of others.[22]

In her thinking, teaching, and writing, Sophia embodied the religious modernist notion that humanity was engaged in a progressive process toward the ultimate and deepest aspects of living.

Progressive Education

Rooted firmly in religious modernism, Sophia was also influenced by the developments in progressive education—the attempts by reformers in the late 1800s to respond through education to the challenges posed by urban industrial expansion and the explosion of scientific knowledge, especially in their goals to improve the lives of individuals.[23] Two themes of progressive education can be readily noted in her thinking and teaching: the experimental school and child-centered education.

The Experimental School

The experimental school was preeminent in Sophia's educational philosophy and practice. Scientific knowledge was advancing rapidly, and as a modernist, she realized that religious education could not hope to keep pace with scientific breakthroughs without its own kind of experimentation. Educators needed to try out new methods, new ways to engage children in wondering and questioning. These new educational methods needed evaluation, reworking, research, reapplication, and further exploration. Religious education would then be as "skilled and fearless" as the instruction "children are getting week-days in the sciences."[24]

Models for this approach existed. John Dewey and Alice Chipman Dewey had organized their experimental laboratory school in Chicago in 1896, in order to test John Dewey's educational theories and to investigate empirically and implement his philosophical and psychological under-standings. The Horace Mann School for Girls, the Horace Mann School for Boys, and the Lincoln Schools were the laboratory schools of Teachers College at Columbia University.[25] The Union School of Religion was modeled after these other "laboratory" schools.[26]

After her graduation from Union Seminary in 1926, Sophia became the principal of the Union School of Religion. For three years she was able, as her biographer Edith Hunter observed, "to put into practice many of the ideas toward which she had been moving in her thinking" over the prior two decades.[27] In contrast to the typical Sunday schools of the day, which Fahs described as trying to teach children about "one great religious experience," the Union School of Religion conceived of religious experience as "growth, widening of horizons, strengthening of wills, adventuring for right, deepening of passion to make this world a better place for every-body to live in."[28] Later, reflecting on the purpose of such an educational process, Sophia wrote:

> The essential harmonizing of religion and science must come, therefore, in the harmonizing of the processes themselves by which both religion and science live. Such an adjustment means the thoroughgoing re-conceiving of religion itself. . . . A religion preeminently of beliefs and moral codes must change to a religion of quest. The essence of the religion of the new day will be found in the process and that must be a process of search into the most intimate and the most perplexing prob-lems of living—the problems of our personal aloneness in this complex universe and of our varied and myriad companionships. It will be con-ceived of as a search for God and for all which that may mean.[29]

This "religion of the new day" needed new methods and new resources to assist in this quest.

Since no set "school curriculum" existed at the Union School of Religion, each year the teachers and supervisors were able to experiment with new approaches and new subjects. Each of the classes helped choose and build their own subject matter and their own ways to explore the theme for the year. Sophia Fahs and Ralph P. Bridgeman described one such class of fifteen-year-old boys:

> At the opening session the teacher is greeted with . . . "My mother signed me up to study the Bible, but I don't care rats about it! The Bible isn't true anyway. Do you think a man could live three days inside a whale?" . . . The teacher returns their fire with a challenge to be shown where the Bible is untrue, or crazy. Jonah seems to worry them most. Clumsily . . . they turn to the book of Jonah. Before long they discover that the book is a novel with a high purpose. By asking whether some races aren't really better than others anyway, one boy precipitates a discussion that lasts several lessons, and finally grows into a consideration of how they should treat Jews and negroes at their schools. So all winter one topic

has grown out of another. Now they are talking about success, what it is, how it can be measured. Their next topic will be the things a fellow should consider in choosing his business or profession. In these latter discussions, Jesus' ideals have been referred to frequently.[30]

The goal of the experimental nature of the curriculum was to engender creativity on the part of the teachers and students. In practice, it also eventually caused those outside the school who had more traditional views of religious education to look harshly upon some of the activities at the Union School of Religion.

In 1928 the president of Union Seminary, Henry Sloane Coffin, brought the popular pastor Reinhold Niebuhr onto the faculty to teach Applied Christianity. This move signaled a shift in the school's theological perspective, away from liberal theology to the new "orthodoxy" gaining popularity with Karl Barth and others in Europe. Sophia continued to pursue her religious modernist and progressive educational ideals. A member of the Union Seminary Board of Trustees and of Brick Presbyterian Church received a copy of a religious questionnaire from the Union School and felt that not enough emphasis on traditional Christianity and biblical studies was included in the queries. He brought his dismay to the attention of President Coffin. In response, Coffin attended an Easter Sunday worship service for the children at the Union School and was horrified to learn that the Union Seminary students under Sophia's supervision refused to acknowledge that Jesus had indeed been resurrected. The resulting controversy between the seminary administration and the leadership of the Union School of Religion forced the closure of the Union School at the end of the school year in 1929.[31]

The official reasons given by Union Seminary for the school's closing were the seminary's financial difficulties and the opening of the Riverside Church, scheduled for 1930. Prior to the construction of the Riverside Church immediately to the seminary's west across Claremont Avenue, there were no liberal churches in the entire Morningside Heights neighborhood. Many seminary officials believed that a religious education program needed to be part of a worshiping community, not an independent school organized by a theological educational institution.[32]

Sophia continued to teach on the faculty at Union Seminary, but her involvement in an experimental school seemed to be over. Then in 1933, Ivar Hellstrom, minister of education at the Riverside Church, invited Sophia, who was fifty-six years old, to become supervisor of the Junior Church School. Here she continued her experimental work with children until 1942, when she retired. Many years later, at the age of ninety-five, she recalled the support for her efforts that she received from Hellstrom:

> The curriculum for the Junior Department had been primarily an introductory study of the Old Testament. I begged for the opportunity to experiment with a broader outlook on the beginnings of religion among

several different peoples, going back even to the days of the first cave men. . . . It was a rare and choice experience to work with a man who trusted and encouraged me in such a new and untried adventure.

Some of the books written later especially for the Unitarians were first experimented with in this Riverside Church School. Had it not been for these first try-outs I would not have been able to do what I did when the Unitarians invited me to become their editor of children's materials. Liberal religious education and I personally owe a great deal to Dr. Ivar Hellstrom.[33]

Child-Centered Education

Child-centered education was the second aspect of progressive education in which Sophia was strongly involved. The child-centered focus of progressive education built upon the foundation established in the kindergarten movement, which took off in the United States in the 1870s. The kindergarten movement emphasized the child's natural inner development and the role of play in assisting with this development.

Throughout her life's work, Sophia stressed that the child was the primary agent and recipient of religious education. The child was important in his or her own right and was the discoverer of his or her own religious meanings and truth. In *A New Ministry to Children* she described this child-centered approach:

> Religion should be something sincerely real in the child's thoughts and feelings. . . . We would give them opportunities to be with baby animals, to plant seeds, and to sense for themselves the mystery in being alive and in growing and learning. We would be companionable and sympathetic, joining the children in their wonderings. We would restrain ourselves for a while from giving them answers in theological language, lest a name be too easily substituted for an experience no word can truly satisfy. We are confident the very nature of the universe is such as to challenge children to stretch their thoughts if only we can be patient and unafraid of children's curiosities.[34]

Not wishing to numb the natural tendencies of the child, Sophia Fahs advocated an approach to religious education that allowed and guided the child's inherent nature to unfurl and to grow.

Sophia Fah's Impact on the Field of Religious Education

Sophia Lyon Fahs had an impact on the field of religious education in two significant ways: (1) as one of the first women on the faculty at Union Seminary and (2) as curriculum editor for the American Unitarian Association (AUA). She was appointed to the Union Theological Seminary faculty as a lecturer in religious education in 1927, when she was fifty-one years old. She and Mary Ely Lyman, lecturer on English Bible, were hired the same year and became the first two women to participate in an academic procession at Union. Fahs taught at Union for seventeen years, retiring when she reached age sixty-eight in 1944.[35]

Fahs played a significant part in shaping the educational understandings of the graduate students who took her courses in the psychology and philosophy of religious education of young children, in curriculum planning, and in such techniques as storytelling, dramatization, and the creative arts. Her course bibliographies included such topics as sex education, religious doctrine and religious experience in children, discipline and freedom, use of Old Testament stories, and the young child and his social order.[36]

Sophia also used the experiences of her seminary students to shape her own educational understandings. One exercise she gave her students was for each to write a spiritual autobiography of his or her earliest childhood memories. The students were asked to recall their childhood dreams; their early fears of the dark, snakes, punishment, death, fire, or failure; their earliest experiences with the birth of babies, human or animal; their curiosity about sex; their earliest memories of Bible stories, pictures or thoughts of God, prayer, and role of Jesus in their lives. Then they were to share their conclusions regarding the effects of these childhood experiences on their self-expectations and their general philosophy of life.[37] Of the written reports submitted by twelve of her students she wrote:

> Years of Sunday school attendance were to some almost a complete blank, except for the receiving of badges, the memorizing of verses, a few Bible stories and perhaps a vague pleasant glow suggesting a happy sort of human contact. Some, who had been accustomed to pray nightly from the time they were first able to lisp words, remembered nothing of the content of their praying. . . . It may be significant that but three of the twelve reported having had, before ten years of age, any satisfying experience of personal relationship to God, while ten recalled one or more experiences pertaining to their thought of God, arousing fear, conflict, worry, anguish or even terror. . . .
>
> One was terrified by fire and another by the wind. These fears were never mentioned to the parents. One child, who was afraid of the dark, reported that her favorite hymn was "There'll be no dark valley when Jesus comes." Several reported great fear of everlasting punishment and dread of the end of the world by fire. One was so obsessed by this thought that a strange fear came over him whenever he saw flame-colored rays in the setting sun.[38]

The responses of twelve students would not be considered a major scientific study, but Sophia was struck by the tone of these recollections. How was it that bright, modern, adult graduate students could still be affected by the painful memories of unhappy childhood experiences?[39] These findings would encourage her to pioneer new approaches to children's religious education.

At sixty-one, Sophia Fahs began a new chapter of professional influence when she became editor of children's materials for the American Unitarian Association. She and her colleague Ernest Kuebler were given a mandate to design new education materials that would reverse the trend of shrinking numbers in the association's Sunday school. Sophia produced fifteen books and teachers guides in the New Beacon Series of Religious Education during her eight years as editor, from 1937 to 1945.

A prolific writer and an energetic thinker, Sophia published thirty-five articles during her career and wrote or coauthored thirteen books for youth and children and four books outlining her educational philosophy. She developed six study guides for teachers and parents, edited numerous other works published in the New Beacon Series of Religious Education, and wrote poetry; four of her poems were even set to music.[40]

Sophia Fahs's Contribution to Feminist Religious Education

Sophia Lyon Fahs retired from active work long before the contemporary feminist movement took hold in the 1970s. She had, moreover, directed her attention toward children, especially those of preschool and elementary age, and was not particularly concerned with the broader social context that disempowers women and children. Nonetheless, her thinking, writing, teaching, and resource editing all provide threads that contribute to a constructive feminist religious education. In the introduction to this text, Barbara Anne Keely identified eight common threads that contribute to the fabric of feminist religious education. I will identify those that are most evident in the work of Sophia Lyon Fahs and that illuminate her legacy for current practice.

First, Fahs believed deeply that experience is central to education. She was strongly opposed to the idea of religious education starting with the subject, whether that be a study of the Bible or a presentation of ethical principles by which one should live. The primary emphasis in religious education, she believed, should be to ask students to explore their own experiences to see what ordinary occurrences called "forth a special wonder or surprise or challenge [to] their liveliest thinking and questioning."[41] Fahs wrote:

> The religious way is the deep way, the way with a growing perspective and an expanding view. It is the way that dips into the heart of things, into personal feelings, yearnings and hostilities that so often must be buried and despised and left misunderstood. The religious way is the

23

way that sees what physical eyes alone fail to see, the intangibles at the heart of every phenomenon. The religious way is the way that touches universal relationships; that goes high, wide and deep, that expands the feelings of kinship. And if God symbolizes or means these larger relationships, the religious way means finding God.[42]

Second, Sophia Fahs, in her writing and teaching, emphasized the grounded nature of all life. She believed that a universal essence connected human, animal, and plant worlds with the source of all life. For Sophia, religion was not dependent on a text or a tradition:

> One's religion, growing from small beginnings, is one's actual philosophy of life seen in the perspective of the greater whole of which one feels himself a part. If real it brings a dynamic quality—certain overtones, certain basic illuminations—into the personal life. A program of religious education . . . should represent an organized effort to encourage and to guide children in building for themselves such personal foundations for worthy living, such supporting philosophies of life as will enhance courage and strengthen high-minded endeavor.[43]

Sophia Fahs believed each individual is inherently religious. Religious education, she felt, is not a process to convert the child to a religious belief, tradition, or practice. It is a process of assisting the child in his or her natural development, a process of assisting the individual in becoming who he or she is.

Third, feminist religious education recognizes the power of language in shaping religious knowing. Sophia Fahs recognized this early in her work with children. Young children did not have the cognitive ability to comprehend the complexity of stories found in the Hebrew Bible or the New Testament. At the suggestion of Frank McMurry at Columbia University Teachers College, she used missionary biography as a way for young children to engage with the missionary's human experiences before attempting to grasp the deeper religious truths. She recounted how this experience with teaching children radicalized her thinking about what to teach.

Sophia utilized stories and cultural myths in most of her teaching and writing. She worked diligently to make her writing accessible to children, through the use of vivid language and imagery related to the child's everyday experiences. Stories, for her, were not "to teach given moral ideals and principles, but to stimulate worthy thinking on the concrete moral problems of life."[44] Sophia was painfully aware of the harm that misuse of language could effect. She tried to foster engagement on the part of her listeners and students, so that they could take an active part in discerning their own meanings and integrated philosophy of living.

The fourth thread of feminist religious education is seen in Fahs's emphasis on the collaborative nature of learning, with both teacher and students actively engaged in the process. Sophia gave great emphasis to the role of the child in his or her own learning. Learning is to "begin where the children live, with the common things and happenings that children have seen and known for themselves."[45] In much of her writing, then, she described what the learning process entailed developmentally for the child. She did not offer specific advice about how teachers were to participate in this process, but she did supply some clues when she and Elizabeth M. Manwell wrote:

> From the teacher's point of view, all that quickens sympathetic imaging, that awakens sensitivity to other's feelings, all that enriches and enlarges understanding of the world; all that strengthens courage, that adds to the love of living; all that leads to developing skills needed for democratic social participation—all these put together are the curriculum through which these children learn. Such learnings are not easily observed or measured; they nevertheless can be planned for, to some extent, and the children themselves can determine in no small measure what the learnings shall be.[46]

The teacher was to be someone who led the child to experiences of wonder, awe, and imagination, rather than someone who gave answers or transmitted cognitive knowledge. The teacher was to be someone who assisted in finding ways for the children to "have a direct experience in finding out something for themselves."[47] In developing her educational philosophy, Sophia gave great weight to the agency of the child. Her deemphasis in her writings on the role of the teacher was, in part, a reaction to traditional religious education's stress on content and instruction and its failure to address the needs of the learner.

Throughout Fahs's work, theory and practice are integrated. This is the fifth thread of feminist work. Sophia supported her theoretical formulations with concrete illustrations from her experimental work at the Union School of Religion or the Riverside Church. Her scholarship embodied her stance toward experimentation and direct experience as essential components in teaching and developing new perspectives and practices. At age ninety-five, she recalled:

> It was primarily because of the opportunity given to me to teach in America's first experimental Sunday School, sponsored by Teachers College and led by Dr. [Frank] McMurry that I developed my first deep interest in children—especially in their religious development. It was then that I saw the basic tenets of John Dewey's philosophy being implemented and became committed [to] trying them out. It was then that I found what I most wanted to do in life, beyond being a wife and mother, and that was to help in reconstructing the processes and the contents of the religious education of children in light of mankind's growing understandings.[48]

Sixth, feminist religious educators believe education leads to liberation. For many contemporary scholars, however, this liberation involves transformation of cultural, social, political, economic, or institutional structures that thwart equality and wholeness of life for women and children. Sophia Fahs, in contrast, conceived of liberation in terms of the emotional and psychological development of the natural person. Hence she stressed the individual learner in most of her work. The goal of religious education with regard to the individual child was to be the nurturing of "the child's religious or spiritual health and growth (if this can be separated at all from the rest of life)."[49] For Sophia, then, liberation might refer to the unfolding of the whole person, as he or she experiences the abundance of life and nature.

The final thread that can be attached to Sophia Fahs's work is that involving the issue of power and the collegiality of laity and clergy. While she rarely referred to power dynamics in her scholarly writing, Fahs nonetheless was aware of their impact on the field of religious education and on her work specifically. When she enrolled in the bachelor of divinity degree program at Union Theological Seminary in 1923, Sophia wanted to gain a thoroughly grounded theological education so that she could be the professional equal of the ordained minister in any church where she might work in the future. If she was to be the sole minister in a congregation, she wanted the ministerial education to enable her to "organize the church on a democratic basis . . . where preaching would be merely an occasional feature of the program."[50]

The one thread of feminist religious education that does not appear in Sophia's work is the emphasis that religious education happens in community. Fahs's focus was directed heavily toward the individual child learner, and she paid little attention to the wider community's impact on the child's religious education.

The Legacy of Sophia Lyon Fahs

On February 8, 1959, at age eighty-two, Sophia Lyon Fahs accepted the invitation of the Unitarian Church of Montgomery County (now Cedar Lane Unitarian Church, Bethesda, Maryland) to be ordained. Characteristic of her outspoken leadership, she preached her own ordination sermon:

> It is because as a church you have discovered that all ministers are educators, and all religious educators are preachers and priests in a broad sense, that you have ordained me to "the ministry" in general. Through this ceremony you are inviting me into full fellowship with them all. This is a truly cherished honor.[51]

Her ordination was a time for setting Sophia Lyon Fahs apart as a minister among all other ministers, yet it was also a time when she chose to challenge the whole church to continue taking the ministry to children seriously. She noted that of the 539 active ministers in the American Unitarian Association in 1959 "there are but six women," and five of these ordained women were retired. She wrote, "The resistance to women as pulpit ministers and as heads of churches is still strong." Yet, she argued, until all the ordained ministers in the Unitarian fellowship were properly trained in relating and ministering to children as part of their theological education, the commitment to children would remain rhetoric and not practice.[52]

As a religious modernist and as a progressive educator, Sophia Lyon Fahs had a profound influence on religious education leadership during the twentieth century. Not content to enjoy the fruits of her labors in one sector of the church's institutional life, whether that be an experimental church school, teaching in theological education, or publishing books for children and youth, she endeavored for her 102 years to help shape the religious and spiritual development of children in every way. Thus she left her stamp on the greater church.

NOTES

1. Edith Hunter's biography *Sophia Lyon Fahs* (Boston: Beacon Press, 1966) has served as the primary source for Fahs's family, educational, and work history.
2. Sydney E. Ahlstrom, *A Religious History of the American People* 2 (Garden City, N.y.: Image Books, 1972), 344–46. The Student Volunteer Movement, made up of college students, formed in 1886 at a Bible study conference at the Mount Hermon School in Northfield, Massachusetts. By the turn of the century, it was at its height of influence and recruited thousands of students as volunteers for missionary work.
3. Hunter, *Sophia Lyon Fahs,* 48
4. Robert T. Handy, *A History of Union Theological Seminary in New York* (New York: Columbia University Press, 1987), 171.
5. Lawrence A. Cremin, *The Transformation of the School: Progressivism in American Education, 1876–1957* (New York: Vintage Books, 1961), 110–15.
6. For an understanding of the significance of the founding of the Religious Education Association, see Stephen A. Schmidt, *A History of the Religious Education Association* (Birmingham, Ala.: Religious Education Press, 1983).
7. Cremin, *Transformation of the School,* 173.
8. Quoted in Hunter, *Sophia Lyon Fahs,* 61.
9. Ruth Miriam Fahs, quoted in Sophia Lyon Fahs, "Our Children's Thoughts of Death," The *Mother's Magazine* (May 1916): n.p.
10. Fahs, "Our Children's Thoughts of Death," n.p.
11. Quoted in Hunter, *Sophia Lyon Fahs,* 130.
12. Handy, *History of Union Theological Seminary,* 125.
13. Harris H. Parker, "The Union School of Religion, 1910–1929: Embers from the Fires of Progressivism," *Religious Education* 86, 4 (fall 1991): 597.
14. Ibid., 600.
15. William R. Hutchison, *The Modernist Impulse in American Protestantism* (Durham, N.C.: Duke University Press, 1992), 2.
16. Sophia Lyon Fahs, *Today's Children and Yesterday's Heritage: A Philosophy of Creative Religious Development.* (Boston: Beacon Press, 1952), 105–7.
17. Ibid., 122–23.
18. Ibid., 8.
19. Sophia Lyon Fahs, "Has Missionary Education Promoted World-Mindedness at Home?" *Religious Education* 21, 2 (April 1926): 176.

20. Sophia Lyon Fahs, "Growth Both Wide and Deep," 1959, Unpublished typed manuscript signed, Meadville/Lombard Theological Seminary Library, Chicago.
21. Fahs, *Today's Children*, 144.
22. Ibid., 135.
23. Cremin, *Transformation of the School*, viii–ix.
24. Hunter, *Sophia Lyon Fahs*, 60.
25. Lawrence A. Cremin, *American Education: The Metropolitan Experience, 1876–1980* (New York: Harper & Row, 1988), 168–70, 501–2.
26. Jack L. Seymour, *From Sunday School to Church School: Continuities in Protestant Church Education in the United States, 1860–1929* (Lanham, Md.: University Press of America, 1982), 79.
27. Hunter, *Sophia Lyon Fahs*, 151–52.
28. Ralph P. Bridgeman and Sophia L. Fahs, "The Religious Experience of Pupils in the Experimental School of Religion," *Religious Education* 20, 2 (April 1925): 106.
29. Sophia Lyon Fahs, "Necessary Changes in Religious Education: Changes Necessary in Elementary Religious Education due to Conflicts between Science and Religion," *Religious Education* 23, 4 (April 1928): 332.
30. Bridgeman and Fahs, "Religious Experience," 101–2.
31. Hunter, *Sophia Lyon Fahs*, 158–61; Handy, *History of Union Theological Seminary*, 172; Parker, "Union School of Religion: Embers," 604–7.
32. Handy, *History of Union Theological Seminary*, 171–72; Harris H. Parker, "The Union School of Religion, 1910–1929: A Laboratory in Religious Education," *Search: Columbia (S.C.) College Bulletin* 17, 3 (July 1968): 33.
33. Sophia Lyon Fahs, "The Future and Religious Education," *Religious Education* 66, 6 (November–December 1971): 457.
34. Sophia Lyon Fahs, *A New Ministry to Children* (Boston: Council of Liberal Churches, Division of Education, 1945), 7.
35. Handy, *History of Union Theological Seminary*, 166, 204.
36. Sophia Lyon Fahs, course bibliographies, 1931–1936, Unpublished typed manuscript signed, Andover-Harvard Library Archives, Cambridge, Massachusetts.
37. Sophia Lyon Fahs, class exercise, n.d., TMsS, Andover-Harvard Library Archives, Cambridge, Massachusetts.
38. Sophia Lyon Fahs, "The Beginnings of Religion in Baby Behavior," *Religious Education* 25, 10 (December 1930): 896.
39. Ibid., 897.
40. See the bibliography of Fahs's published works in Hunter's, *Sophia Lyon Fahs*, 266–70.
41. Fahs, *Today's Children*, 179.
42. Ibid., 179–80.
43. Sophia Lyon Fahs, "Religion in the Public Schools . . . Values at Stake," *Childhood Education* 18, 6 (February 1942): 245–46.
44. Sophia Lyon Fahs, "Some of the Unsolved Problems Inherent in Children's Worship Services," *Religious Education* 20, 5 (October 1925): 383.
45. Fahs, *New Ministry to Children*, 6.
46. Elizabeth M. Manwell and Sophia Lyon Fahs, *Consider the Children, How They Grow* (Boston: Beacon Press, 1940), 182.
47. Sophia Lyon Fahs, *Beginnings of Life and Death: A Guide for Teachers and Parents* (Boston: Beacon Press, 1939), 9–10.
48. Fahs, "The Future and Religious Education," 457–58.
49. Fahs, "Growth Both Wide and Deep," 6.
50. Quoted in Hunter, *Sophia Lyon Fahs*, 130.
51. Fahs, "Growth Both Wide and Deep," 2.
52. Ibid., 2–3.

Hulda Niebuhr

≋

TEACHER AS ARTIST

Elizabeth Francis Caldwell

As believer, the teacher is part of a community that lives in response to God's claim upon it, teaching of God's grace, probably unconscious of the fact that any teaching is going on.[1]

It is certainly true that one can learn how to teach. But some people are born with natural gifts for teaching, for enabling learners to make connections between theory and practice, for stirring imaginations and challenging assumptions. Clara Augusta Hulda Niebuhr was that kind of teacher.

She was born into a family with deep theological roots. Her mother, Lydia Hosto Niebuhr, was the daughter of a pastor in the German Evangelical Church. Lydia Hosto was working with her father in San Francisco when she met and married Gustav Niebuhr, a young pastor assigned to help her father with ministry to the growing numbers of German immigrants arriving in California in the 1880s. The German Evangelical Church environment in which they lived and served and by which their beliefs were formed was strongly committed to religious education for all ages, an ecumenical church consciousness, care for and ministry to persons with illnesses or handicapping conditions, and a zealous piety.[2]

Hulda was born in 1889, the first of four children. The explicit teaching of her father and the more implicit learning opportunities provided in their home by her mother were evident in the Christian formation of the children. A faithful and practicing piety—in the church, in the world, and at home—is clearly evident in the vocational journeys of Hulda and two of her brothers, H. Richard Niebuhr and Reinhold Niebuhr.

Hulda was a bright student, graduating with honors in 1906 from Lincoln High School in Lincoln, Illinois. Continuing her education was not an option allowed by her father, who believed that a college degree represented a woman's desire for emancipation and who said, "What the emancipated woman really desires is neither scientific nor spiritual development, but rather enjoyment, respect, freedom and sport, together with freedom from all the burdensome duties and responsibilities. For the taproot of all emancipation is egoism."[3] The emancipation that Gustav imagined his bright young daughter would discover in college would thus prevent her from becoming a good "marriage prospect for an educated younger man."[4] He did not fear this emancipation for his sons, who were sent to college immediately after high school.

Hulda made her own comment about this when she was asked to respond to her brother Reinhold's interpretation of her father's effect on her education, which was included in June Bingham's biography *Courage to Change: An Introduction to the Life and Thought of Reinhold Niebuhr*. In a letter to Bingham written after Hulda read a draft of the biography, Hulda took issue with Reinhold's statement that she had to wait until after her father had died in order to continue her education:

> I attended Lincoln College in his [Gustav's] time for courses. My professional career I'm said "to have always wanted" was slow coming into picture. If my aim had been what it sounds here, I might have achieved it sooner. College was not as generally assumed for both boys and girls in those days as a few decades later. I was very fully occupied.[5]

Bingham is correct when she comments that "in regard to his only daughter, it simply never occurred to Pastor Niebuhr that a girl might be interested in the kind of professional training he was planning for the boys."[6]

For Gustav Niebuhr, the realm of acceptable vocations for his daughter was contained by the church. Hulda began teaching at the elementary level of her church's parochial school and later worked at a newspaper, saving money for her education. In 1912 she enrolled at Lincoln College, but her studies were interrupted by the death of her father in 1913, when she and Lydia were left without any financial support.

After moving with her mother to Detroit, where they worked in religious education at Bethel Evangelical Church, where Reinhold was the pastor, Hulda decided to complete her college education. She moved to Boston in 1918, completing her bachelor and master of arts degrees at Boston University in the School of Religious Education and Social Service. Hulda was an instructor in the school's Elementary Education Division while working on her M.A., focusing on courses in teaching methods, child development, school administration, and the supervision of teachers. In 1927 she was one of three female assistant professors on the school's faculty. It is clear that Hulda had both named and claimed her identity and authority in her vocation as religious educator.

In terms of practical experience as a religious educator, the most formative period in Hulda's life were the years 1928 to 1945, when she lived in New York City. She began, but did not complete, graduate study for a doctorate in the joint program of the Teachers College of Columbia University and Union Theological Seminary. When explaining to the president of McCormick Theological Seminary in Chicago in 1945 why she did not finish this degree, Hulda wrote, "I had done most of the work needed for a Ph.D. except the dissertation, but Teacher's College was in an era when everything had to be proven by questionnaires and I was not interested in taking a good year out of my life to work on anything that suggested itself within the limitations."[7]

The focus for Hulda's vocation was "practical work in the church," as she called it. From 1930 to 1945, she was employed as a religious educator at Madison Avenue Presbyterian Church, a large urban congregation. "Though her work began as a part-time position with special emphasis on the approach to religion through the arts, by 1941 it had evolved into a position as Associate Director of Religious Education, including partial supervision of four assistant directors of religious education."[8]

In this period, Hulda published material that had grown out of the practical experiences she had gained while writing church school curriculum and teaching in her home church in Lincoln, Illinois; in Bethel Evangelical Church in Detroit, where Reinhold was pastor; and in Boston. She wrote two books—*Greatness Passing By: Stories to Tell Boys and Girls* (1931) and a collection of plays, *Ventures in Dramatics: With Boys and Girls of the Church School* (1935)—and she contributed four articles to the *International Journal of Religious Education*. From 1938 to 1946 she served as an adjunct faculty member at New York University, teaching courses in curriculum, teaching the Bible to children and worship in the church school, and supervision of teaching in the church school.

When the Presbyterian College of Christian Education, associated with McCormick Theological Seminary, contacted her in 1945 about a teaching position as instructor in children's work, Hulda Niebuhr had a wealth of both education and experience at her fingertips. She joined the faculty of the college at age fifty-six, as associate professor of religious education and when the college merged into the seminary in 1949, she became a regular member of the faculty teaching in the Division of Christian Education and Social Work.

In 1953, Hulda Niebuhr became the first woman inaugurated as a full professor. The question that she believed offered the greatest challenge to the field of Christian education at that moment was the one she spoke to in her inaugural address, "A Seeming Dilemma in Christian Education": "Is it possible that a Christian teacher of his religion can do more than merely tell and yet not indoctrinate?"[9]

Her reply was her life's example. Hulda's passion and commitment to nurturing the growth in faith of children and adolescents through religious education, worship, stewardship, and mission are the truest answers to her own question. At a memorial service after her death in 1959, in the chapel on the campus of McCormick Theological Seminary, Clara Augusta Hulda Niebuhr was remembered this way: "Into all of her teaching she put intelligent and helpful Christian concern for the life of the Church and the growth of her students. . . . Professor Niebuhr gave dignity and distinction to the calling of the teacher."[10]

Scholarship and Teaching

Like other women in this book, Hulda Niebuhr's journey to teaching had its foundation in her practice of religious education. In a letter to Harry Cotton, the president of McCormick Theological Seminary, she said:

> I have come to a tested philosophy of religious education that I am in the process of writing down, have developed our own curriculum here [Madison Avenue Presbyterian Church], and I have thoroughly enjoyed the teaching I have done in the latter years in New York University for now I feel I am not talking out of notebooks, but I have hammered out a position that I feel is mine, out of years of experience with many people.[11]

Hulda's work in religious education in three congregations, her teaching experience in two theological schools, her doctoral study, and her writing (articles, books, and curriculum) provided a rich variety of experiences that served as essential preparation for the last leg of her vocational journey. Her path to this vocation, like those of other women in religious education, was not a straight one from a doctoral program to teaching but followed a more circuitous route, with stops along the way.

Though certainly different from the academic norm, Hulda's journey ensured that her teaching and her scholarship were drawn from experience and reflection on the theory and practice of religious education. Her contributions to the field of religious education are more clearly evidenced by the students she taught than in the body of writings that she left. Just as her parents formed her in knowledge and practice of the Christian faith, so she sought to form her students in their role as "sprititual progenitors" of those they were preparing to teach and to lead.

The tenets of faith basic to the German Evangelical tradition in which Hulda's parents raised her became foundational to her theory of religious education. These included the beliefs that (1) the Bible is the Word of God, which can be understood by children, young people, and adults when taught with appropriate methods of instruction; (2) faith is concerned with how a person lives and relates to others; and (3) faith is a concern of both the church and the home and cannot be nurtured and grow without this partnership, so that instruction and experience are as natural during the week as on Sunday.[12]

Hulda Niebuhr's scholarship and teaching provide an excellent example of what would now be identified as a praxis model of education—that is, a model that requires dialogue, reflection on experience, and action in response to that reflection. For Hulda Niebuhr, "talking out of notebooks" would have been unimaginable. Her significance as a teacher and a scholar lies in her choice to invest herself in her teaching and in her students. Her reflection on experience and her writing were important to her but were not her major contribution to religious education. Her mark in this field is evident in her commitment to "educating women and men who would possess the educational abilities to serve the church and the world with a vision for God's realm."[13]

Three concepts served as the priorities for Hulda's teaching and philosophy of religious education: (1) intentional religious nurture, (2) age-appropriate methods for teaching and learning, and (3) the role of the teacher as artist.

Intentional Religious Nurture

When Lydia Hosto Niebuhr received an honorary degree from Lindenwood College in St. Charles, Missouri, in 1953, Hulda Niebuhr delivered a Founders' Day address on the topic of "Spiritual Progenitors." In speaking to the issue of how we share faith with another person, Hulda asked the question "Do we really stand in that line of parents, pastors, teachers, neighbors, citizens whose influence was of such order that they may be thought of as spiritual progenitors, ancestors, forebears, people whose faith kindled the faith of others?" She believed that the role of *spiritual progenitor* was not a matter of age. She contrasted this term with *nominal Christians,* for whom Christianity described their identity but not their practice. Hulda Niebuhr believed that nominal Christians, in their conformity to the world, had the right form but lacked the spirit of their beliefs:[14]

> To say that we are living in a day when we are especially tempted to live conventionally respectable lives, says in effect that we are living in a day of conformity. The rewards seem to go, in many communities, to the teacher, the minister, the politician, the voter, commentator, playwright, who takes no risks in moving counter to prevalent trends.[15]

These thoughts were more than words for Hulda Niebuhr. Madison Avenue Presbyterian Church, where she worked for more than ten years, was actively involved in changing attitudes in the area of race relations. It was in the forefront of social activism on issues of labor, peace, and justice for people. This church held a belief that "a church ought not to be Christian at arm's length"—a belief that extended to the educational priorities of its associate director of religious education, Hulda Niebuhr.

The home of Hulda and her mother, Lydia, was a welcome place, with invitations extended to children of church members as well as to children from the neighborhood. Hulda described their household hospitality in this way:

> These youngsters, mostly from the over crowded homes on the East side, were often in our apartment, serving each other Sunday luncheons, responsible by groups for different courses, or possibly slumber parties. Any trips of mine out of the city were signal for a looked for slumber party—then there was room in the apartment for more girls.[16]

The connection of private and public faith was essential to her belief that "the obedience God asks is seldom something separate from our relations to others."[17] The church and its curricula of worship, education, mission, and stewardship were the context of the living and witnessing community of faith in which Hulda believed it was possible for form to be alive, and not just nominal.

Hulda Niebuhr believed that nurture in Christian faith was a partnership between the church and the home. She addressed the issue of the role of parents in religious education by identifying three kinds of church-school parents. The first group consists of those whose lives are so busy that they leave the religious education of their children to the church, with no recognition of their part in the educational process. "They have eyes to see but see not what is going on in their children's lives or if they do see, they do not realize that there is anything they can do about it. . . . No one has helped them to know the adventure and profit of such an experience."[18]

The second group is made up of those for whom the daily necessity to feed, clothe, and house their children demands everything they have. "They have the best intentions to be good parents but have no time or energy to learn to be intelligent educators and no opportunity to be with the children sufficiently to use what understanding they may have achieved."[19] The call of the church in relation to these parents, Hulda believed, is social before it is educational. "It [the church] must address itself to changing a social order in which privileges are so uneven."[20]

The third group of parents consists of those who "take their work as educators seriously, though at the same time joyously and in the spirit of adventure."[21] Parents such as these, she noted, are involved in a variety of ways in the life and ministry of the congregation.

Hulda Niebuhr wrote the article that delineates these groups, "Parental

Education and the Church," in 1929. The authority of its analysis of parental models of commitment to spiritual formation is still clear today. The description of "harassed parents who must live a tread-mill existence" unfortunately now applies across class lines in this culture.

> We say, we church school workers, that we want the creative cooperation of the home in the religious education of the children. We know that without such cooperation we will not achieve the aims we project, that without close touch with the pupil's home life our teaching will not have root in everyday realities. We recognize that the school has no magic by which the effects of faulty home training can be nullified, that at best we can be only helpers to the home. We understand very well, theoretically, that it is wasteful for us to be about our task in a manner as if the home did not exist. Practically we are likely to ignore it.[22]

For Hulda Niebuhr, it was the partnership of Christian formation in the home and in the church that made possible the unity of the form and spirit of Christian faith, which leads to faithful Christian presence and leadership in the world.

Age-Appropriate Teaching

Hulda Niebuhr was one of the pioneers in thinking about methods of teaching and learning that are appropriate to the age of the learner. She believed it was essential that the congregation "minister to all its constituency."[23] In her practice and teaching of religious education, she found the use of two particular methods of teaching and learning to be most appropriate to children: drama and stories "that will capture the imagination, interpret the biblical text, and open the doors of faith to the children."[24] According to Hulda, the task of Christian education is "to furnish imaginations with the story of salvation so that it may become a part of each individual's own history, absorbed into the context of his own particular life, be he young or older, rich or poor, from east or west."[25]

Hulda believed that the methods a teacher uses to communicate the biblical stories matter greatly in Christian education, and that how liturgy is designed gives clear indications as to whether the congregation wants "to be the church in relation to all its members."[26] She made the latter point most clear in her adamant belief that the analogical children's sermon is "a misdirected effort because it is not understood by children."[27] She contrasted this with "junior sermons," where a good biblical story is simply told. "Through stories, boys and girls identify themselves with people whose experience clarifies, heightens, or interprets their own. They also make their own applications, an opportunity denied them in sermons given to moralization."[28] Her statement that "we bemoan the fact that our church members do not know the Bible, while at the same time we waste opportunities to make it available to them" is unfortunately still true.[29]

The Teacher as Artist

This chapter began with a statement about the difference between innate teaching ability and what can be learned. Some teachers move us by the power of their presentation, their style of communicating information. Hulda Niebuhr modeled her conviction about the role of the teacher as artist in the learning processes that she designed for her classes. Her students remember her well. Reverend Richard Wylie has said, "I knew then she was a pioneer in classroom involvement, and inter-relationships. No assignment was made in isolation from involvement. Students interacted with each other as well as with her. Everything was on a shared basis."[30] Another of Hulda's students, A. Wayne Benson, recalls his frustration about how few notes he was taking in class. He was convinced that he was going to learn nothing. He observes that Hulda's method "was to get us to do our own research and study; not to spoon-feed us."[31]

In advocating the teacher as artist, Hulda Niebuhr sought to engage a student not by telling her or him about a topic but by making it "come alive by leading into experience of that subject."[32] This praxis model of education, which requires students to name their own "knowing" and to reflect on that knowing in light of their experiences, represented a way of learning different from the normative experience of most students at that time. Hulda Niebuhr's student, Mary Duckert, recalls that "she insisted, to the dismay of many, that we operate within an arena of responsible freedom. It was the freedom, not the responsibility, that vexed students accustomed to doing prescribed assignments step by step."[33]

When one examines the connections between what Hulda said about teaching and how she taught, her consistency is obvious. The teacher acts "to help the pupil make the gospel experience his own, its historic context invading the pupil's own, so that the pupil can live in that context, can snare it in imagination and discover for himself its meaning.[34]

Hulda encouraged her students to use their gifts in religious education in service to the church. Her guidance and inspiration have provided the Presbyterian Church with a generation of faithful leaders who have served as educators, ministers, curriculum editors, judicatory leaders, and seminary professors. Robert Worley was one of Hulda's students at McCormick, who returned to teach in the field of religious education. Reflecting on Hulda's legacy as an educator, he said that "she gave a vision of what teaching should look like. The teacher as artist illustrates how she saw everything as having potential for learning: nature, art, drama, story, music. The teacher's role was to put reality together so that students could discover it and make it their own."[35]

The Teacher as Maternal Thinker

A major purpose of this book is to identify the nature and practice of a feminist approach to religious education through the examination of the lives, teaching, and writing of twelve women. For some of these women, including Hulda Niebuhr, *feminist* would not have been used as an adjective to describe their philosophical and methodological approaches to religious education. In writing of them, it is important to name their approaches to the teaching of religious education and to interpret their priorities for teachers and learners in light of those characteristics that are identified in this book as feminist threads.

A Partnership of Teacher and Learner

When asked to recall Hulda Niebuhr's style of teaching, students describe it as "different." The dominant mode of teaching in use during her tenure in theological education (1938–1959) was the lecture. Students were trained to sit, listen, and learn the information that was presented. In contrast, Hulda Niebuhr believed that informed and prepared discussion, based in experience and reflection on experience, was an equally appropriate method for teaching and learning in theological education. One of her students has recalled, "I do not remember a lot of lectures. I do remember that she provided a wide range of experiences, projects, and resources, which we undertook and shared. There was no question about her authority and expertise, but she seemed to be in the role of a fellow learner."[36]

A "maternal thinker" can be defined as one who focuses on three concerns: "preservation of the learner, enabling growth, and nurturing the movement of a learner into the world."[37] Hulda Niebuhr is a vivid example of a maternal thinker. She made her classroom a place of connection, where learners were expected to work as intentional partners, with one another and with the teacher, in a communal commitment to the processes of learning. She believed in the integrity and potential of each learner in her class. One student recalled:

> There was an atmosphere in the class that education was growth and must be related to experience (doing). There was a high regard for the importance of each member of the class—often our projects would be evaluated by our peers. I do not recall anyone ever being humiliated in class. Also, we were encouraged to get out of the class what we put into

it—nothing came from just being there. Consequently, we all learned from our outside reading, from doing our projects, and from each other. Creativity was encouraged, imagination was stimulated.[38]

Hulda Niebuhr's authority as teacher was not claimed in traditional ways, which emphasize the teacher's own knowledge and the power of personality in communicating course content. Rather, it was named and evidenced in her expectation that adult learners be responsible members of a learning community. She advised teachers in the church school and learners in her classes to "know your pupils." She knew her own students through class discussions, assignments, papers, consultations in her office, and informal conversations in her home.

A maternal thinker is also concerned with helping learners to claim their own authority and abilities and to move into the world. Hulda's achievement in this area through her partnership with learners is evidenced by the church educators, lay leaders, seminary professors, judicatory leaders, pastors, and curriculum editors who recall vividly the ways in which she encouraged their thinking and development.[39]

Integrating Life Experiences and Classroom Learning

From her experience as a religious educator in a congregational setting, Hulda Niebuhr knew it was imperative for seminary students to move beyond the classroom in order to learn about theories of religious education in congregational settings. An experiential model of teaching religious education was obviously at the core of her philosophy. For example, a class on adolescents would require, among other things, observation in juvenile court and conversations with attorneys, judges, and social workers about their perspectives on the needs of young people.[40] If a student had an assignment to write a drama for Christmas, she or he was expected first to observe such a drama performed in a congregation. Hulda observed and then gave prompt critique to those of her students who were teaching in a field placement in a congregation. Theory and practice were tightly woven together in her philosophy of religious education.

After her curriculum for junior high school students, *The One Story,* was published for the Christian Faith and Life Curriculum of the United Presbyterian Church in the U.S.A., Hulda responded to the church's need for future writers by selecting a group of students to form a class on curriculum writing. At the end of the class, students were put in contact with curriculum editors in the church, and several class members went on to become curriculum writers.[41]

When Hulda Niebuhr was considering her move to McCormick Theological Seminary in Chicago, she speculated about the challenge of teaching "a homogeneous group of young Presbyterians."[42] She went on to describe the variety of adults in one of the curriculum classes she was teaching at New York University, which included

> a missionary from Latvia, one from Indo-China, the promotion secretary of the Church of the Brethren, a major in the Salvation Army who is supervising the religious education of the Army in eleven states, and the Salvation Army head of the educational work in New York City, . . . a Lutheran and a Methodist deaconess, the supervisor of weekday religious education in Salem, Oregon, herself a Methodist lay preacher, . . . a 40 year-old policeman, . . . an elderly industrialist widow who is superintendent of a Junior department; a young Norwegian who broadcast religious messages to Norway under the OWI during the war, a teacher in the Missionary Alliance Training School.[43]

In her teaching at McCormick Theological Seminary, she worked to ensure that learning experiences beyond the school would enrich the classroom teaching just as they had in the variety of life situations she had encountered among her students in New York City.

Learning Beyond the Walls

Hulda Niebuhr instinctively knew that the invitation to learning cannot be bound by the walls of a classroom. Hospitable learning space emerges wherever teachers are open to the varieties of contexts and spaces for hearing, silence, and speech.

In the Introduction to this book, Barbara Anne Keely suggests that one of the contributions women bring to feminist approaches to scholarship is the unity of teaching, learning, and living, that the contexts of learning extend far beyond the formal classroom setting. An important connection exists between who we are as women and our religious education theory and practice. I am first a daughter, a woman; then a teacher, educator, pastor; and then the appropriate descriptors are added—sister, spouse, mother, friend, niece.

Hulda Niebuhr and her mother made their home together in New York City and on the campus of McCormick Theological Seminary in Chicago. Their practice of inviting students to their house for informal gatherings continued after they moved to Chicago. Children from the seminary community and surrounding neighborhood were often invited to work on art projects with Lydia Niebuhr.

Georgie Frame Madison, who worked as a fieldwork supervisor with Hulda's students, recalls conversations about Chicago politics and Hulda's great enthusiasm for Eleanor Roosevelt and the emergence of the United Nations Committee on Human Rights. She also remembered how "we'd hear about our McCormick/Chalmers Place neighborhood beyond the classroom, especially about the faculty children and their doings, for both Mrs. and Miss Niebuhr were greatly endeared to the children. There were always several sitting on their doorstep."[44]

Hulda often invited students over for refreshments when Reinhold and H. Richard Niebuhr were in town for a visit. In these informal gatherings, space and time for conversation were shared with her quite notable brothers. She shared with her pupils her interests in art and politics and demonstrated her commitment to the smallest residents of the community. She lived what she believed about learning within and beyond the walls of theological education.

A Feminist Legacy

Hulda Niebuhr lived and taught in the male world of theological education. She was different not only because she taught using a variety of methods but also because she was the only tenured female faculty member at McCormick Theological Seminary in the 1950s.

A feminist approach to religious education assumes the authority and power of voice, even when it is singular, female, or spoken in softer or quieter tones. Entitlement, right, and authority have not historically been granted to women and minorities in this culture. Hulda Niebuhr had to use her voice to demand what was hers, both professionally and personally.

By 1946, Hulda had worked professionally in congregational religious education for over fifteen years. She had an equal number of years of experience as a member of the faculty of Boston University and as a lecturer at New York University. The job she was offered in Chicago, at the mature age of fifty-six, was as an instructor in children's work. Her response to the job offer was forthright. She replied that though she felt "that the limitation of 'children's work' you speak of is interesting to me, I feel it a limitation as I like a wider range and have given much time to adolescents and youth."[45] As a result of these negotiations she was hired as associate professor, with salary, housing, pension, and moving expenses provided.

The personal issue that required her explicit voice pertained to housing offered her. Four-story row houses for faculty and administrators surrounded the seminary campus on the north side of Chicago. The dean of the Presbyterian College of Christian Education assumed that since there was not a faculty house available and since Hulda was a single woman, she could live in the dorm with female students.

Hulda began corresponding with the president, Harry Cotton, making it clear that with anticipated visits from her brothers and their families, "we are really not a family of only two," and that the seminary's expectations for her to live in the dorm were not acceptable.[46] Within a year of their move to Chicago, a faculty residence became available for Hulda and Lydia Niebuhr—a home whose hospitality forever changed the nature of relationships among those living in the seminary community.

Hulda Niebuhr died at age seventy on April 17, 1959, a month before her retirement. In a statement that had been prepared for her retirement celebration, Arthur McKay, then president of McCormick Theological Seminary, described Hulda in terms of the marks of a good teacher: "She has been a shining example of the creative and imaginative scholar. Hulda Niebuhr has touched the lives of her students with kindness and generous self-giving."[47] It is significant that a woman in a vocation that was considered traditional for women was recognized by her colleagues as a scholar, whose creativity and imagination would stand as a legacy to all who follow her.

NOTES

1. Hulda Niebuhr, "Is Christian Education True to Its Reformation Heritage?" *McCormick Speaking* 10, 8 (1957): 10.
2. Elizabeth F. Caldwell, *A Mysterious Mantle: The Biography of Hulda Niebuhr* (New York: United Church Press, 1994), 9.
3. William Chrystal, *A Father's Mantle: The Legacy of Gustav Niebuhr* (New York: Pilgrim Press, 1982), 39.
4. Ibid.
5. Hulda Niebuhr, letter to June Bingham, 5 April 1959, *Archiver*, McCormick Theological Seminary.
6. June Bingham, *Courage to Change: An Introduction to the Life and Thought of Reinhold Niebuhr* (New York: Charles Scribner's Sons, 1961), 57.
7. Hulda Niebuhr, letter to Harry Cotton, president of McCormick Theological Seminary, 2 March 1945, in Archives, Jesuit-Krauss-McCormick Library, McCormick Theological Seminary, Chicago.
8. Caldwell, *A Mysterious Mantle,* 59.
9. Hulda Niebuhr, "A Seeming Dilemma in Christian Education," *McCormick Speaking* 7, 1 (1953): 6.
10. "Professor Hulda Niebuhr: In Appreciation," memorial service, April 20, 1959, in Archives, Jesuit-Krauss-McCormick Library, McCormick Theological Seminary, Chicago.
11. Niebuhr, Letter to Cotton, 2 March 1945, 80, 81.
12. Caldwell, *A Mysterious Mantle,* 116.
13. Ibid.
14. Ibid., 91.
15. Hulda Niebuhr, "Spiritual Progenitors," *The Pulpit,* no. 266 (June 1955): 3.
16. Hulda Niebuhr, letter to Ted Braun, 3 February 1959, in Archives, Jesuit-Krauss-McCormick Library, McCormick Theological Seminary, Chicago.
17. Niebuhr, "Spiritual Progenitors," 4.
18. Hulda Niebuhr, "Parental Education in the Church," *International Journal of Religious Education* 6, 1 (October 1929): 13.
19. Ibid.
20. Ibid.
21. Ibid.
22. Ibid.

23. Hulda Niebuhr, "Know Children as Persons," *Christian Century* (3 April 1947): 423.
24. Ibid.
25. Hulda Niebuhr, "Communicating the Gospel through Christian Education," *McCormick Speaking* 11, 6, (1958): 15.
26. Ibid.
27. Hulda Niebuhr, "Red Roses and Sin," *The Pulpit,* (June 1958): 13.
28. Hulda Niebuhr, "Junior Sermon," in *Twentieth Century Encyclopedia of Religious Knowledge* (Grand Rapids: Baker Book House, 1955), 620.
29. Niebuhr "Red Roses and Sin," 13.
30. Richard Wylie, letter to the author, 6 January 1988.
31. A. Wayne Benson, letter to the author, 20 February 1988.
32. Niebuhr, "Is Christian Education True to Its Reformation Heritage?" 15.
33. Mary Duckert, "Interpreters of Our Faith: Hulda Niebuhr," *A.D.* (September 1976): 36.
34. Niebuhr, "Is Christian Education True to Its Reformation Heritage?" 15.
35. Robert Worley, interview with the author in Chicago, Illinois, 29 April 1987.
36. W. Douglas Sampson, letter to the author, 21 April 1987.
37. Sara Ruddick identifies these qualities in her article "Maternal Thinking," *Feminist Studies* 6, 2 (1980): 342–67.
38. Norman D. Nettleton, letter to the author, 28 December 1987.
39. I was teaching a workshop at a judicatory event in Dallas in 1989, and a man came up to me and said, "I'm Norman Nettleton." Norman had been corresponding with me about his memories of Hulda Niebuhr as his teacher, which were still fresh in his mind after thirty years. He told me that his granddaughter, a teenager, had been elected an elder in her church. He thought Hulda Niebuhr would have been proud.
40. Sampson letter.
41. This story was shared by Paul Krebill, letter to the author, 13 April 1988.
42. Hulda Niebuhr, letter to Harry Cotton, president of McCormick Theological Seminary, 11 December 1945, in Archives, Jesuit-Krauss-McCormick Library, McCormick Theological Seminary, Chicago.
43. Ibid.
44. Georgie Frame Madison, letter to the author, 4 April 1988.
45. Niebuhr, letter to Cotton, 2 March 1945.
46. Hulda Niebuhr, letter to Harry Cotton, president of McCormick Theological Seminary, 29 January 1946, in Archives, Jesuit-Krauss-McCormick Library, McCormick Theological Seminary, Chicago.
47. Arthur R. McKay, "Hulda Niebuhr as Teacher," *McCormick Speaking* 12, 4 (1959): 20.

Nelle Morton

A RADICAL JOURNEY

Elizabeth Francis Caldwell

Maybe "journey" is not so much a journey ahead, or a journey into space, but a journey into presence. The farthest place on earth is the journey into the presence of the nearest person to you.[1]

The hills of east Tennessee; the academic environment of Madison, New Jersey; and the women Nelle Morton nurtured in her retirement community in Claremont, California, were all features in the landscape of the journey that she called home.[2] A lifetime of engagement with people, educational institutions, and issues of power and powerlessness convinced her that a new image of "journey" needed to be articulated. Rather than conceiving of journey as a movement toward a destination or goal, Nelle believed it was essential to reverse the process, so that "road-building becomes inseparable from the journey itself."[3] Home for Nelle was not a sentimental return to roots in a particular place but "a movement, a quality of relationship, a state where people seek to be 'their own,' and increasingly responsible for the world."[4]

Nelle Morton was born on January 7, 1905, in the mountains of Sullivan County, Tennessee, and was raised in Kingsport, Tennessee. The house in which she lived with her parents and two sisters and to which she returned as an adult in the late 1940s is more than two hundred years old, built on land passed down through maternal generations.

NELLE MORTON

After graduation from Flora MacDonald College, Red Springs, North Carolina, in 1925, Nelle taught art in the public schools of Kingsport. From 1929 to 1931 she attended Biblical Seminary in New York City, graduating with a master of religious education degree. She worked as a religious educator in congregations in New York and Virginia from 1931 to 1937 and then was called to Richmond, Virginia, where for seven years (1937–1944) she was assistant director of youth work for the Board of Christian Education of the Presbyterian Church in the United States. It was in these formative experiences that her roots in religious education firmly took hold.

Nelle's work in race relations in the South developed in the years from 1945 to 1949, which she spent as general secretary of the Fellowship of Southern Churchmen. The Fellowship was an organization that began in the South in the mid-1930s as an interracial and interdenominational group of women and men who met for discussion, prayer, and reflection about cultural and political issues. By the time of Nelle's leadership, the Fellowship had assumed a more activist role, working in the specific areas of race relations, labor, and rural reconstruction in the South.[5]

After completing her work with the Fellowship, Nelle returned home to her family's Tennessee farm. From 1949 to 1956 she wrote several books and articles, taught physically handicapped children, and developed educational programs for severely mentally challenged children in Bristol, Tennesse.[6] In 1956 she joined the faculty of the Theological School of Drew University in Madison, New Jersey, to teach in the field of Christian education; she remained there until her retirement in 1971. It was at Drew that the evolvution of her faith and experiences took expression in her response to "the woman movement," as she called it. With her own growing awareness of and anger over the position of women in the culture at large and the church's role in discrimination against women's leadership, the focus and direction for Nelle's teaching, writing, and speaking changed.

In *The Journey Is Home,* Nelle documented almost a decade of her thinking related to women, theological language, and the church. In commenting on this work, Rosemary Radford Ruether said that it contained "the best of her spirit, both radical and rooted."[7] Nelle's journey from religious educator to feminist theologian was a natural evolution of her work with students, with women at Drew, at conferences, and of her own thinking and reflection on her experiences as a female theological educator.

Nelle was fifteen years old when, in 1920, the U.S. Congress enacted legislation giving women the right to vote; forty-nine when, in 1954, the Supreme Court declared that segregated education was unequal; and sixty when, in 1965, the former Presbyterian Church U.S. ordained the first woman, Rachel Henderlite, to the ministry of Word and sacrament.[8] During the fifteen years she taught in the Theological School of Drew University, she was the only tenured female faculty member but was never promoted to the rank of full professor. She also knew that, for many years, her salary was lower than that of her male colleagues at the same faculty rank. This was a point of particular irony and a source of great anger to her: "It came clear to me that discriminations I had experienced all my life were not because I was incompetent but because I was a woman."[9]

Nelle's prophetic words and actions have their foundation in her concern with the role of the church in social change, both within itself and in its engagement with the culture. Whether her work was in the peace movement or in racially integrated summer camps for children, families, and college students in the 1940s and 50s, whether it involved the education of mentally and physically handicapped children or confronting the church about patriarchal images and practices that denied women's voice and role in leadership, Nelle's experiences shaped her educational theory and her theology. The roads that Nelle began to build in the areas of race relations, religious education, and the role of women in ministry are far from complete.

Scholarship and Teaching

Many of the theological educators whose stories are told in this book shared two vocational foundations, as did Nelle Morton.[10] The first of these vocational foundations is experience in local church education. Nelle's work as a local church educator both before and after graduate school provided practical experience in working with congregations and their models of Christian education. This is most clearly evident in her leadership of vacation church schools in rural churches in Sullivan County, Tennessee, in 1925 and in Virginia in 1927. The knowledge gained during these summers doubtless influenced her choice of a thesis for fulfillment of the master of religious education degree from Biblical Seminary in New York, "A Synthesis of Theory and Practice in the Evolution of a Daily Vacation Bible School Program."

The second vocational foundation for theological educators is curriculum writing. Creating a variety of curricular resources for use with children and youth was a major focus of Nelle's work from 1949 to 1953, while she lived on the family farm. During 1950 and 1951 she wrote worship resources for junior high school youth in a regular column in the *International Journal of Religious Education*. (As assistant director of youth work for the Presbyterian Church U.S. from 1937 to 1944, she had developed a junior high school camping program.) The Christian Education Press published her curriculum *Living Together as Christians: A Guide for Camp Leaders on Creating Christian Community* in 1952.

Like other women in this volume, Nelle Morton served in the only field that theological faculties would invite a woman to join—Christian education.[11] Transforming this field was a major goal in her agreement to teach in the Theological School of Drew University. She was concerned that traditional Christian education had failed to keep up with modern biblical scholarship: "It had evaded the theological implication of the tradition and had missed the ethic. . . . I believed firmly that there are so many stories in the Bible that are mythological stories and characters, that communicate something that you can't explain, adults don't understand them, but so many children just love them." Nelle was concerned that in the need to tell children the biblical story in terms they could understand, much of the Bible becomes "watered down."[12]

Two factors in particular influenced Nelle's decision to teach at Drew. The first was the commitment of the Theological School to rethinking the field of Christian education and its curriculum. The other deciding factor was her friendship with Alex Miller, who headed the Southern office of the Anti-Defamation League. Her friendship and conversations with Miller reinforced her conviction that the leadership of clergy in local communities was essential to social change. Nelle's passion for religious education and her conviction of the importance of the church's role in confronting and changing discriminatory practices intersected as she designed courses and taught seminary students who were preparing for their roles as religious leaders.

Nelle paid her dues. By the time she joined the faculty at Drew, she had a wealth of experience in both practical work and writing. The foundational work she had completed in education in general and in religious education in particular, as well as her commitment to social change in the area of race relations in the United States, served as essential background for the final focus of her work, from 1968 until her death in 1987: women's issues.

Nelle's unique contributions as scholar and teacher are evident in three areas: (1) the role of listening in learning and teaching, (2) images and concepts in teaching and learning, and (3) the responsibility of the church in general and religious education in particular to work for social change in the culture.

Listening and Becoming

At the heart of Nelle's philosophy of education was a commitment to the activity of listening. Notice the qualities she identifies in this 1960 article:

What does it mean to listen to a child, or to any person, for that matter? When we listen, we extend to a person the courtesy of being attentive and receptive when he talks. . . . One has to be secure enough to afford listening—even to a child. For listening is more than being quiet in order to hear the sound of words, or to give another a chance to express himself. Listening includes respecting another person as a human being and receiving in trust the gift of himself that he offers. . . . In listening one risks becoming involved. Genuine listening invites change. When a person is received as a person it means his side of the communication is carefully considered. His ideas may be approved or they may be rejected, but in either case meeting has taken place.[13]

Implicit in these words that Nelle wrote for teachers and parents of children in the church school are two themes that were foundational to her theology of religious education. The first is God's power and presence realized in moments of real listening. God's grace transforms the conversation partners in their moment of meeting. The second is equality. Inherent in Nelle's belief in the church as a community of faithful people was the concept of mutuality:

> The communal nature of the church itself, includes both the adult and the child in a mutual ministry which the Word brought into being and to which the Word speaks. Therefore listening becomes as important for the adult's becoming as for the child's. Listening to a child may be a means by which God's grace and judgment impart themselves to self-sufficient and pride-prone teachers and parents. It may involve being delivered from exalted self-images and entering the very life of the other.[14]

It is clear that the basis for Nelle's most quoted phrase had its origin in her work with children; in 1974, speaking about the work of women doing theology, she said, "We began hearing one another to speech. We experienced God, as Spirit, hearing human beings to speech—to new creation."[15]

Transforming Images

During a sabbatical year in Geneva in 1962/63, Nelle studied with the Swiss developmental psychologist Jean Piaget. It was during this time that she became convinced that "we live out of our images; not out of our concepts or ideas."[16] She wrote that her research on infant baptism at the Ecumenical Institute at Geneva "led me to the heart of the way symbolic ritual comes alive as participated in by an entire community, including children, before there is comprehension."[17]

Nelle recognized the positive and negative power of symbols and imagery. She believed they had the potential to liberate people as well as to indoctrinate and oppress them. Consider her comments on the power of a transforming and liberating image when it is related to the biblical story and how the Bible is read and taught to children:

> Is the Bible allowed to be biblical? Is it allowed to function as story? As the Bible? Or on the other hand is it literalized by having it parroted back or illustrated? Is it sold short by moralisms and applications? When the wholeness of the story is allowed to become a gift and to do its own work with the child in the child's own way it can become a transport of the Word itself, and its own interpreter.[18]

For Nelle Morton, religious education had the potential to transform lives. Paying careful attention to the images used in teaching was essential. In thinking about teaching and learning with regard to mentally challenged children, she commented on the role of teachers who wait: "They do not talk, they listen. . . . Teaching in this sense as ministry is engagement, a two-way process; teaching is living, exposing, participating, involving."[19]

As with the first concept inherent in her philosophy, listening and becoming, Nelle's work with transforming images in relation to religious education with children became an essential conceptual frame for her feminist theology. "Doing theology is a process of transforming images and symbols so that they can function in the world in which we live, function to heal, redeem, reshape, reforge. Doing theology is acting on the conviction that we have been called to our present time and place to take responsibility for the world and for history."[20]

Prophetic Religion and Social Change

Nelle once told a story of working during the depression in the Plymouth Congregational Church in Brooklyn, New York, after graduating from seminary. Her job as parish assistant in this large, wealthy congregation was to minister to the growing immigrant community that was moving into the church neighborhood. The church had been the pulpit of Henry Ward Beecher. Its rich history, which included the desk on which Harriet Beecher Stowe had written *Uncle Tom's Cabin,* stood in sharp contrast to its present practices toward the poor and oppressed who lived in its neighborhood. Nelle understood that she had been hired to minister to immigrants moving into the community so that the other ministers could "take care of the wealthy people who would commute in."[21]

An important part of Nelle's work was selecting children from the community to attend fresh-air camps sponsored by the Brooklyn Sunday School Union. She made her choices without regard to race, and when she took a group of twenty children to meet a boat that would take them to camp, one child from Jamaica, Verna, was refused permission to go because she was black. Nelle stormed into the church "to get the whole church to protest the Brooklyn Sunday School Union for this discrimination and to withdraw funds. The church wouldn't do it."[22]

The assistant minister and the organist immediately resigned in protest, but Nelle later recalled that the senior minister never made contact with Verna's family to offer the support of the church in this act of discrimination. Nonetheless, he persuaded Nelle to continue in her work until Verna was confirmed, arguing that receiving Verna into the church would be an important step in working against racial prejudice. In reflecting on her decision to remain, Nelle said:

I don't know why I did. . . . When Verna finished confirmation class the board of trustees and the elders of the church would not let her join the church, saying that she would be happier with her own kind. Well, I'll tell you, I just bellowed and I made so much stink that I was fired immediately, they knew that I would ruin all of them if I stayed on. I never had heard that expression before, "they will be happier with their own kind."[23]

For Nelle, it mattered greatly that the church act prophetically in response to injustice as near as its own front door. Her actions in Plymouth Congregational Church in the early 1930s demonstate her beliefs about religious education and prophetic faith. Twenty-five years later she wrote these words:

God has acted. God continues to act . . . through the earthy, prejudiced-prone institution—the Christian church. . . . Response in faith to God is always response in action. Response and action are simultaneous. It is not a matter of achieving a faith and then applying it. . . . But if God is at work reconciling the world then it follows that response is at one and the same time entering into participation in God's activity. Churches become activity-centered when the demands of God's activity are too radical. . . . The wholeness of the church is present where the Gospel is communicated.[24]

History reveals the boundaries and constraints that have sought to keep women and minorities in the place to which the dominant white male culture has assigned them. In both her scholarship and her teaching, Nelle worked consistently to open windows of fresh ideas that would bring new images for all of God's faithful people.

Radical Feminist Threads

When commenting on the impact of "the woman movement," as she referred to it, which emerged in the United States in the late 1960s, Nelle Morton said, "My whole life just fell open."[25]

I was well into my second decade of teaching . . . when the woman movement crested and its profound theological implication dawned on me. The very foundation of my earth shook. Then the pieces of my life began to come together and make more sense than they had ever made. Feminism was not a new cause to me any more than the race issue and the peace issue had been causes for me and the youth people in the South. It merely set me at a new cutting edge to view myself, the universe, and other human beings on this globe in a more radical way, and to raise theological questions I had never dreamed of before.[26]

The Introduction to this book identifies eight threads that contribute to feminist approaches to religious education. These threads describe the realities of the purpose of religious education, the setting in which it takes place, the methodology inherent in the practice, and the goals or expectations for learning. Nelle Morton brings color, texture, and depth to six of these feminist threads while adding a thread of her own to the fabric of theological education.

Integration of Life and Experience

For Nelle Morton, life and faith were inextricably woven together. Her commitments were clear, and she always acted on them. She expected the same from others. Many have called her thinking and acting "prophetic." It is interesting that those who seek to educate the whole person and to live in response to a biblical commitment to which they are called are seen as prophets. We need more prophets like Nelle, to remind us of the radical nature of the biblical faith and God's call to us to integrate what we believe with how we live and act in the world.

An article on "Notable Presbyterians of 1949" in *The Presbyterian Outlook* included Nelle Morton as one of the twelve persons recognized by the Presbyterian Church U.S. She was selected as notable for her leadership and work with the Fellowship of Southern Churchmen. The story concluded in this way:

> Nelle is bored to death by the clap-trap that glorifies the prophets but has lost their source of courage and their power to fit positive and permanent Christianity to the day in which we live. . . . She has had run-ins with complacent individuals which are understandable. But as she has found dormant churches that love the sound of taps more than reveille, Nelle wonders, as do others, Why? In the name of God, Why?[27]

Feminist Religious Education Happens in Community

In 1969 a new course, "Women in Church and Society," appeared in the catalog of the Theological School of Drew University—a course that was very different from those historically offered in the field of religious education.[28] Some have said that this course, taught by Nelle, was the first one offered in a theological school that explicitly affirmed the presence and leadership of women in the church. A student who was in that first class remembered Nelle's effort and courage in teaching the class, as well as the radical step she took by teaching it in the milieu of an all-male faculty and a general lack of consciousness regarding the role of women as leaders in the church:

> As Nelle began to tackle the fundamental issues of discrimination against women and the justice issues raised by this discrimination, the men in the class, and a few of the women, moved from discomfort, to anger, to hostility, to attack. Nelle remained respectful, didn't respond to the per-

sonal aspects of the attacks and continued focusing on the fundamental issues that needed to be addressed. . . . Those of us lucky enough to be in that class were learning a methodology for dealing with differences whether they be sexual, racial, ethnic, or theological, and we learned this not just from the content of the course but from how Nelle treated differences in the course.[29]

Grounded in the Partnership of Teacher and Learner

In 1990, *The Christian Century* published an issue on the topic "In Praise of Teachers." Nelle Morton was the only woman among the nine people who were recognized for their abilities as teachers. Catherine Keller, a professor of theology at Drew University, wrote about Nelle's influence on her life. Keller recalled an academic discussion group on women and religion in Claremont, California, of which she and Nelle Morton had been a part. In speaking of Nelle's presence, she said, "Perhaps I would have become a feminist theologian anyway. But without her it would be a more insecure, more superficially intellectual pursuit, one undernourished by self and by relations."[30]

In recalling Nelle's gifts as a teacher, Keller contrasted her "quiet, sharp, instructive but never dominant presence" with her "deep fidelity to her own questions and communities," which Keller believed "was inseparable from a never-ending process of inquiry, self-critique and transformation."[31] Nelle's commitment to "hearing others to speech" required that she empower the learner's naming of questions and struggle with answers. But equally important in Nelle's role as teacher was her own continued growth, which ensured that the activity of teaching and learning was truly a partnership.

Language Shapes Religious Knowing

Churches have made only slow progress in recognizing and affirming the contribution women have made in leadership, as both clergy and laity. Some changes in thinking and practice have been made concerning language for God and inclusive language used in liturgy. Much slower progress has been made on the issue of how God-language shapes how we name, perceive, and understand God in relationship to humankind. The educational task of exploring how language shapes knowing has fallen far behind feminist theological constructive thinking about God.

When Nelle decided to join the faculty at Drew, she said that she was concerned about the gap between biblical scholarship and the teaching of the Bible in congregational programs of Christian education. During the fifteen years she taught there, another gap became obvious to her: the one that exists between feminist theological perspectives and Christian education.

51

Language for God and the use of image and metaphor became primary issues for Nelle in the last decade of her life, as shown in the essays in her book *The Journey Is Home*. One of the clearest examples of her thinking about how language shapes religious knowing is found in a graduation address, "Holy Spirit, Child Spirit, Art Spirit, Woman Spirit," that she gave at the Pacific School of Religion in Berkeley, California, in 1976. This address is significant in the way in which it illustrates her role as a feminist theological educator. She concluded her speech in this way:

> The prime metaphor of the Biblical confession is "The Word became flesh." But image-wise we made the word a man to symbolize the core of this humanity—this whole people. We pierced his side as living proof that the rib of man, and not the womb of woman, produced the water and blood of birth. The early patriarchs knew the power in blood and sought it in a sheep without blemish or in a man rather than hear or accept the woman in their midst. They perceived man a little lower than God, woman lower than man, and child lowest of all. The illegitimate child who could not trace blood lineage directly through a man was lower than other children. But the male illegitimate ranked lower than the female illegitimate. The female could legitimate blood lineage for her children through marriage and redeem herself. The male child, never! To pursue the image further; it was in the lowest of the low that God came present in this humanity. But the early church fathers could not bear so great a salvation. It would have meant the end of their rulership and dominance. The whole patriarchal structure would have had to crumble so that the one at the bottom could be free to free the whole people. Metaphor shatters the old perception and frees the experience to enter the lives of the most dispossessed of the earth, not in any paternalistic way, but in a way that would hear them to *their own* speech and *their own* autonomy. Jesus said it loud and clear, "Those who have ears to hear let them hear!"[32]

Liberation/Transformation of Church and Culture

The current agenda for Christian religious education appears to emphasize curricula and programs for congregational members. Rather than focusing on the curricula of the church—community, teaching, service, stewardship, prayer, and proclamation—many congregations view Christian education much more narrowly, in terms of church school and youth groups.[33] A holistic understanding of the relationship between religious education, cultural issues, and societal transformation seems to have a low priority for many churches today. Nelle would not have fit into this mold.

In presenting Nelle Morton to the Theological School of Drew University on the occasion of awarding her the doctor of humane letters degree, on March 8, 1984, David Graybeal, a faculty colleague and friend

A Radical Journey

of Nelle, introduced her as "Theologian Teacher of the Church Prophet of God."

> Nelle's lifelong ministry thus has been a ministry of advocacy—for children, for the mountain people, for blacks, for labor, for women. She has sought to "hear into speech" those who could not yet find their voices. Her lifelong style has been confrontational. She has spoken truth to authority, and she has never suffered fools gladly. Generations of students squirmed under her penetrating questions, then went to their tasks sobered and strengthened. Colleagues learned quickly that condescension to her was unwise. Her lifelong calling has been to the role of a prophet. She has been ahead of her time on most issues, calling for an inbreaking into the present of that which is long overdue.[34]

Nelle's embodiment of the intimate connection between religious education and personal and social transformation serves as a model for those children, youth, and adults who are called as leaders for the church into the twenty-first century.

Mutuality in Ministry

One of the first descriptions of the early church can be found in Acts 2:43–47. It describes a time when the believers were "together and had all things in common; they would sell their possessions and goods and distribute the proceeds to all, as any had need. Day by day, as they spent much time together in the temple, they broke bread at home and ate their food with glad and generous hearts, praising God and having the goodwill of all the people."

Noticeable in this biblical passage is the lack of hierarchy. The people who gathered were called *believers,* a word that gives us no indication of sex, age, race, or educational status. We know that in its struggle to survive as a minority group, the early church quickly appointed leaders and offices. Consider the church today in comparison to congregations of the first century. Who is called to be a leader? Whose call to leadership and ministry is not welcomed or recognized in the church? Hear Nelle's words:

> It was out of the radical feminist perspective that I began to see racism, war, poverty, anti-Semitism, class, economics, compulsory heterosexuality, and politics as connected and interconnected for all these are women's issues.[35]

Nelle believed that the church faced a critical crossroads with regard to leadership, youth, women, racial minorities, gays and lesbians. In speaking of the invisibility of women, Nelle argued that what was at stake in the church was not merely reform or improvement: "The stake is far more revolutionary—the recovery of the spiritual and the survival of humankind."[36] Perhaps the thread that impassioned Nelle throughout her life and work, even to the end of her days, was this belief in the equality of all people called for ministry in God's realm.

The Artistic Method
in Teaching and Learning

In the Introduction, Barbara Anne Keely notes the important thread of the integration of theory and practice in feminist teaching. Holding together the content and the processes of teaching is an explicit priority of the theological educators described in this book. Part of this feminist methodology is a very specific approach that has been and continues to be a priority for several of the foremothers in this book—the artistic.[37]

A course taught by Nelle Morton at Drew, "Some Contemporary Expressions of the Church's Ministry," explored the theological dimensions of story, drama, dance, art, and role-play and the relationship of these methods to ministry. Nelle's early work as a teacher in art education, her use of art in teaching mentally challenged children, and her personal love and enjoyment of artistic expression found their way into her writing and teaching in Christian education.

Consistent with her prophetic voice, Nelle examined drama, literature, and the relationship between the church and the artist in an article titled "The Drama of Social Protest":

> Theater audiences seem strangely troubled that all is not well as the contemporary dramatist seeks to articulate in his own paradoxical way what is happening. Perhaps middle-class resistance to modern drama of protest reflects a widespread confusion of religious with the American Way of Life both within and without the church. When a church loses the cutting edge of ministry it loses at the same time any alternative to an offensive attitude toward realistic drama. On the political and national scene, when leaders employ religious terminology they tend to delude people into believing that ideals, long dead, still live. In view of this situation, many saw prophetic action, rather than sophistication, in the late President Kennedy's effort to bring the arts to the White House.[38]

Commenting on the dramatist's commitment to truth without compromise, Nelle said, "A minister may lose churches in loyalty to the Word of God, or jeopardize 'the good he may do' by refusing to ride the structure on a watered-down proclamation; or he may not, and still remain a 'minister of the Gospel.' Some ministers are convinced the *laity* can bear to hear the Gospel and hear it whole."[39]

Consistent with her thinking and writing about issues of race, peace, mentally and physically challenged children, and the voice of women in the church and the culture, Nelle held in tension the prophetic and the artistic. "The true prophet exposes the condition of the situation and the ambiguity of the human heart in such fashion that no one escapes. Every human motive, every human act, the prophetic drama would affirm, manifests in one way or another its own self-seeking and prejudice. Every order in time makes known its own relativity to the extent that judgment hangs over every nation under the sun."[40]

A Feminist Legacy

An essential step in biographical research is identifying those places where the subject is quoted. The genre of writing in which Morton is most often cited is feminist theology, and the phrase most frequently mentioned is "hearing to speech." This phrase captures the essence of Nelle's lifelong commitment to the empowerment of people's voices. Whether she was working for the education of mentally challenged children, the civil rights of African Americans in the South, or the liberation for leadership in the church and the world of all those to whom the church has attempted to deny voice—women, young people, gays and lesbians—Nelle Morton spent a lifetime "hearing people to speech" and thereby to responsible living and acting as agents of change in a world constructed to deny voice to those groups.

But her feminist legacy cannot be limited to that image. Nelle knew from experience that hearing people to speech was but a step in the process of confronting images, contexts, and powers that work to dehumanize human beings. Once a person was heard to speech, she or he was expected to move out from that hearing. The quote at the beginning of this chapter illustrates the consistency of Nelle's thinking, being, and teaching, which is probably her greatest legacy as an educator. The moments of meeting between human beings, regardless of age, sex, color, or physical or mental challenges, have the potential for real hearing, presence, and dialogue. They are the basis for reflecting on thinking and actions in relationship to calls to Christian presence in the world. For Nelle Morton, journeys were not about physical distance on a map but rather about the development over a lifetime of a person of faith, for she believed that "the farthest place on earth is the journey into the presence of the nearest person to you."[41]

Nelle Morton died on July 14, 1987. In her obituary, the *Claremont Courier* described her as a "pioneer feminist, early civil rights and anti-war advocate . . . respected theologian and educator."[42] Her legacy is truly that of being rooted in faith and community and radical in her expectations of those who call themselves faithful. She was an iconoclastic prophet. But as her friends Adrienne Rich and Michelle Cliff remembered, she was equally endowed with the spirit of a "compassionate and courageous warrior . . . a true revolutionary, filled with a love of life and respect for human beings, who dedicated her extraordinary energies to change the social and political injustices of others. . . . Nelle worked from the heart and the mind."[43]

NELLE MORTON

In her book *The Journey is Home,* Nelle said, "I am convinced that to see violence and injustice demands a passionate, forgiving, and committed love. It demands a new way of perceiving and a new way of hearing, which women are already beginning to experiment with boldly."[44]

The last twenty years of Nelle's life were formative in bringing her feminist voice to the church, both locally and globally. Her initiative and guidance in naming the patriarchy that prohibited feminist theology, imagery, and leadership brought the "woman movement" in the American culture squarely into dialogue and confrontation with the church and its unexamined images for God and the role of women.

Even in her retirement at Pilgrim Place in Claremont, California, Nelle's visions and hopes continued to expand. "In living out our vision in the present, we create a new reality for all the past and the future is there."[45] Whether it was challenging norms for dress, seating, and prayer at meals at her retirement community; nurturing young feminist scholars in the Claremont community; or her search for patriarchy-free worship experiences, Nelle was tireless in her commitment to opening windows for new forms of thinking and acting to enter. In 1978 she wrote:

> Now when along the way, I pause nostalgically before a large, closed-to-women door of patriarchal religion with its unexamined symbols, something deep within me rises to cry out: "Keep traveling, Sister! Keep traveling! The road is far from finished."[46]

These words still inspire women and men to challenge assumptions, examine symbols, and hold each other and the church accountable in order to make possible a new world order. This is the feminist educational legacy of Nelle Catherine Morton and still the task of religious education today.

NOTES

1. Nelle Morton, *The Journey Is Home* (Boston: Beacon Press, 1985), 227.
2. See the title of her collection of essays, *The Journey Is Home.*
3. Morton, *The Journey Is Home,* xviii.
4. Ibid, xix.
5. John A. Salmond, "The Fellowship of Southern Churchmen and Interracial Change in the South," *North Carolina Historical Review* 61, 2 (April 1992): 180.
6. The books Nelle Morton wrote during this period include *The Church We Cannot See* (New York: Friendship Press, 1953) and *The Bible and Its Use* (St. Louis: Bethany Press, 1955).
7. Rosemary Radford Ruether wrote this about Nelle's book; it was quoted by Betty A. Thompson in the article she wrote on the occasion of Nelle's death, "Nelle Morton: Journeying Home," *Christian Century* (August 26, 1987): 711.
8. I share similar roots with Nelle, in the South and in the Presbyterian Church. I was in high school in 1964, when the leaders of the congregation where I was a member voted to refuse membership and the opportunity to worship to persons of color. This church was a part of the Presbyterian Church U.S. Re-

fusing to recognize the ordination of women, the congregation left the Presbyterian Church (U.S.A.) in 1989.

9. Morton, *The Journey Is Home*, 191.

10. Hulda Niebuhr, Rachel Henderlite, and Sara Little, as well as Estelle Rountree McCarthy, coauthor of Chapter 4, all brought to their college and seminary teaching experience a practical background in local church education and curriculum writing.

11. It was not until the mid- to late 1980s that theological faculties began to reflect the diversity of the wider culture.

12. Nelle Morton, unpublished interview with Adrienne Rich, (Feb. 19, 22, 24, 1984 at Nelle Morton's house at Pilgrim Place, Claremont, California). Used by permission.

13. Nelle Morton, "Listening to Children," *International Journal of Religious Education* 36, 11 (July–August 1960): 12, 13.

14. Ibid., 76.

15. Morton, *The Journey Is Home*, 82.

16. Nelle Morton "How Images Function," in *The Journey Is Home*, 31.

17. Ibid.

18. Nelle Morton, "Ministry and the Retarded," *Religious Education* 60, 6 (November–December 1963): 441.

19. Ibid.

20. Nelle Morton, "Myths and Truths in Theology," *Presbyterian Survey* (November 1984): 21.

21. Morton, interview with Rich.

22. Ibid.

23. Ibid.

24. Nelle Morton, "Toward the Church's Self-Understanding in Race Relations," *Drew Gateway* 30 (autumn 1959):20–21.

25. Quoted by Karen McCarthy Brown in her introduction in the *Leader's Guide* to the videocassette, *The Journey Is Home* (Louisville, Ky.: Presbyterian Church [U.S.A.], 1989), 20.

26. Morton, *The Journey Is Home*, 191.

27. "Nelle Morton," in "Notable Presbyterians of 1949," *Presbyterian Outlook* 131, 10 (March 7, 1949): 7.

28. The course was described as "an exploration into the rising and persistent question regarding the place of women in church and society. Once the hierarchical structures of ecclesiastical life are called into question, the freedom of men and women to come into a new humanity is opened up. An attempt will be made to examine biblical images that perpetuate the stereotype at the same time that the basic biblical confession transcends them." The course title is important because it reflects Nelle's movement within the field of practical theology. Other courses she taught in Christian education that were in the Drew curriculum include: "The Bible and Christian Education," "Trends in Christian Education," "Race and the Church's Educational Ministry," "Some Contemporary Expressions of the Church's Ministry," "Learning in the Christian Fellowship," "The Church's Ministry and Children," "Worship and Christian Education," "Environmental Learning," and "The Faith of a Child."

29. Diane Deutsch, "Memories of Nelle," in *Leader's Guide* to the videocassette, *The Journey Is Home*, 36.

30. Catherine Keller, "Nelle Morton: 'Hearing to Speech,'" *Christian Century* (February 7–14, 1990):143.

31. Ibid.

32. Nelle Morton, "Holy Spirit, Child Spirit, Art Spirit, Woman Spirit" (graduation address given at the Pacific School of Religion, Berkeley, California, May 29, 1976).

33. Maria Harris identified five curricula of the church in her book *Fashion Me a People* (Louisville, Ky.: Westminster/John Knox Press, 1989). I have added a sixth curriculum of the church, stewardship.

34. David Graybeal, (presentation of Nelle Catherine Morton for the honorary degree of Doctor of Humane Letters awarded by the board of trustees of Drew University) March 8, 1984, in Drew Theological Seminary Archives, Drew University, Madison, New Jersey.

35. Morton, *The Journey Is Home,* 191.

36. Ibid, 197.

37. Attention to the artistic method in teaching and learning, both in theological education settings and in the local church, is also evident in the teaching of Hulda Niebuhr and Maria Harris.

38. Nelle Morton, "The Drama of Social Protest," *Social Action* 32, 4 (December 1965): 10.

39. Ibid, 17.

40. Ibid, 18.

41. Morton, *The Journey Is Home,* 227.

42. "Nelle Morton," *Claremont Courier,* 18 July, 1987, 6.

43. Michelle Cliff and Adrienne Rich, tribute sent to Nelle Morton's memorial, 12 September 1987.

44. Morton, *The Journey Is Home,* 178.

45. Ibid, 198.

46. Ibid.

Rachel Henderlite

A LIFE LIVED
IN RESPONSE

Carol Lakey Hess and Estelle Rountree McCarthy

R achel Henderlite's life was a response to the grace of God, and
that response took on many manifestations.[1] Rachel was a pioneer who cleared many paths for women. She was the first
woman ordained as minister of Word and sacrament in the Presbyterian Church in the United States; she was the first full-time female
faculty member at a Presbyterian Church, U.S., seminary; and she was
the first female president of the Consultation on Church Union
(COCU). Although Rachel did not name herself a feminist, her approach to Christian education includes most of the "common threads"
of a feminist approach, such as that described in the Introduction.

Rachel Henderlite's Life and Work

In an interview conducted toward the end of her life, Rachel stated
that she could not imagine anyone being interested in a lengthy treatise about her life and work—"perhaps a pamphlet," she suggested.[2]
When one looks at the course of her life, one finds that it does seem
often to lack the drama that makes a "good read." A "child of the
manse," she was born in Henderson, North Carolina, on December
31, 1905. From her "growing-up" years on into young adulthood she
lived in Gastonia, North Carolina. Her father, James Henry Henderlite,
was pastor of First Presbyterian Church in Gastonia, and her mother,
Nelle Crow Henderlite, was an active member. Her sister, Virginia,

older by two years, remained a lifelong best friend—even though she humorously noted that the two sisters "could never agree even on how to make up a bed!" Rachel's brother, Jim, was younger than her by four years. The interplay between a loving and stimulating home life and a nurturing congregational life enabled Henderlite to proclaim, "I was a P.K. and I thank God for it."[3]

Rachel's father was her most important mentor, and she was grateful all her life for his part in the shaping of her faith. She enjoyed "many intensive conversations at the dinner table, in [my father's] study, and in the little Chevrolet he used for parish visiting."[4] No doubt some of those informal forums centered on her father's involvement in an early interracial commission that worked to improve the schools that black children attended and on his advocacy for the reunion of the Northern and Southern Presbyterian churches.

In the mid-1920s, Rachel attended Mary Baldwin College in Staunton, Virginia. After two years she transferred to Agnes Scott College in Decatur, Georgia, to be educated in a less confined and restricted atmosphere than was Mary Baldwin's during those years. Though she characterized much of her life up to then as somewhat conservative, at Agnes Scott College she began to encounter folks "who had the gift of flinging open windows and doors to questions" that had never come up before. She recalled how "startling new ideas would sweep in . . . shattering the protective covering of my unquestioning childhood."[5] After a bout with serious illness that was diagnosed as tuberculosis, Rachel graduated with an English major and returned to North Carolina for two years to teach and work with her father. She then completed a master's degree in Bible at the Biblical Seminary in New York (now New York Theological Seminary).

Rachel's faith continued to be broadened by the people she encountered and the material she studied at Biblical Seminary. Her education in biblical studies was particularly exhilarating and, upon her graduation in 1936, "drove" her into teaching. She spent several years "seeing other people captured by the same magnetism that had caught me up in my own study." She taught in camps and conferences, Sunday school classes, women's circles, and she led a businesswomen's class. During the late 1930s she was professor of Bible at two different Presbyterian junior colleges: first at Mississippi Synodical College in Holly Springs, where she was also dean; and then at Montreat College in North Carolina. When she returned home in 1941 to care for her dying father, she also taught in two nearby high schools.[6] It was her experience teaching high school that led to her first two publications. Targeting football players who saw Bible as an easy course, Rachel developed two workbook-style resources: *Exploring the Old Testament* and *Exploring the New Testament*.[7]

Rachel grew increasingly uncomfortable with what she perceived to be her lack of a deep and broad theological education. Bible study had thus

A Life Lived in Response

far been separated from other disciplines of study. "I was hankering to be changed—hungering for something that had been left out of my experience," she explains.[8] After her father's death in 1942, she entered the doctoral program at Yale Divinity School, seeking to provide for herself a stronger foundation for teaching and, in particular, to "see what the Bible meant to the world."

At Yale she was steered in the direction of Christian ethics, which was a major turning point in her life. Her study in this area set the path for much of her later work as a teacher, curriculum director, author, and church leader. She was thus—"blessed day!—put in the tutelage of H. Richard Niebuhr"[9] and his colleagues Robert Calhoun and Liston Pope. Though she felt at sea in her first months at Yale, this was a transforming time for her. Whereas former schooling had been beneficial in supporting and lending strength to what she already knew and believed, Yale was a radical new departure intellectually, and she blossomed in the school's academic rigor and relentless pursuit of truth. Of the time with her mentors she recalled:

> I had never known anything like their lectures. Manifesting ranges of thought and mastery of detail I had never dreamed of, they both destroyed me and re-created me. . . . Then things began to fall into place, and what I had taken with me to New Haven was restored and supported and enlarged.[10]

Rachel's study of Horace Bushnell's *Christian Nurture* validated both the "borrowed faith" of her childhood and her own developed faith that had been enriched by her expanding experiences. Her lifelong trust in the grace of God, God's sovereignty, and God's transcendence coupled with God's immanence was both challenged and filled with more complex meaning. Her mature faith embraced ambiguity and paradox as she struggled to reconcile the judgment of God with God's love, the importance of conviction with the value of openness, and the worth of the individual with the pursuit of truth.

To the disappointment of one Yale professor who tried to steer Rachel in the direction of a university-level teaching position, she accepted an invitation in 1944 to teach as professor of Applied Christianity and Christian Nurture at what was then the General Assembly's Training School for Lay Workers (ATS; now the Presbyterian School of Christian Education) in Richmond, Virginia. At that time ATS was primarily a graduate school, offering bachelor of arts, master of arts, and master of religious education degrees. The majority of students were women training for various non-ordained ministries in the church. Likely her Yale professor's disappointment arose from the fact that she had chosen "typical woman's work" rather than a position at the university level, the more highly valued men's arena.

As professor of Applied Christianity and Christian Nurture, Rachel always felt her most important contributions to ATS were her courses in

Christian ethics, though she had to push to have them included. For many years, ATS was the only Presbyterian Church, U.S., theological school with such courses. During certain faculty sabbaticals at Union Theological Seminary in Richmond, Virginia, she was invited to teach ethics there—rare for a woman in those days.

Rachel's years at ATS embraced some of the most significant events in her career. It was during those years that she wrote what she felt was her most important book, *A Call to Faith* (1955). She further was an organizing member of the first predominantly black Presbyterian Church, U.S., congregation in Richmond, All Souls Presbyterian Church, and became friend and colleague of the pastor, Mike Elligan, whom she named as an important mentor. During her time at ATS, she took part in the civil rights marches on Washington, D.C. (1963), and from Selma to Montgomery (1965). It was also during this time that she was invited to become the first female member of the St. James Society, a prestigious informal group of Presbyterian professors and ministers in the Richmond area.

In Rachel's view, her most significant contribution to the church began during her tenure at ATS. After serving on a committee to form a new Christian education curriculum for the denomination, she was asked to come to the Presbyterian Church, U.S., Board of Christian Education as director of curriculum development (1959–1965). Her leadership in the Covenant Life Curriculum (CLC) is everywhere evident—in its foundation papers, its scope, its design, and its final shape.[11] Rachel recalled that her role in this curriculum development "called for everything I knew and had to give." One of the unique features of this new curriculum was its emphasis on Christian life in addition to the standard emphasis on Bible and church history. This emphasis on Christian life was to play a significant part in drawing the denomination out of the tendency toward "spiritualizing" the gospel, and it would help equip its members to face the oncoming civil rights struggle.

In 1965, while Henderlite was still at the Board of Christian Education, a committee from Hanover Presbytery (Richmond, Virginia), came to her suggesting that she seek ordination to the ministry of Word and sacrament. The Presbyterian Church in the United States had just opened ordination to women, and it was widely recognized that it would be altogether appropriate for Rachel Henderlite to be the first woman ordained. The service of ordination took place at All Souls Church on December 12, 1965, with an overflow crowd of worshipers. Rachel mused later in her life that she heard almost no negative reactions to her ordination, other than from "an old man who must have been a minister in South Carolina who use to send me an unsigned postcard every year in his wavering handwriting, lamenting that I had violated the canons of the Almighty."[12]

Although Rachel considered herself to have been spared grievous discrimination, she did experience poignant moments of gender bias. While teaching at ATS, Rachel was invited to present a prestigious lecture in a local church. The previous lecturers had all been distinguished men. Although she was judged the intellectual peer of the men who preceded her, on the morning of the lecture her gender posed a problem for the church. The men had all given their lectures from the pulpit, which was situated in the center of the sanctuary; but it was deemed inappropriate for a woman to address the community from this exalted vantage point. A makeshift podium, placed at ground level and off to the side, was set up for Rachel, and she was asked to wear a hat. The committee wanted her to offer her recognized expertise without transgressing her station as a woman. Although Rachel didn't balk at the request, she didn't forget the incident. Years later, she was called back to the church to give a baccalaureate address. After ascending the pulpit, she recalled before her audience the time when she was asked to speak and not allowed to speak from the pulpit; she stressed how nice it was *this* time to be able to speak *from the pulpit*.

In 1966, Austin Presbyterian Theological Seminary in Texas asked Henderlite to join its faculty as professor of Christian education. She moved to Austin, and there she continued to live out her concern for the equal rights of ethnic minorities as persons and citizens. Rachel worshiped regularly in a Mexican-American church, and she marched in solidarity with the United Farm Workers on more than one occasion. The embodiment of her life and beliefs is further evidenced by her courses on and involvement in the ecumenical movement. Rachel became deeply involved in the ecumenical movement through her appointment in 1966 to the first Presbyterian Church, U.S., standing committee of the Consultation of Church Union (COCU); she later was appointed one of the denomination's delegates. Although she didn't know about it until years later, she "unwittingly created what was almost a catastrophe" because of her ordained status. Because the Episcopal Church was not yet ordaining women, there had been an unwritten gentlemen's agreement "that none of the churches would send an ordained woman as a delegate to COCU" until the Episcopalians could work it through.[13] Because this hadn't been written down, however, the Southern Presbyterians knew nothing about it. Rachel's presence paved the way for other ordained women to be included in COCU. In fact, ten years later, in 1976, she broke another barrier by being elected the first female president of COCU.

Rachel retired from Austin in 1971 and was made professor emeritus, a singular honor for one who had taught at the seminary for only a few years.[14] For a number of years she lived quietly in Austin with a friend, participating in seminary occasions, especially festive ones. Her health progressively declined, and she died in Austin in 1991, at the age of eight-five.

Themes in Rachel's Writings

There are three themes in Rachel's writings that can be compared with threads of feminism. First, she emphasized community life as the locus of the educational ministry. Second, she pressed for the integration of theology and life. Third, she insisted that the Christian church be a socially sensitive transformer of culture. Included in all these themes is a concern that Christian education, too often taken hostage by a limited notion of "Sunday school," be understood broadly. Rachel further resisted defining the academic discipline of Christian education too precisely. In protest over Campbell Wycoff's attempt to define the field, Rachel wrote that she felt "the strictures of sharp definition coming at me like a vise." Throughout her career, she insisted that "Christian education by its own nature must always be in flux,"[15] and her inaugural address at Austin delivered March 7, 1967 insisted that "We Can't Go Home Again" to the education of yesteryear.

Education Happens in Community

Rachel was deeply concerned that community life be understood as the principal educator for a congregation.[16] She was impatient with Christian education programs that took the "marginal strategies" of the "marginal institution" of the Sunday school as the starting point for faith education.[17] "In my judgment, the only way in which such faith as this can be elicited is through inclusion in a community of faith where the whole life of the community is shaped and governed by the community's commitment to its Lord."[18] This conviction—shaped by her own positive experiences of congregational life (and her experience of Sunday school as inconsequential) as a pastor's child,[19] her work as a teacher and curriculum writer, her research interest in Horace Bushnell's theory of Christian nurture,[20] and her studies at Yale—pervades her writings. "At every age the child will be picking up theological concepts simply from living within the community of faith," she recognized.[21] At the end of *Forgiveness and Hope,* subtitled *Toward a Theology for a Protestant Christian Education,* Rachel challenged churches to take seriously the role of congregational life in an overall program of Christian education:

> This requires that the church think of the curriculum of Christian education as a congregational curriculum, in which the worship and work of the congregation becomes the context and means of nurture. . . . It supports the work of the Sunday school by providing through other channels of the church's life the reality which may be the object of study in the church's school.[22]

The community was, she recognized, a fallible educator. Indeed, along with the possibility of the congregation educating comes the danger of the

A Life Lived in Response

congregation *mis*educating. "And what of the life of the congregation?" Rachel asked. "In what ways does this inform children of Jesus Christ? Is the church split by the difference between its word and its deed?"[23] Henderlite was quick to point out that "our theology is not what we *say* we believe . . . ; our real theology is what we act on."[24] The congregational life is a key curriculum in the education of its members. If there is a disparity between what we say and what we do, what we do is more likely to be internalized, according to Henderlite. She was quite critical of mainline churches that touted a grandiose proclamation devoid of both life and knowledge— plenty of words but little energy, plenty of moralisms but bad theology.[25] "I have never felt the need to apologize for the Christian faith—although many times for the Christian church," she wryly remarked.[26] Presbyterian Sunday schools, with their "extravagant paraphernalia," embarrassed Rachel not only because they were ineffective but also because they reflected a "Bourgeois structure of education" that contributed to the Presbyterian "class church" culture.[27]

Rachel did not give up on the notion of church school, however. She pushed for rethinking its purpose and professionalism. She was bothered that expensive buildings were erected while "we set lower educational standards for the director of education than we do for the preacher" and "keep them [directors of Christian education] out of the official courts [presbyteries] of the church."[28] Rachel, in fact, encouraged women to seek ordination in order to increase their own possibilities for church service. Urging those concerned about the church school to start working out a statement of what transforming faith is, Henderlite advised, "If you believe the educational work of the church has anything to do with shaping this faith, you will already have a clue to the nature of education in the church."[29] She admonished:

> The school will take different forms according to the congregation's need. *When* it meets is not important. What gadgets it has or does not have are of little importance. The significant thing is to recognize the school of the church as the occasion for men and women of faith to come together with their children to reflect upon the meaning of these events in human history through which God has made himself known and through which he has called this fellowship of faith into being.[30]

By exposing the potentially "miseducating" effects of community, Rachel opened the door for naming and fighting the pervasive and corrupting effects of sexist practices. Rachel's consciousness about the miseducational effects of sexist language was raised after her ordination, on an occasion when she chose to use the hymn "God Himself Is with Us." Reflecting on her growing concern for inclusive language for humankind, she admitted that it was still "very difficult to say anything but 'he' about God," due to habit. "The problem," she said, "lies in the limitations of our language. We do not have a personal pronoun that transcends sex." She related how, in a communion service she had recently participated in, she was bothered by continual references to God as "Father". "I found myself wondering whether I ought to say 'Father/Mother God' or every now and then say 'Mother God' instead"—though she concluded that either solution would be difficult for her.[31]

The Integration of Theology and Life Practice

The second theme that Rachel emphasized might now be called "practical theological reflection" in the congregation. She stressed very strongly that a congregation should know its theology and should use that theology in all its decision making and mission. Raised in faith and immersed in the Bible in seminary, she was "eager to open this new world of Biblical thought to other people as it had been opened to me."[32]

Rachel deplored the "lack of theology" that pervaded the Sunday school environment, which stressed good behavior, pious attitudes, and obedience to higher authorities.[33] She wanted to see faith taught, struggled with, and lived. She sought to help Christians clarify both their thinking about theology and their understanding of what contribution theology makes to life.[34] The Bible studies she wrote were clearly devoted toward equipping the community of saints for theological reflection. While not abdicating her authoritative teaching role, she always directed the learner back to her or his own critical interpretive powers. Her guides were "a means to an understanding and enjoyment of the Bible and not an end in [themselves]."[35] Not only did she teach and provide resources for Bible and theology classes in every capacity possible, but her most influential works were a theology of the Christian church for laypersons[36] and two theologically based treatises on Christian education.[37]

In advocating careful theological reflection in the church, Rachel was challenging the status quo. She saw that the church was slipping back "to the medieval concept of equipping the minister to know in order that the people shall not need to know, of urging [the minister] to act in order that the people may be relieved of acting."[38] She perceived that there was a fresh and desperate need to herald the Reformation claim "that the whole church must know the gospel"—and not only know it but live according to their knowledge of it.[39] What was needed for "an appetite for theologizing" to develop was a context in which theology developed "through radical experiments in living."[40] This would empower the whole community rather than exalt the clergy.

As noted, Rachel insisted that a theological orientation necessarily included an ethical impulse. Christian ethics, however, was not a legalistic venture for Henderlite. Though she perceived guidelines, she offered no rigid pronouncements. Christian ethics was a "practical wisdom," in which Christians responded to God's call with discernment in the midst of their lives. And it was based not on righteousness but rather on forgiveness. At the heart of theological vision for Henderlite were love, forgiveness, and hope, all of which were brought to us through the incarnation. It was in Jesus Christ that God both announced the divine love for humanity and showed humanity how to live in a broken and fragmented world. It was by the incarnation, the indwelling with humanity, that God expressed the relationship between faith and life:

> What is the religion of the Incarnation? It is a religion in which because of this central event of history all of our silly distinctions between sacred and secular have to be broken down. It is a religion in which we see that *all* of life is God's, to be transformed by His Spirit. There is nothing so humble, so dirty, that He will refuse to come down to meet it. The stable in which He began life shows us that. It is a religion in which there is no Sunday and weekday, no religious activities and irreligious, no chosen people and unchosen.[41]

It is the guarantee of God's love that frees humanity to acknowledge at the same time its unsuitability and yet its availability for ethical response in life. Grace sets one free *from* the "insatiable yearning to control" and *to* love.[42]

Education for Transformation and Liberation

Rachel believed that a Christian education program that equipped people to think theologically could not be inward-looking, static, moralistic, sheltered, or provincial. She pressed for the "kind of Christian education that will make perfectly clear the relevance of the Christian faith to the overwhelming burden of political and economic problems that face us today, and that may develop a body of responsible citizens, ready to tackle these problems in a revolutionary way."[43] She saw the church as a transforming power in society, and she envisioned Christian education as the primary vehicle for shaping and equipping the community of saints for such a transformative presence.

Although the compelling social issues of the 1960s intensified Rachel's concern that faith be responsive and responsible, the theme of personal struggle and committed response is reflected in her earliest curricular writings.[44] Her tripartite description of Christian faith—God's work for humanity, God's work in humanity, humanity's work with God—culminated in human response to God's activity and initiative. "A call to faith is a call to work in response to God's own work." A call to faith is a call to make a difference in the world, to make theology incarnate—even "a prolongation of the incarnation."[45]

The influence of her mentor H. Richard Niebuhr's paradigm "Christ the transformer of culture," combined with Rachel's earlier predispositions, ultimately evolved into her firm conviction that "the church is for the sake of mission."[46] Mission, she argued, should be understood "in comprehensive terms, as the concerns of God for the world are comprehensive. It covers the whole of life—the spiritual and the physical, the individual and the social, the private and the public, the national and the international, the relationships of [people] and the hard structures of economic and political reality within which relationships occur."[47]

Rachel stated that "Christian education must be education for mission, or it is not Christian education."[48] And she saw that this could only come about with a new vision of the nature, process, structures, and program of Christian education. Despairing of an educational program that for too long had merely preserved the status quo, Henderlite shared glimpses of an educational program designed for living in the world with transforming hope and practice. "Too long have we played at school while the world moves from crisis to crisis," she reproached—but not to dishearten. With positive candor she went on: "I have no doubt that the same resources we have used to play could, if channeled toward equipment for mission, be the means of a radical renewal of the church."[49]

An important event at the COCU led Rachel to be cautious of any attempts to parcel out mission energy. Paul Lehmann, professor of Ethics at Princeton Theological Union in New York, was invited to present an address on racial concerns in COCU, and "he made the remark early in his address that he did not consider the women's problem to be anything like as significant as the race problem." Encouraging COCU not to steer interest away from the race problem by tackling the women's problem, he provoked an uprising among the women. "This is ridiculous; while maybe men can't give attention to more than one problem at a time, women can and it's really all one problem—the problem of liberation," the women protested. Thus was born the Women's Task Force of the COCU.[50]

In her last book, *The Holy Spirit in Christian Education,* Rachel argued for a more prophetic and revolutionary Christian education that depends on the power of the Holy Spirit. Though such education would still focus on the scripture and the practices of the church, it would do so with an intentional openness to the Spirit as God's presence in the world today. She asked:

> Cannot the school of the church become a school of the prophets—
> opening up for disciples, young and old, radical new meanings of life
> under the Lordship of Christ? Can we not teach them to read the letters
> of Paul with eyes that are open at the same time to the pains of our rest-
> less world? Can we any longer play paper dolls at church when the world
> cries out for the Spirit of God?[51]

Henderlite put forth her most visionary proposal for Christian education in her article "Christian Education and Christian Social Ethics," published in 1968. Sounding somewhat battered by the years of "irrelevance" that had prevailed in the Christian church, she felt at the same time renewed by the

Conference on Church and Society, an ecumenical conference sponsored by World Council Churches in Geneva in 1966, which declared the gospel "relevant to the mammoth problems of this century." She looked with renewed hope to "a day in which Christian education and Christian social ethics may come together to assist the Christian layman to make an impact upon this chaotic world." Education in the church was to take four forms: theological education, economic education, political education, and social education.[52] Aware that only a minority might enter her vision, Henderlite was satisfied that such could "serve as agents of a permanent revolution under the Lordship of Christ."[53]

Concerned that we not be imprisoned by the past, Rachel was reluctant to share too explicitly her concrete dreams for Christian education. "Dreams put on paper today will be useless in churches tomorrow," she counseled.[54] Though it may have been true, as she acknowledged, that "the patterns of Christian education that are needed today have not yet been dreamed of," the dreams and patterns Rachel envisioned for a "permanent revolution under the Lordship of Christ" remain useful. Feminists today dream of communities that educate people in justice and liberation, construct patterns for an integrated life of theology and practice, and boldly seek to "make an impact on this chaotic world."[55]

"Miss H." The Teacher

Teaching was the primary way in which Rachel Henderlite understood her life to be a response to the grace of God.[56] Her teaching both issued forth from and embodied the central role of "forgiveness and hope" in her theology of education:

> Teaching can never be defined as simply telling the learner the profound truth the teacher has learned. Nor is teaching simply pointing the learner to where truth may be found. Teaching requires the teacher and pupil to join hands and go out in search of truth together, the pupil set free to search by the teacher's respect for him and confidence in him. The teacher identifies himself with the learner, and is himself ready to learn. . . . This means that the teacher can teach now with humility and boldness. . . . The bitter rivalry that characterizes those who do not know the secret of God's grace is now removed. The fear of losing face is gone, for each one wears his own face no longer, but all wear the face of Christ. A band of self-acknowledged sinners can listen together to the Word of God and search fearlessly for its meaning for their lives, supporting one another in the search, reaching out to include any other sinner who may wish to come up.[57]

Her students' great affection for her resulted in the nickname "Miss H.," a name by which those she taught still refer to Rachel Hendelite. In the classroom Miss H. combined a relentless and reverent search for truth with an unwavering respect for each student in all her or his uniqueness. She echoed themes from her earlier Bible studies when, in a 1989 interview, she talked about the way in which she taught:

> I think what I try to do when I teach is to line up the central issue, the "fors" and the "againsts" of some truth . . . and then let the class see what that issue is and then . . . to try to help them see all the things that were involved in making a decision about it, but to try very hard not to steer them in one direction or another, so that what they come out with will be theirs forever, until they find reason for changing it."

Closely linked with her concern for truth was Miss H.'s insistence on conceptual clarity. She was opposed to language that "covered up" rather than "uncovered." She constantly pushed her students for precision, often reminding them in her own concise prose that "if you can't say a thing three ways you probably don't know what you're talking about!"

One of her great gifts as a teacher lay in evaluation. She had an uncanny ability to discern the quality of the work being presented and to weigh that quality along with the student's ability and the amount of effort expended. Thus she pushed those of both moderate and above-average abilities to work to their *particular* capacity and thereby to experience a sense of accomplishment and self-worth that was specific to them.

In nonclassroom settings, whether at a gathering in her home or at an appointment in her office, Rachel's presence as a teacher was evident and yet not intrusive. And her method in these situations, as in the classroom, was coherent with both content and context. A former student from the Deep South recalls talking to her in the mid-1950s about her discomfort in a yearlong fieldwork assignment at a predominantly black congregation. Actually, the student had come to get Miss H.'s blessing on a change of location. As the student remembers it, Miss H. listened attentively as the student expressed one weak justification after another, until the student's own words convicted her of her irresponsible attempts to avoid some hard moral issues. Miss H. said nothing of any substance the entire time; she simply served as a catalyst to let the student teach herself.

In the final analysis, Rachel Henderlite's power as a teacher both inside and outside the classroom emanated from her own integrated life. She was true to one of her most cherished convictions: "Christian people are tired of their own words when they are not expressions of real life."[58] Similarly, she might have said that Christian teachers are tired of their teaching when it is not an expression of genuine "presence" (Nelle Morton). The partnership of teacher and learner was important to Rachel. The words of the citation she received when awarded the Union Medal by Union Theological Seminary in New York capture this very well:

A Life Lived in Response

In you the grace of good teaching seems naturally akin to the graces of Christian discipleship. Your students may have come to study "under" you, but they stayed to study with you, for that was the only way in which you permitted them to stay.[59]

The Future of Education and the Response of Play

In the last section of *A Call to Faith,* capping off her discussion on Christian response, Rachel introduced "the response of play." "The response of service finds itself supplemented and brought to completion finally in the response of play," she proclaimed.[60] Becoming like little children, in play we allow ourselves to appreciate and rejoice in the beauty of creation, the differences of personalities, and the re-creative embrace of God's nurturing love. "In play, as in worship, we are raised to the highest level of which we are capable—the surrender of ourselves to the world, to our fellow human beings, and to the God who created us."[61]

The category of play resonates very deeply with feminist aims, and perhaps here more than anywhere else Rachel's vision illumines our future. Education for the appreciation of creation, diversity, and re-creation is needed in a world where the earth has been raped, xenophobia reigns, and weariness threatens to overwhelm us. Perhaps the patterns that are needed in Christian education today *have* been dreamed and lived. Perhaps the day is here when we can move "play" from the sidelines and place it more fully in the center of education. Such would be a fitting response to the legacy of Rachel Henderlite.

NOTES

1. See Rachel Henderlite's *A Call to Faith* (Richmond: John Knox Press, 1955), where she develops an understanding of "the Christian ethic of response."
2. In addition to the published works cited, the biographical material in this article is drawn from three sources: (1) Extensive interviews conducted by Robert H. Bullock, Jr., in February and March 1980. Bullock is a former student of Rachel Henderlite's at Austin Theological Seminary. He is currently serving as editor of *The Presbyterian Outlook.* Transcripts of these interviews are available from the Historical Foundation in Montreat, North Carolina. (2) Interviews conducted by Estelle Rountree McCarthy in January 1989, which remain in her possession. (3) Personal recollections by McCarthy.
3. Rachel Henderlite, "Reflections of a P.K.," in *What Faith Has Meant to Me,* ed. Claude A. Frazier (Philadelphia: Westminster Press, 1975), 77
4. Ibid., 77.
5. Ibid., 78.
6. Ibid., 79.
7. These were published by John Knox Press (Richmond) in 1945 and 1946, respectively.

71

8. Henderlite "Reflections of a P.K.," 80.
9. Ibid., 80.
10. Ibid., 80
11. Henderlite was the final writer for Foundation Paper 5, "The Teaching-Learning Process to Be Used in the Educational Work of the Church," put out by the Presbyterian Church, U.S., 1961 Board of Christian Education.
12. Lois A. Boyd and R. Douglas Brackenridge, "Rachel Henderlite: Women and Church Union," *Journal of Presbyterian History* 56 (1978): 14. See also Rachel Henderlite, "Musings on Christian Education [Upon Receiving the Union Medal]," in *Rachel Henderlite: A Pioneer Ministry* special volume of *Austin Seminary Bulletin: Faculty Edition* 99 (May 1984): 10.
13. Boyd and Brackenridge, "Rachel Henderlite," 17.
14. Ibid.
15. Rachel Henderlite, "Elements of Unpredictability Which Create Difficulties in a Precise Definition of Christian Education," *Religious Education* 62, 5 (1967):405–10.
16. It should be noted that Sunday school, the time-honored occasion for Christian education, was never significant in Henderlite's life. She had no memorable teachers, and she much more valued the occasions for informal teaching that took place in her own family circle.
17. Rachel Henderlite, "We Can't Go Home Again," *Austin Seminary Bulletin: Faculty Edition* 82, 7 (April, 1967): 19.
18. Rachel Henderlite, "Asking the Right Questions," in *A Colloquy on Christian Education,* ed. John H. Westerhoff III (Philadelphia: Pilgrim Press, 1972), 204.
19. Henderlite, "Reflections of a P.K." 76–84.
20. Henderlite's doctoral dissertation at Yale was "The Theology of Christian Nurture," a "study of the theology which underlay Horace Bushnell's doctrine of Christian nurture." She wrote this under the supervision of H. Richard Niebuhr.
21. Henderlite, "We Can't Go Home Again," 24.
22. Rachel Henderlite, *Forgiveness and Hope: Toward a Theology for a Protestant Christian Education* (Richmond: John Knox Press, 1961), 116.
23. Henderlite, "We Can't Go Home Again," 25.
24. Henderlite, *A Call to Faith,* 14.
25. Ibid., 12.
26. Henderlite, "Reflections of a P.K." 81.
27. Henderlite, "We Can't Go Home Again," 21.
28. Ibid., 9.
29. Henderlite, "Asking the Right Questions," 203.
30. Ibid., 206.
31. Boyd and Brackenridge, "Rachel Henderlite," 15.
32. Henderlite, "Reflections of a P.K.," 79.
33. Henderlite, "We Can't Go Home Again," 13.
34. Henderlite, *A Call to Faith,* 15.
35. Henderlite, *Exploring the New Testament,* 3. See also Rachel Henderlite, The Epistle of James, Theology Today, vol. 3 (o.s. 60), no. 4 (October 1949) 460–76; idem, *The Church, the Body of Christ: A Guide to Bible Study* (Richmond: Presbyterian Church in the United States, Board of Christian Education, n.d.); idem, *Paul, Christian and World Traveler,* student's book and teacher's guide (Richmond: John Knox Press, 1957).
36. Henderlite, *A Call to Faith*
37. Henderlite, *Forgiveness and Hope;* idem, *The Holy Spirit in Christian Education* (Philadelphia: Westminster Press, 1964).

38. Henderlite, "We Can't Go Home Again," 23.
39. Ibid.
40. Ibid., 28.
41. Henderlite, *Forgiveness and Hope*, 82–83.
42. Ibid., 71.
43. Rachel Henderlite, "Christian Education and Christian Social Ethics," *Austin Seminary Bulletin: Faculty Edition* 83, 7 (April 1968):29.
44. For example, *Exploring the Old Testament* and *Exploring the New Testament*.
45. Henderlite, *A Call to Faith*, 181.
46. Rachel Henderlite, "Mission in the Church of Christ Uniting," *Austin Seminary Bulletin: Faculty Edition* vol. 86, no. 4, (December 1970): 57–70.
47. Ibid., 68.
48. Henderlite, *The Holy Spirit in Christian Education*, 16.
49. Henderlite, "Mission in the Church of Christ Uniting," 70.
50. Boyd and Brackenridge, "Rachel Henderlite," 17.
51. Henderlite, *The Holy Spirit in Christian Education*, 46.
52. Henderlite proposed that such education be *theologically sound* (listening to the word of God that speaks in the present); directed toward the *equipping of the laity* in God's redemptive work (exploratory rather than transmissive); *professionally done* by educated leaders (those trained in theology, the social sciences, and education); *ecumenically based* (preparing Christians for a world vision); *locally based* (not a canned program but one responding to the local situation and immediate problems); and *flexible in organization* (allowing for a variety of patterns of study and action). See her "Christian Education and Social Ethics." 29–41.
53. Ibid., 43.
54. Henderlite, "We Can't Go Home Again," 27.
55. Ibid.
56. Much of the material in this section is drawn from the McCarthy interviews and Estelle Rountree McCarthy's own recollections.
57. Henderlite, *Forgiveness and Hope*, 60–61.
58. Henderlite, *A Call To Faith*, 11.
59. John Jansen, "Rachel Henderlite—Christian Educator," *Austin Seminary Bulletin: Faculty Edition* 99, no. 8, (May 1984): 24.
60. Henderlite, *A Call to Faith*, 195.
61. Ibid., 198.

Iris Cully

IMPARTING THE WORD

Joyce Ann Mercer

Iris V. Cully—Christian educator, theologian, writer—is an unusual kind of feminist. In a time when feminist theologians stress the immanence of God, she talks about God's "otherness." While some feminists seek to leave religious traditions behind in their quest for a nonpatriarchal spirituality, Iris celebrates the rhythm of the liturgical calendar in spiritual life. In an era when ordained office has become both possibility and norm for many feminists who feel called to work in the church, Iris chooses to be a laywoman. And while some feminists of faith treat the Bible with caution and suspicion, she claims that the Bible is at the center of Christian education.

When asked recently about herself in relation to feminism, Iris responded without hesitation, "Yes, I consider myself a feminist. But the question is, would other people? I don't put much of it in my books. I just do it."[1] Much of "just doing it" for Iris involves important "firsts": the first woman in her family to go to college; the first woman to be awarded the doctorate in religion from Northwestern University; the first woman with faculty status at Yale Divinity School; the first woman professor at Lexington Theological Seminary and on any Disciples of Christ faculty; the first woman president of the Association of Professors and Researchers in Religious Education (APRRE).

Iris Cully's Life and Work

Iris Virginia Arnold Cully was born in 1914 and grew up in New York City. She credits her father, James Aikman Arnold, with fostering her appreciation of music and the arts. He involved her in the arts at an early age by taking her to ballet performances, opera, and piano concerts. Iris credits her mother, Myrtle Marie Arnold, with instilling in her a love of drama and theater. This interest in the arts shows up in her later writings on method and curriculum in Christian education.

Iris was baptized in the Methodist Episcopal Church. She identifies as a turning point in her faith journey the moment when Miss Isabelle Kerby, teacher of her Sunday school class when Iris was ten or eleven years old, offered a prayer at the end of class. "Suddenly God became real to me," Iris says.[2] She names Miss Kerby as her first mentor. Kerby's name appears along with that of an eighth-grade public school teacher, Anne G. Hughes, on the dedication page of Iris's 1962 book *Imparting the Word: The Bible in Christian Education*.

In the book's preface Iris explains this dedication, saying, "Through [Kerby's] words and actions God in Christ shone forth, calling the listening child. To do for other children what had been done through her became the background of a vocation. . . . Under [Hughes's] guidance, horizons enlarged. . . . One thinks of these two women with the hope that all Christian teachers may be like them. True teachers impart the gospel of God through their very selves."[3] This understanding of teachers and the teaching vocation runs throughout Iris's writings.

When her family moved to the suburbs in 1928, during her high school years, Iris became active in a Dutch Reformed church that had called a Presbyterian as its pastor. "During high school and college he had me working in every part of the church—perhaps a little too much," she notes. She described the growth-filled struggle that took place for her as she sought to reconcile her personal appreciation for this pastor with her emerging sense that his orthodoxy could not adequately address her questions about Christian faith. "Religion and science were issues for young people at that time," she recalls, "and in college we studied Albert Schweitzer and *The Quest for the Historical Jesus*. That and Christology became my fascinations then." Why did she personally become interested in those topics? "Well, isn't it always the work of the Holy Spirit that draws us to certain things?"[4] She became the first woman on either side of her family to attend college. Iris graduated from Adelphi College in Garden City, New York, in 1936, with a major in English and a minor in religion.

Young Adulthood

During Iris Cully's junior year in college, she says, "it suddenly came to me that I did want to do religious education as a career." She enrolled in the School of Religious Education at the Hartford Seminary Foundation in Connecticut, graduating with a master's degree in 1937. She describes the school as "completely steeped in liberalism"[5] and a good place to learn about religious education. She studied with A. J. William Myers and Edna May Baxter, who, she recalls, "taught the 'how to' courses—seems to be what women did, while the men taught the theory courses." She adds that classes in meditation from Quaker scholar Harnell Hart provided her with techniques she continues to use today in contemplative prayer.[6]

While at Hartford Seminary, Iris met Kendig Brubaker Cully, who earned his bachelor of divinity degree in 1937 and completed his Ph.D. in 1939, both from Hartford. In the interim between her graduation in 1937 and their marriage in 1939, Iris worked as "a D.C.E. [director of religious education] and church secretary combined, because that's what women did then," at Hollis Presbyterian Church on Long Island.[7] Writing about this work she comments, "It was a strenuous experience—as I am sure the first job is for every young person—but it gave me a sense of independence and achievement, a good preparation for equal marriage."[8] During the years Iris and Kendig lived in Massachusetts, their two daughters, Melissa Iris and Patience Allegra, were born. The family later moved to Evanston, Illinois when Kendig took a position on the staff of the First Methodist Church there.

At the time of their marriage, Kendig was ordained as a Congregational minister, and so, Iris says, "I became a Congregationalist. Later, when he was ordained an Episcopal priest, I became an Episcopalian. I had to then. In those days a wife took her husband's religion, especially if he was a minister."[9] The latter change was more difficult for her because of her discomfort with "the Anglo-Catholic attitudes of the Episcopal Church in Chicago toward other religions."[10] She was confirmed by Bishop Stephen Keeler of Minnesota during the Second Assembly of the World Council of Churches in Evanston, Illinois.

In the end, Iris came to value two elements in particular from her Episcopal Church tradition. The first is what she calls "living the church year" through observing the liturgical calendar. This appreciation shows up in her writings, which otherwise have a fairly strong tone of Reformed Church influence. Second, Cully values the Episcopal celebration of the Eucharist on a weekly basis, with its historic liturgy of adoration and praise.

A Theological Education of Her Own

Around 1950, Iris began to think about pursuing Ph.D. studies of her own. When the family moved to Evanston, Illinois, she began studies at Garrett Theological Seminary (B.D., 1954) and in its joint program with Northwestern University (Ph.D., 1955). "I was one woman in a class of one hundred men," she remarks about her time at Garrett. "I don't remember them, but you can be sure as the only woman in the class that they remember me!"[11]

It was at Northwestern that Iris encountered biblical theology through the teaching of her mentor and professor of historical theology, David Shipley. She describes the days of her graduate studies at Northwestern as times of great excitement, in which she and Kendig would sit at the lunch table after her classes, discussing lectures about and readings from the works of John Calvin, Reinhold and H. Richard Niebuhr, Rudolf Bultmann, and Martin Buber. This theological scholarship grounded her work in Christian education, with its focus on the Christian kerygma and the Bible. As Iris puts it, "I appreciate many things about my exposure to liberalism, but I am primarily biblical in my orientation. There's more depth there. . . . I have a greater sense of the otherness of God. The immediacy and immanence of God takes on a sense of wonder in light of the transcendence of God."

Iris was the first woman to graduate with a doctorate in religion from Northwestern. Her doctoral dissertation was titled "A Kerygmatic Approach to Christian Education with Special Reference to Implications concerning Writing Curriculum for Children Ages Three to Eleven," and it became the basis for her book *The Dynamics of Christian Education*.

Pursuing Her Vocation
to Teach and Write

Throughout her years of graduate studies, teaching, and work in churches, Cully wrote curriculum for various denominations, including The United Presbyterian Church in the U.S.A. (now part of the Presbyterian Church [U.S.A.]), the United Church of Christ, and the United Methodist Church. She wrote for the Christian Education: Shared Approaches curriculum and the Christian Faith and Life series.

After her family's move from Evanston to New York City in 1964, Iris taught religious education in several schools (Union Theological Seminary, Yale Divinity School, New York University, and Drew University in Madison, New Jersey). In 1965 she began to teach at Yale Divinity School on a part-time basis. Eventually Cully became the first woman to have faculty status at Yale Divinity School, where she taught as associate professor of religious education until 1972.

In 1971, Iris and Kendig moved to Vermont, where together they founded and edited the *Review of Books and Religion*. In 1976, Iris received an invitation to teach the spring term in religious education at Lexington Theological Seminary in Kentucky. Recalling their decision-making process as a couple, Iris says, "Kendig and I said that whoever had something come first, something full-time, that's where we'd go."[12] After four months as visiting professor, Iris became the Alexander Campbell Hopkins Professor of Religious Education at Lexington Theological Seminary and the first woman on the faculty of any Disciples of Christ seminary.

In addition to those schools where she held a faculty appointment, Iris taught at many other institutions, including Fordham University in the Bronx; Pacific School of Religion in Berkeley, California; St. Meinrad School of Theology in St. Meinrad, Indiana; and the School of Theology at Claremont,

California. The courses she taught were always determined by the people she was teaching. "I have always taught on the Bible and on children. For a while I sort of got typed with that. Later I moved more into 'minister as religious educator' sorts of courses because that was the interest at Lexington."[13]

Iris describes her nearly ten years at Lexington and her work with student ministers there as the high point of her teaching career. There she saw her role as helping these students to see themselves as teachers. Iris is fond of reminding listeners of the Presbyterian designation of ministers as *teaching* elders, as a way of emphasizing the teaching vocation of pastors.[14]

In 1985, Iris and Kendig moved to Pilgrim Place in Claremont, California, launching their retirement by co-editing the *Harper's Encyclopedia of Religious Education.* After a lifetime of partnership that included writing five books together and being founding co-editors of the *Review of Books and Religion,* the *Harper's Encyclopedia* became their final shared work. Kendig died of cancer in March 1987, the volume yet unfinished.

Finishing the *Encyclopedia* in 1990 finally allowed Iris to complete her grief. That is also the event by which she dates her turn toward a more contemplative spirituality. Cully is a member of a lay order of Episcopal women, the Society of Companions of the Holy Cross, who gather each year at their retreat house in Massachusetts and carry on a continuing practice of intercessory prayer throughout each year. Iris Cully's 1984 work *Education for Spiritual Growth* is dedicated to this community "who for a century have both practiced and shared the spiritual life."[15]

Iris names the present time in Christian education and curriculum work "an in-between time," in part because of the current resurgence of interest in the spiritual life. "Everyone is interested in this, but can it be *taught?*" she ponders.[16] Cully asserts that "the spiritual life is nurtured. . . . Persons become nurturers by living in caring communities. . . . Nurturing happens gradually."[17] She remarks further, "A spiritual director is not a teacher but a guide and mentor. Perhaps educators as mentors may be the next wave in religious education."[18]

Iris Cully has traversed many denominations and served in a variety of capacities within the church. Throughout it all, and in spite of her extensive theological education, she has not sought ordination. She states her reason directly and concisely: "My call is to be a layperson *and* a theologian."[19] According to Cully, Protestant women largely abandoned the field of religious education when ordination to parish ministry became open to them. She notes this situation as a necessary reality for women seeking to work in the church, because "after the war, churches had more money and so they wanted someone ordained to do the work. Ordained women tend to leave the field of religious education. Now, of course, the churches have two ordained people—one man and one woman—and the woman will always be the educator, but she isn't necessarily trained for it. And there is no place for the layperson in church work, period."[20]

And yet Iris Cully has clearly made a place for herself, both in the church at large and in the field of religious education. Her impact there and her contributions to scholarship and teaching are far-reaching. She has written eleven books herself and coauthored or edited six others with her husband. In addition, Iris has written numerous book chapters, journal articles, curricula, and book reviews.

A Theorist with Practical Sensibilities

Iris Cully's most significant contributions are twofold. First, she has developed a distinctively *theological* framework for Christian education. This effort comprises one of the earliest theoretical contributions to the field of religious education by a woman. Iris not only generates a theological understanding of the content, method, and context of Christian education but also develops a distinctive theological perspective on teaching. Throughout all of her writings, she calls on Christian educators to utilize the Bible as the Christian community's primary text in church education, educating themselves about scripture with the best of current biblical studies.

Second, Iris's work integrates theory and practice in a purposeful effort to strengthen the educational ministries of the church. For instance, she addresses curriculum issues in terms of the total system of the congregation, against tendencies to think atomistically about curriculum as educating individual learners. She calls for the Christian education program to be a fully integrated part of the church. Finally, she brings together a theoretical perspective on child development with a practical concern for nurturing children in the church.

Let us now consider these contributions to the field of religious education through several key themes from her writings. As these themes unfold, many of the eight threads of feminist approaches to religious education that are identified by Barbara Anne Keely in the Introduction will also manifest themselves.

Kerygma as the Content of Christian Education

It could be said that Iris Cully's 1958 book *The Dynamics of Christian Education* serves as the theoretical grounding for her approach to Christian education, while her subsequent books constitute practical application of that approach to a given area of education, such as children's ministry or curriculum. *Dynamics* puts forth her assertion that proclamation of the good news of God's activity in Jesus Christ—the kerygma—constitutes the foundation of Christian education and is the norm for its content. Education should be about teaching and conveying this message, so that God's action in Christ becomes real both in the lives of individuals and in the world.[21]

The methodology behind Iris's approach holds in tension the liberalism of her religious education studies in Hartford and the neo-orthodoxy of her theological studies at Garrett and Northwestern in a way that relativizes each one. For example, she represents the kerygma as centering on God's initiating action toward humanity, stressing God's freedom and "otherness" in relation to human persons. This neo-orthodox emphasis stands in contrast to liberalism and experience-oriented education, with their starting point in human persons and their present experience.

At the same time, however, Iris's kerygmatic approach does not ignore human needs and experience as critical for education. These play an important part, for example, in choosing a particular artistic medium as a way to invite creative participation among learners. In her approach to religious education, a learner's experience is not limited to the immediate present but includes a sense of history. Iris also utilizes developmental psychology. For her, though, psychological and educational theories are not the starting point for education. Instead, they function as part of the understanding of the total human environment, in which the Spirit of God works.[22]

Participation as the Method
of Christian Education

Iris emphasizes an educational methodology rooted in proclamation and witness to the good news that happens through persons' *participation*. That is, people understand the reality of the gospel as they participate in it and live it out with others. She adopts the language of Martin Buber to describe her relational method of participation, in which learners are subjects rather than objects as teachers engage them in an "I-Thou" relationship. This relationship is patterned on the I-Thou relationship between human persons and God's self-disclosure in Jesus Christ. By participating in that relationship, persons incorporate the gospel message into their lives not simply as cognitive affirmation but as a reality that results in a new way of living.

Iris's educational method of participation and her understanding of teaching exhibit two threads of a feminist approach: partnership between teacher and learner and education as involving the whole person in an integration of life and experience.

Faith Communities as the Context

The church is the context for Christian education, teaching through its worship and its work. Through participation in the church—in its worship and liturgy, fellowship, and service in the world—persons are nurtured in faith. The church context gives Christian education a distinctively theological agenda that differs from "cultural school" education, with its endeavor to prepare good citizens. Christian education, by contrast, is concerned with the nurturing of faith, so that persons can live out their vocations in relation to God's calling.[23] Iris Cully's attention to faith communities as contexts for Christian education reveals another thread of a feminist approach to religious education, namely, that it takes place within a community.

Iris views the church as a community that makes central "the story of God's love made known in creation and redemption through the people of Israel and through the life, death, and resurrection of Jesus Christ."[24] That necessarily places the Bible "at the center of Christian education. . . . This story is our story. It is the foundation and continual support of the church, the Christian community."[25] Whether she writes about curriculum, revitalizing a church education program, or children in the church, Iris always stresses the importance of the Bible in Christian education.

Biblical Scholarship as the Practical Approach

The Bible in Christian Education is Cully's most recently published book. Its title is the subtitle of an earlier work, *Imparting the Word: The Bible in Christian Education.* Of the relationship between these two works she quips, "I had this feeling I had to write it again!"[26] Both books explore the place of scripture in Christian education and call for teachers to employ the best of biblical scholarship toward their own understanding and interpretation of scripture, so that they might provide learners with tools to make the Bible come alive.

Such urgings demonstrate another strand of feminist religious education, namely, the integration of theory and practice, as Iris calls on teachers to connect their theoretical learnings about the Bible with their teaching practice so that the story can be heard and told anew. Her interest in teaching the Bible also implicitly draws forth another strand of feminist religious education: the awareness that language shapes religious knowing. Iris contends that the church possesses a unique set of narratives in scripture that shape the identity of the community sharing those stories. The scriptural narratives thus constitute a particular "language" that shapes religious knowing.

Teachers as Mediators of the Gospel

Teachers are persons who mediate the gospel by being guides and fellow participants with learners in the story of God's redeeming grace. For that reason, the church teaches in part through the participation of children and adults together in the total life of the Christian community. Such a view of teaching assumes that the teacher is a person of faith, not simply one with an intellectual interest in religious ideas. Iris stresses that only a person whose own life has been transformed by the good news can mediate that message to another. Teaching therefore is not a role to be put on but a calling to act as guide and mentor to others within the faith community. It is a vocation. And "teaching is not a task for everybody."[27]

Cully contends that Christian education will not improve until some changes occur in the system of volunteer teaching used by most churches. To make her point, she often invokes the comparison between choir members and church-school teachers: "Choirs rehearse for two hours a week to prepare for that one hour of worship on Sunday morning, yet teachers are often recruited with assurances that it won't take much time or preparation. We need to be honest that good teaching requires preparation time, and then teach people how to do it."[28]

This view of teaching manifests two threads of feminist religious education. First, one can see in the teacher-student relationship a partnership. Second, her model integrates the life experience of the teacher as a person of faith with the activity of teaching, instead of separating what teachers teach from who they are.

Children and the
Church's Educational Ministries

In 1960, Iris wrote *Children in the Church,* in which she "approach[ed] the task of Christian teaching from the position of the parent and the teacher trying to understand both the child and the Christian faith."[29] Similarly, her 1979 work *Christian Child Development* [30] holds together studies on children's development and learning with the concern about how to nurture religious development in children. This is a practical agenda, but Iris integrates into it both a theology and a theory of childhood. She writes of children as first and foremost created by God for the purpose of growing into their vocation as persons who live lives in relation to God. Children are full participants in the church's worship and sacraments and persons who can contribute to the work of the church. Cully's writing on children is distinctive in that it holds together theological and psychological perspectives on childhood.

These concerns about the religious education of children again demonstrate the integration of theory and practice that is a thread of feminist religious education. They also attend to power issues, as Iris advocates that children have a full and significant place within the church. In addition, she challenges those who would trivialize the significance of work with children by continuing herself to write, teach, and theorize about children's ministry.

Curricula in Relation to
the Educational Process

In her book *Planning and Selecting Curriculum for Christian Education,* Iris Cully's approach to educational curricula in the church calls for viewing education in a system. This includes (1) planning and evaluation, (2) certain theological and educational assumptions, (3) teaching and learning opportunities, (4) material resources, and (5) leader development and support.[31] The whole educational process can be hurt by a weakness in any of its parts. Cully develops this extension of systems theory in relation to Christian education and then offers practical help for using such an approach in a church's education ministry.

In addition to the "nuts and bolts" of curriculum selection, Cully also raises the issue of a church's theological and biblical perspective. Within denominations, she writes, there is too wide a range of constituencies to have a single perspective for all in one curriculum. But both children and adults experience confusion when incongruity occurs between the theological and biblical perspectives preached from the pulpit and experienced in the liturgy and those taught in the Christian education program. "The final question to ask is who sets agreed-upon theological interpretations for the curriculum—the teacher (who wants materials that are theologically agreeable), the religious education committee, parents (who have convictions they think should be in the material), or the minister (who is theologically educated)?"[32] Iris Cully thereby raises questions of power in the church's selection and use of curriculum, another aspect of a feminist model of religious education with which religious leaders continue to grapple.

Gender Issues in Religious Education

Although it is not the central topic in most of her writing, Iris Cully attends to the subject of women and education frequently. In *Change, Conflict, and Self-Determination,* for example, she includes a section about women in her discussion of changes within the church. Women may well be in positions of power in smaller churches, she writes, but "not where large sums of money are handled."[33] She notes that when women, ordained or otherwise, are employed by the church, their opportunities for advancement remain limited and their salaries fall below those of men. Always with an eye toward the practical consequences for the church, Iris concludes, "One of the more specific tasks is to rewrite curricular materials in such a way as to change the male and female stereotypes. Another is through broader sharing of working roles in the life of the church. Women will persist in seeking responsibility and power and will refuse to do only traditional work, until a balance is achieved. If women should stay away from the church in protest, the emptiness would be obvious."[34]

In the 1970s, Cully focused directly on the issue of gender in two articles. The first, her presidential address to the Association of Professors and Researchers in Religious Education, calls into question the popular assumption that Christian education is a female-dominated field. She notes the dearth of women professors in graduate programs and professional schools. While women may dominate the ranks of volunteer teachers, "they have seldom been numbered among the theorists who shape the future for religious education"[35] except for children's work and curriculum. She calls on women scholars to embrace the field of religious education: "Since they have never had very much it is foolish for them to scorn what they have while reaching for what they have not had."[36] And she calls professional societies to provide more encouragement for women members.

Iris Cully's writings on women exhibit several threads of a feminist approach to religious education. Feminist religious education leads to liberation and is therefore political. Iris clearly advocates changing the positions of women within the church, society, and the profession of religious education. Another mark of a feminist approach, as mentioned earlier, concerns issues of power. In her attention to the problems women face in the field of religious education and to the portrayal of women in curricular materials, Cully makes constructive proposals for change that would redefine gendered power relations. Such an approach is therefore highly political, although in Iris's case the language of her call for change is more likely to be feisty than acerbic.

A Legacy of
Shaping Feminist Approaches to Christian Education

Iris Cully's legacy can be seen in at least four areas. The first is the continuing presence of women as religious educators and the increase in women professors of religious education in theology schools. Nearly two decades ago, Iris urged women not to abandon this field and prophetically called on professional organizations and seminaries to make the necessary changes to support and encourage women in religious education. She continues to be involved in APRRE and is a mentor to younger women in the profession even after her retirement from teaching.

Second, Iris never allowed the stereotyping of children's education as "women's work" (by implication inferior) to sway her commitment to writing in that area. Today, a new generation of feminist theologians and educators focuses its attention on the marginal status of children in church and society. Renewed energies have emerged around child advocacy among persons working in parent education, children's justice issues, and feminist liberation theologies. Through her consistent efforts to help parents and the church better understand children and faith, and by continuing to write about children during the 1960s and 1970s, when some feminists eschewed the association of women in the church with children's work, Iris Cully kept the door open for the present generation of educators and theologians to focus on children.

A third aspect of Cully's legacy concerns her ecumenism. Her own journey has involved participation in and work with multiple denominations. In her writing she draws from the riches each offers. Thus, for example, she shows a Presbyterian and Reformed appreciation for strong preaching in worship and for giving scripture a central role in education. From her Episcopalian involvement she draws a keen sense of aesthetics in liturgy and a valuing of the rhythm of living out the liturgical calendar. Her interest in Orthodox spiritual practices shows up in her writings on spirituality, as well as when she reminds readers of the power of art in education, with its ability to evoke the ineffable and mysterious aspects of religious consciousness. In an era of increasing denominational retrenchment, her legacy invites contemporary feminist religious educators to engage in a healthy pluralism that celebrates the multiplicity of faith communities and faithful learning.

Fourth, the integration of Cully's life with her ideas provides a model for feminist educators concerned with helping people in churches to negotiate changes in gender roles and to balance the conjoined vocations of career, family, and church participation. For example, the word *partnership* comes up frequently when Iris talks about her marriage. She describes a mutuality in that relationship similar to the kind called for in her theory of teaching—in which both parties learn from and contribute to each other's well-being—and in her view of the church as community. This legacy invites contemporary feminist scholars to integrate what we write about and how we live.

Iris Cully's passions for teaching, writing, and theology are her gifts to the church and the world. She continues to offer these gifts, even in her retirement from professional teaching, as she mentors a new generation of Christian educators through her involvement in professional organizations such as the Religious Education Association and the Association of Professors and Researchers in Religious Education. Cully's contributions to emerging feminist paradigms of Christian education undoubtedly will continue to unfold for years to come.

NOTES

1. Iris Cully, telephone interview with the author, 16 September 1996. Undocumented quotes throughout this essay are from this interview with her. Many of the details of this interview with Dr. Cully may also be found in three sources she generously provided for my use in preparing this chapter: (1) Iris V. Cully, "Persons, Places, and Ideas That Have Influenced Me," *Lexington*

Theological Quarterly 13 (July 1978): 65–74; (2) videotaped interview with Iris Cully, *Alan Moore's Oral History Project,* School of Theology at Claremont, California, 13 April 1987; (3) videotaped interview, *Iris V. Cully and Randolph Crump Miller—Interview at School of Theology, Claremont: Currents in Religious Education in the Twentieth Century,* School of Theology at Claremont, California, 26 October 1992.

2. Cully telephone interview. See also Cully, "Persons, Places, and Ideas," 66–67.
3. Iris V. Cully, *Imparting the Word: The Bible in Christian Education* (Philadelphia: Westminster Press, 1962), 10.
4. Cully telephone interview.
5. Cully's use of the term *liberalism* differs from its contemporary meaning as the opposite of *conservatism.* As she uses it, liberalism denotes a particular theological and philosophical tradition in the United States in which philosophy, various theories of human experience, and the emerging sciences of human development and psychology played a primary role in religious thinking. Theological liberalism stresses divine immanence and harmony between God and humankind. Liberalism in religious education emphasizes the centrality of human experience and humanitarianism, is optimistic about human progress, and places a high value on change. The tradition stands in contrast to *neo-orthodoxy,* which sought to use scripture as its Archimedean axis, emphasized the limits to personal growth and individualism, and stressed divine transcendence. For helpful summaries of both currents of thought in relation to religious education, see W. R. Rood, "Liberalism," and W. Klempa, "Neoorthodoxy," in *Harper's Encyclopedia of Religious Education,* ed. Iris V. Cully and Kendig Brubaker Cully (San Francisco: HarperCollins, 1990), 378–79 and 449–50.
6. Cully telephone interview. See also Cully, "Persons, Places, and Ideas," 68.
7. Cully telephone interview. See also Cully, "Persons, Places, and Ideas," 69; and videotaped interview with Cully, *Alan Moore's Oral History Project.*
8. Cully, "Persons, Places, and Ideas," 69.
9. Cully telephone interview. See also Cully, "Persons, Places, and Ideas," 71.
10. Ibid.
11. Ibid.
12. Cully telephone interview. See also videotaped interview with Cully, *Alan Moore's Oral History Project.*
13. Cully telephone interview.
14. Iris Cully, "Pastors as Teachers," *Religious Education* 74 (March–April 1979): 121.
15. Iris Cully, *Education for Spiritual Growth* (San Francisco: Harper & Row, 1984), dedication page.
16. Cully telephone interview.
17. Cully, *Education for Spiritual Growth,* 166–68.
18. Cully telephone interview
19. Ibid.
20. Ibid. See also Iris V. Cully, "Women in Religious Education: An Overview," *Living Light: An Interdisciplinary Review of Christian Education* 12 (spring 1975): 12–13.
21. Iris Cully's theory appears most fully in *The Dynamics of Christian Education* (Philadelphia: Westminster Press, 1958). See also Iris V. Cully, *Children in the Church* (Philadelphia: Westminster Press, 1960), 55–70 and 118–42, for a practice-oriented restatement of her basic ideas.
22. See Cully, *Dynamics of Christian Education,* 83.

23. Ibid., 29.
24. Iris Cully, *The Bible in Christian Education* (Minneapolis: Fortress Press, 1995), 1. Elsewhere, Cully writes, "The spiritual life is nurtured within community. This does not require living a dedicated life within an enclosed community . . . . For most people life 'in the world' is their existence. Their spiritual life develops within the parish congregation" (*Education for Spiritual Growth*, 136).
25. Cully, *Bible in Christian Education,* 1.
26. Cully telephone interview.
27. Cully, *Children in the Church,* 50–54.
28. Cully telephone interview. See also Iris V. Cully, *Planning and Selecting Curriculum for Christian Education* (Valley Forge, Pa.: Judson Press, 1983), 47; videotaped interview, *Alan Moore's Oral History Project.*
29. Cully, *Children in the Church,* 12.
30. Iris V. Cully, *Christian Child Development* (San Francisco: Harper & Row, 1979).
31. Cully, *Planning and Selecting Curriculum,* 67.
32. Ibid., 82.
33. Iris V. Cully, *Change, Conflict, and Self-Determination: Next Steps in Religious Education* (Philadelphia: Westminster Press, 1972), 110.
34. Ibid., 111.
35. Cully, "Women in Religious Education," 17.
36. Ibid., 18.

Norma H. Thompson

COMMITTED TO INTERRELIGIOUS DIALOGUE

Sherry H. Blumberg

Norma Hoyt Thompson is best described by the Yiddish word *mensch*—a full human being, one whose life is filled with the richness of giving to others. In person, she is an exceptional presence. Humanness, warmth, intelligence, and openness all radiate from her smiling face. She is a woman of faith, a woman of devotion, and a woman of both the practical and the academic world of education. An account of her life and work through the present day and an examination of her writings can only touch on the truly special woman whom these attempt to characterize.

During her exceptional career, Norma Thompson has served as secretary, supervisor of vacation Bible schools, director of children's work, executive director of an ecumenical religious organization, instructor, director of the religious education program at New York University, and professor. This variety of positions represents both the wide range of her interests and her willingness to do whatever is necessary and responsible. She has also written widely and participated in many of the cutting-edge movements in religious education during the latter half of the twentieth century. She has explored the boundaries of interreligious dialogue and has developed a remarkable religious educational approach in a time of unprecedented religious pluralism.

Norma has learned from all of her experiences. Her life experience and her passion for learning have combined the themes of ecumenism, interreligious dialogue and understanding, a passion for both the whole person and the institution. While much of her religious educational experience has been created and developed in community, she has never stopped focusing on the importance of the individual.

While she would not necessarily call herself a feminist, Norma exemplifies rather than espouses the causes that feminists have fought for. She has been a working woman and very respected in her field, as well as the first full-time woman faculty member in the religious education program at New York University. She has used methods that are consensual and relational, rather than competitive, in most of her work.

Her belief that language shapes religious knowing and that religious education occurs in a context that extends beyond the classroom led her to explore religious educational practice from the broadest of perspectives—that emphasizing the whole person, the whole institution, and people's relationships in their own religious community and in the larger, more diverse global religious community. It is one of the reasons that she worked to change the identification of professors of "Christian education" to that of professors of "religious education."

Yet Norma's work was done not as a feminist but as a deeply committed Christian educator, with the feminist principles as a subconscious part of her being. She was aware that how she treated her students and colleagues and how she worked with both lay and clergy within the churches and synagogues was as important as what she taught. These themes formed much of the basis of her life and work, as we shall see.

Early Religious and Educational Experiences

Norma Hoyt was born in 1915 in the small Missouri town of Burlington Junction. She was a child from the middle of the United States, born into a large farming family (she was the third of eight children) of fairly meager means that knew the meaning not only of economic struggle but also of Christian faith and enduring love.

Her earliest religious experiences in her family were varied. Her mother's family belonged to the Reorganized Church of the Latter Day Saints, the group of Mormons who, after the death of Joseph Smith in 1844, rejected the leadership of Brigham Young and his call for a mass emigration to Utah and chose to remain in western Illinois and Missouri. The church's values included the importance of family and community responsibility. Although the family did not attend a church of her mother's denomination, those Mormon values nevertheless became guiding forces in Norma's life.

Her father's family were Methodists. Norma remembers her small Methodist church with its beautiful stained-glass windows. Her aunt taught Sunday school. It was there that Norma developed a wonderful and fundamental connection to Jesus that has sustained her even as her faith has matured and her image of God has changed.

Her parents taught her the importance of loving and helping everyone. Although they lived on a small farm and could not often get to church, Norma was baptized when she was seven or eight years old, in a big lake near the property they farmed. Her memories of that moment, which held enormous power for her, include her recollection of Brother Okerland, who came in a big car and stayed with the family for two to three days. She had expected to "hear the voice of God" as she was dunked,[1] but Norma recalls that she felt special even without such a specific revelation. The baptism and her parents' early teachings reemerged during her career as she blended her life experience and learning.

Norma recalls her love of reading, made difficult by the kerosene lamp in her home and the problem of finding time to study while caring for her younger brothers and sisters. This experience translated into Norma's later patience and understanding for those students of other cultures for whom finding quiet times to study was a challenge.

Even with her family responsibilities, Norma was valedictorian of her school. Although she might have gone to college on scholarship after high school, she decided against it at that time. No one in her family or community expected a young person to attend college. Most girls got married, and most of the boys worked on farms.

Norma took a job with a family that lived six miles from her home, caring for their two children and an aged grandmother. She started a correspondence course to learn shorthand, finance, and typing so that she might find work in a larger town, but she discovered that her eyes were bad and reading was difficult. She also discovered that she needed to study in a more organized and structured environment.

In the spring after her high school graduation, Norma attended the Jackson School of Business in Chillicothe, Missouri, and also worked by caring for two small children. Although her responsibilities left her with little free time, she developed close friendships and met Paul Thompson, who later became her husband. Norma describes Paul as "one of the major religious influences of my life."[2] They shared both a religious journey and a marriage that was almost unique for its time: after twenty-two years it became a commuter marriage, as both partners pursued careers they loved.

Religious Formation and Education

After business school and before they married, Norma and Paul moved to Kansas City to find work, which was difficult at the end of the depression. Because Paul came from a Southern Baptist family, Norma and Paul attended the Centropolis Baptist Church in Kansas City. For Norma, this was "the first experience of hearing about Jesus Christ as a Savior for life after death, saving one from hell and destruction."[3] Her family had always placed an emphasis on how one lived life, and so, Norma says, she "embraced this Jesus as Savior, and became quite a radical follower."

It was also at Centropolis that she met a missionary couple who had been in Africa. Inspired by their work and their faith, Norma would have gone with them when they returned to Africa, to be a missionary, throwing herself into what seemed to be responsible and vital work with human beings who needed the kind of patience and love she had to offer. The couple told her that she needed theological training before she was ready to go with them.

To get that training, Norma and Paul went to the Moody Bible Institute in Chicago. Though Norma received a diploma from Moody, the institute was an uncomfortable fit.[4] Norma remembers Moody's rigidity, particularly its rules against makeup and bobby socks. Acknowledging that she really did learn Bible, which was well taught there, she reflected sixty years later that "rigidity never seemed to be a proper part of what human beings ought to be."[5]

Norma realized while she was at Moody that she would not be able to fulfill her desire to be a missionary in Africa because her life would be with Paul. She began studying Hebrew culture and the Bible in Hebrew. Then she shifted to Christian education. Before attending Moody she had taught in Kansas City at the Centropolis Baptist Church, and after her move to Chicago she taught at an evangelical Lutheran church.

Norma was a successful student at Moody and was chosen to be the speaker for its class of women, but she was unwilling to sign a statement of belief demanded by the faculty and, if not for her election by the women, might not have been allowed to graduate. Paul also refused to sign and so could not graduate. The two began to search for a theological school where Paul's desire to be a minister could be realized and where he could go to college.

The school they chose was St. Lawrence University, a Universalist seminary in Canton, New York. One of Norma's earliest formative experiences there had nothing to do with the educational life of the college but rather with the societal realities experienced by many individuals with whom she would later work. When she arrived, she had no money; in fact, she had sat up all night in the bus terminal in New York City, waiting for her bus. She began working as a secretary for the dean of the seminary, Dr. John Atwood. Too proud to acknowledge her need and ask for help, she had nothing to eat until she received her first paycheck, three days after she began.[6] Until then, Norma had not known what real hunger meant.

A liberal seminary, St. Lawrence had a different atmosphere from Moody. The quality of the teaching was comparable, but the faculty's openness to ideas about evolution and science was exhilarating to the couple. Dr. Atwood was one of the great influences on Norma's growing theology and style of teaching; she both worked for him and took courses from him.

Norma credits his kindness, gentleness, and scholarly guidance as being profoundly important to her. Even though financial problems meant that Paul and Norma only stayed one year, Norma acknowledges this as a turning point in her formation as a Christian educator.

During their year at St. Lawrence, Paul and Norma returned to Centropolis be married in the Baptist church there. Norma recalls that her wedding was a large one, with about six hundred people attending the church's evening service. The wedding was a real family affair, and even the honeymoon that followed was spent with the family.[7]

Since Paul still maintained his desire to be a minister and Baylor University in Waco, Texas, offered free tuition for those going into ministry, the couple moved again.[8] Norma attended classes for a year at Baylor (Paul was not happy with Baylor's fundamentalism), and found work at the Missouri Kansas and Texas Railroad, where she worked in the roundhouse. Still thinking about the ministry, Paul and Norma then moved to New York City so that Paul could attend Union Theological Seminary. Norma attended Hunter College and finished her A.B. in psychology and philosophy in June 1946. She graduated magna cum laude and was elected to Phi Beta Kappa. The couple lived in the dorms at Union.

While a student at Hunter, Norma worked at the Greater New York Federation of Churches supervising the vacation church schools and the weekday church schools. She served from 1944 through 1947 in this capacity, helping to train teachers and sitting in on classes to evaluate the teaching and courses. Norma described the work as something she loved; she had very strong ideas about how teachers should use games and other techniques to make the material appeal to the students. She had taken several classes in Christian education at Moody and St. Lawrence, so here she put into practice her ideas and training.

In Norma's work with vacation church schools, she worked for the first time with African Americans and Eastern Europeans. Her introduction to the variety of peoples and cultures active in the church helped shape her pluralistic approach to religious education, which is reflected in her later writing.

From 1944 to 1945, Norma also worked at the Fifth Avenue Presbyterian Church as director of children's work and assistant director of youth work. This was one of her first experiences with children of the wealthy and privileged, and it furthered her understanding that all people had similar needs and desires. She taught kindergarten and supervised the other grades, working with children of all ages. She discovered that while she loved to work with any age group, she especially enjoyed working with the teachers.

It was here that she discovered the work of Sophia Lyon Fahs, one of the most profound influences on her philosophy of religious education.

Norma described Fahs's writings, the textbooks for Beacon Press, and her ideas about religious education as a "wave of fresh air to my soul."[9] Fahs's ideas helped move Norma toward her more liberal views about religious education. Fahs's theories of religious education fit with Norma's theological position, which was most influenced by Henry Weiman. His theory of religious naturalism, in which God is part of the cosmos experienced in human freedom and morality, appealed to Norma. She states that her concept of God is that God is "the creative force and origin of love in the universe."[10]

To add more religious education theory to the work that she had begun, Norma enrolled at Union Theological Seminary[11] to study with Harrison Elliott and Frank Herriott, as well as Paul Tillich and Reinhold Niebuhr. Dorm rules allowed a husband who was a student to live in the dorm with his wife but would not allow a wife who was a student to live in the dorms with her husband. Thus, Norma and Paul were forced to move out of the dorms. Although she took several courses over the next few years, the financial impact of this move meant that she could not continue full-time studies.

Career Beginnings: Blending Work and Academic Experience

In 1947, Norma was asked to serve as the executive secretary of the Bronx division of the Protestant Council of the City of New York. This position helped shape her ability to work with a wide variety of cultural, ethnic, and racial groups, as she worked with both the poorer churches of Harlem and the wealthy churches of the white community. While executive secretary, she also organized several large ecumenical meetings that brought together different denominations and ethnic groups.[12] This work honed her administrative skills.

It was also during this time that she felt especially challenged by some of the neo-orthodox writings of Karl Barth and Emil Brunner,[13] and so she continued her education at Columbia University Teachers College, where she was awarded her M.A. in 1955. Soon afterward, Norma began a Ph.D. at New York University under D. Campbell Wyckoff and Lee Belford. She recalls D. Campbell Wyckoff as the person who invited her to teach part time at New York University (NYU). He had been helpful to her in many ways, as colleague, friend, and teacher when she worked for the Episcopal diocese and when she began to study at NYU. When Wyckoff moved from New York University to Princeton, Norma joined the faculty at New York University at his suggestion. He continued to influence her with his teachings about the relationship between religious education and humanism during a scientific age.

NORMA H. THOMPSON

A Career of Service

In 1954, Norma joined the religious education faculty at New York University as an instructor. She joined Lee Belford and Sam Hamilton and became the first full-time woman professor on the faculty.

When she completed her doctorate in 1961, Norma became assistant professor; in 1972 she became a full professor. She taught and worked at New York University for twenty-nine years. During that time, the program at NYU changed from an undergraduate to a graduate program as the priorities of the university changed. This change meant fewer students, but Norma continued to teach and work with any who wanted to study and learn. Her courses included "Principles of Religious Education," "Theory and Practice of Religious Education," "Curriculum," "Fine Arts and Religious Education," "World Religions," "Psychology," and "Sociology of Religion." A normal teaching load was six courses a semester. In addition to her teaching, Norma was the faculty adviser to the Religious Education Fellowship.[14]

Despite her heavy workload and shepherding dozens of students a year through the thesis program, Norma's teaching did not become stale. She incorporated a variety of teaching methods, both in the classroom and in the field, taking advantage of unique situations. An older evangelical student, whom the others called Yaweh, was a "preacher" who would speak the "truth" at Times Square on weekends. He sometimes would listen patiently in her "Sociology of Religion" class but at other times would have outbursts of sermonizing about the "truth." Norma tolerated his behavior and remembers another course he took with her, in which she wanted the students not only to read from books but also to meet the people whom the theory affected. In his Rolls Royce, Yaweh drove all the students out to meet with migrant workers, to see how religious education could serve their needs. The mixture of his zeal, the variety of beliefs that filled her classes, and the irony of riding to a migrant camp in a Rolls Royce made a lasting impression.[15]

In September 1974, Norma became director of the program in religious education at New York University. She developed the Ph.D. program and continued to run a school in which students from many different religious traditions and diverse cultural and ethnic backgrounds could come together to learn from her and from one another. She taught, advised, and counseled hundreds of students.

Gabriel Moran taught with Norma after Lee Belford retired. He described Norma as one of the most patient, dedicated teachers he had met and praised her work with students who had serious difficulty writing their dissertations because of the language and cultural barriers they faced. She never lost her calm or resented the extra work that it took to help the student. She had built a vital department that attracted many foreign students, but since it got little support from the university, there were many frustrations. Dr. Moran described how she helped him find time for his own research, writing, and teaching, often protecting him and his time from the numerous administrative duties that could become so consuming.[16]

While at NYU, Norma won the Professor of the Year Award in the late 1970s, given by students and faculty of the School of Education, Health, Nursing and Arts Professions in recognition of her dedication to individual students and of her innovative classes. In 1983 she retired and became professor emeritus; for a long time after her retirement from teaching, she continued to work with her dissertation students until they all had completed their work.

Norma's educational mission included foreign travel, and she lectured at a number of universities. Many of the trips were arranged by former students who wanted her to teach in their native lands, such as Japan, Taiwan, Hong Kong, Thailand, India, and Lebanon.[17]

Major Contributions

One of Norma's contributions to religious education was her ecumenism, that is, her ability to work with and accept all Christians and, later, people of all faiths. She did much of her teaching and writing about interreligious dialogue. Her later work moved beyond dialogue to encourage the acceptance of religious pluralism as a positive force in this world. While she credits this impulse to her parents' "love of everyone," she acknowledges that her contacts with diverse groups were limited for many years; she did not know any Jews or African Americans until she was an adult. Her willingness to be in dialogue with everyone, learning from them as she taught them, created openings for true dialogue between the diverse religious education students at New York University and in the organizations of which she was part. She encouraged the Religious Education Association to be more open to Jews, and as president of the Association of Professors and Researchers in Religious Education from 1976 to 1977, Norma brought a consciousness of religious pluralism to the wider religious education community.

Her work in the area of Christian-Jewish relations included membership on the Committee on Jewish-Christian Relations of the Episcopal Diocese of New York. She also served as a member of the board of directors for the Center for Jewish-Christian Studies and Relations at General Theological Seminary in New York City[18] and was a member of the Commission on Muslim, Jewish and Christian Relations of the National Conference of Christians and Jews.

Norma's work in religious pluralism reached beyond the university and community of scholars in religious education to include the U.S. military. In a speech to the army's yearly conference for chaplains, Norma admitted that religious pluralism was not "a situation that we [Christians and Jews] have chosen. It is something that is happening."[19] In this speech, as elsewhere in Norma's work, part of the power comes from her description of how she herself has had to change when truly encountering the other. Just as she examined her own Christology in the light of her new ability to accept other religions (namely, Judaism) as living religions of today, she suggests that others do the same.

Writings

Norma's writings focused on the whole enterprise of religious education in community, the clarification of the role of theology, and the vital need for religious tolerance and genuine dialogue. Her first published article, "Christian Education Where You Find It," appeared in 1964.[20] In it her holistic approach to religious education and teaching shines through, as she describes the ushers, the choir, and the sexton as all participating in the teaching process. She uses examples of the teaching that goes on in the church doorways and kitchens as well as in the classrooms. Her major points are that (1) the leader's or teacher's words and actions must be in harmony, (2) the whole church and its membership are part of the enterprise of education, and (3) the concept of Christian education needs to broaden to include both the formal and informal aspects of the educational system. This theme was recently repeated in a joint conference of APRRE and REA in New Orleans in 1996; Norma was very much ahead of her time.

To explore the impact of theological positions on religious education, Norma edited the volume *Religious Education and Theology*.[21] She wrote the initial article, which outlined the history and development of the role of theology in religious education and identified the four most important issues in the book: (1) the relationships between theology and religious educational content, methodology, curriculum, and administration; (2) the problems of communication and language between the two fields of study; (3) the impact of the educational process itself on theology; and (4) the growing reality of religious pluralism and how it affects both religious education and theology.

The power of Norma's introduction comes in her affirmation of the term *religious education* to encompass the many terms that various religions traditions use. She acknowledges the reader's emotional attachment to words while still positing a "commonality in religious education which cuts across faiths."[22]

Continuing the theme of the commonality in religious education, in 1982, Norma wrote on "The Covenant Concept in Judaism and Christianity."[23] Here Norma demonstrated her scholarship, tracing the history and writings of the early Abrahamic covenant through the covenant with Jesus, and her consideration of the issue of whether there was "one true" covenant or many. Norma was convinced that the covenant was repeatedly renewed by God, from the time of Noah through Abraham, Isaac, Jacob, on to Jeremiah and then Jesus. Her belief in the renewal of this covenant, the feelings of some Jews that the creation of the State of Israel after the Holocaust was like a new renewal, and the connection of all people to the God of Sinai convinced her to focus on Christian-Jewish dialogue in her work.

Fighting anti-Semitism and prejudice was at the heart of *The Future of Jewish-Christian Relations,* which Norma edited with Rabbi Bruce Cole in 1982,[24] a volume published to honor the work of her NYU colleague Lee Belford. In her introduction, Norma was able to see the irony that churches could condemn anti-Semitism and yet use scripture passages in worship and study that bred or enforced anti-Semitism when read without guidance about their possible misinterpretation. Norma brought an optimism and a faith that raising the consciousness of the synagogue and church about these problems and recalling them to their common prophetic goals of mercy and justice would move Jewish-Christian relations in positive directions.

The same spirit of care and concern for scholarship moving us in the direction of working together in this world is found in *Religious Pluralism and Religious Education,*[25] to which Norma contributed a chapter on "Future Directions." In one of her most summary statements, she noted:

> We occasionally feel the exhilaration of appreciating and understanding the meanings, the values, and the ideas of another religious group. We feel at peace, and the tension drops away. Of course our understanding is fragmentary, and tomorrow we may think we have not understood at all. But a frontier has been crossed, and we can never be the same again.[26]

Her emphasis on dialogue, and on going beyond dialogue to develop courses on world religions is coupled here with her approach of living creatively with the myriad of issues that religious pluralism raises. Norma speaks of her commitment and concern for creating in students and in readers those exhilarating moments that change us forever from persons of faith in our own truth to persons of faith in communication with others of faith.

A Life Worth Living, a Faith Still Growing

Norma continues to be a mensch. Her retirement is not quite what she expected or envisioned (her Christmas letter asks, "Where is the rocking chair on the front porch?"), and she still has an active mind and a soul that shines with great beauty. At over eighty years of age, she has both the wisdom of her age and the unique charm that comes from a life well lived.[27]

It seems fitting to end this essay with one of her favorite biblical quotes: "Not that I have already obtained this [resurrection] or have already reached the goal; but I press on to make it my own, because Christ Jesus has made me his own" (Phil. 3:12).

NOTES

1. Norma Hoyt Thompson, speech presented at a meeting of the Professors of Religious Education on the Eastern Seaboard during the late 1980s. Her words were: "As I was being dunked I half expected to see the skies open and God speak, since I was quite aware of Jesus' baptism." Found in notes she had saved.
2. Norma Hoyt Thompson, interview with the author, September 19, 1996, Great Barrington, Massachusetts.
3. Norma Hoyt Thompson, paper presented at a meeting of the Professors of Religious Education on the Eastern Seaboard.
4. Norma recalls that Paul worked during the evening and attended school during the day, whereas she worked during the day and went to school at night. Because Moody did not allow dating during the first semester, the two would meet and talk at the post office on campus or would attend church together. In spite of not dating, she and Paul became engaged during this first semester.
5. Norma Hoyt Thompson, interview with the author, August 19, 1996, Great Barrington, Massachusetts.
6. Norma knows, on reflection, that the Atwoods would have helped her with money, because they were very generous. The Atwoods became like parents away from home to the couple, and for Norma's wedding, the family bought the materials for the wedding dress and the Atwood's daughter made it. From Thompson interview, August 19, 1996.
7. Norma's sister was a bridesmaid. Paul and Norma borrowed her mother's ring, since they had no money to buy a ring. They had stayed with Paul's family that Christmas until their marriage on December 28, and then they took Paul's little sister and brother with them to her family. There they picked up two more children and so had five little children with them on their honeymoon. From Thompson interview, August 19, 1996.
8. Paul's theological beliefs were already very influenced by his love of and interest in science. At Baylor, Paul began to study theology and Bible but found he could not continue. He moved to Baylor's physics program, where he earned his degree in physics and also worked as a student assistant.
9. Thompson, speech presented at a meeting of the Professors of Religious Education on the Eastern Seaboard.
10. Norma Hoyt Thompson, interview with the author via telephone, 9 December 1996.
11. During this time, Paul was teaching at Columbia University and taking more courses in math and science.
12. At one of the meetings, Mrs. Eleanor Roosevelt was presented with a copy of the Revised Standard Version of the Bible. Norma remembered this especially because she, too, received her copy at this meeting.
13. Norma talked about these developments in religious education and the publication of Randolph Crump Miller's book as the stimuli that motivated her to

edit the volume *Religious Education and Theology*. From Thompson, speech presented at a meeting of the Professors of Religious Education on the Eastern Seaboard.

14. The Religious Education Fellowship was a group of alumni and students who would meet several times a year and hold programs emphasizing challenging new ideas and techniques in religious education and suggestions on how to get published. They would even celebrate many different holidays together.

15. Thompson interview, 9 December 1996.

16. Gabriel Moran, interview with the author, 1 December 1996, Montauk, New York.

17. She also taught at three South Korean universities in 1983. This was a return to the Far East for Norma; in 1965 she had gone to Thailand under the sponsorship of the World Council of Christian Education. She had co-workers and former students all over the world.

18. Norma was awarded an honorary doctor of divinity degree by New York Theological Seminary for her work in this area.

19. From a draft of a speech in Norma Thompson's files, delivered to the U.S. Army conference for chaplains after she retired in 1983.

20. Norma Thompson, "Christian Education Where You Find It," *International Journal of Religious Education* 41, 3 (November 1964): 6–8+.

21. Norma Thompson, ed., *Religious Education and Theology* (Birmingham, Ala.: Religious Education Press, 1989).

22. Ibid., 15.

23. Norma Thompson, "The Covenant Concept in Judaism and Christianity," *Anglican Theological Review* (1982): vol. XLIV, no. 4, 502–24.

24. Norma Thompson and Bruce Cole, *The Future of Jewish-Christian Relations* (Schenectady, NY: Character Research Press, 1982).

25. Norma Thompson, *Religious Pluralism and Religious Education* (Birmingham, Ala.: Religious Education Press, 1988).

26. Ibid., 301–2.

27. Norma's retirement has not been inactive. She and Paul finally live together full time, in their beautiful old home in Great Barrington, Massachusetts. While Norma was based in New York, Paul was a professor in Georgia, and so they had an early commuting marriage. They both worked at their jobs and would meet on weekends in New York and then later at their home in Great Barrington. They had no children of their own, at a time when marriage almost inevitably resulted in children (although they have become like parents to many of their students), and they even had a foster child, Kim Yung, whom they helped for many years. They have kept up the close relationship with her to this day. She and Paul were very busy with careers and with their research and teaching until they retired and it is now, when others are letting go of household work, that Norma fills her time with "cooking, cleaning, yard work, and other mundane chores."

Norma and Paul's home reflects their vitality, scholarship, and warmth. There are beautiful carved wooden pieces of furniture; books; musical instruments; records, tapes, and CDs; clocks; telescopes; and artifacts from their world travels. Often they open their home to visitors from around the world and to the civic activities that they sponsor. Paul plays tennis, as he long has, and Norma is vitally active in both the Great Barrington Historical Society, where she has worked to include minority members on the board, and the interfaith committee of her local church.

Olivia Pearl Stokes

A LIVING TESTIMONY OF FAITH

Yolanda Y. Smith and Mary Elizabeth Mullino Moore

My first lesson in race relations came when I was about five years old on my family's 300 acre farm in North Carolina. Mother told my brother and myself that we didn't have to carry drinking water to the hired farm hands on our farm if they said nasty words to us or called us ugly names. Those farm hands were local white men working for the Stokeses on nine family farms, most frequently called "The Stokes Place." Mother meant if we were called "niggers." That experience was my first conscious lesson in human dignity and racial difference.[1]

With these words, Olivia Pearl Stokes introduces herself. Throughout her life, Olivia embodied both her mother's lesson of human dignity and the strong faith commitments of her family. In this context of family and faith, Olivia grew to be a woman of strength, and a woman who would give her life to enhancing the dignity and worth of others.

Roots and Education

Born on January 11, 1916, Olivia grew up on the Stokes Place, her identity planted in the soil of Middlesex, North Carolina, where she spent her earliest years. She knew from an early age that her identity was tied to that of her family. She said of those years, "We were Stokeses and were to be treated with dignity, equality, worth and human kindness."[2] The values of the Stokes family were evident everywhere she turned.

100

A Living Testimony of Faith

Olivia also knew early that Christian faith was central to her family and to herself. Her grandfather had donated the land for the Stokes Chapel—a strong Baptist church in Middlesex (and a historical landmark today). Olivia's grandparents, aunts and uncles, parents, and extended family made up the core of the church's five-hundred-member fellowship. When Olivia's father died she was only seven, and shortly thereafter, her mother decided to move the family to New York so that the children could get the best education available. The first thing they did in New York was join the Abyssinian Baptist Church, which came to be the center of their life. When Olivia's mother remarried, her stepfather, also a strong Baptist, would take the children to his church (Union Baptist) as well, introducing them proudly.

The church was always at the hub of Olivia's life, and it shaped her course toward ordination as a Baptist minister and lifelong ecumenical leader, serving first as director of the Department of Education for the Massachusetts Council of Churches and later as associate director for urban education for the National Council of Churches. Despite the importance of these institutional relationships, however, Olivia was always guided by the early teachings of her mother: "My mother taught me that being a Baptist was fine, but that would not get you to heaven. You have to be a Christian."[3]

Olivia has always loved people. One recent interviewer described her in this way: "Olivia Pearl Stokes believes that there is a great future in every child, and all it takes to get that goodness out is a little love."[4] Perhaps this is not a surprising description of a woman who experienced an abundance of love in her own family and community life. She identifies many individuals and institutions who were influential in her life, including her parents, William Harmon and Bessie Thomas Stokes, whose attention to their children, stress on education, and leadership in the community (as a gentleman farmer and schoolteacher, respectively) were exemplary. She remembers her stepfather, Lester Lee Van, as a man who "was proud of us four children."[5] She also recalls the African-American principal of Public School 89, Gertrude Ayers, and the director of religious education at the Abyssianian Baptist Church, Horatio Hill.[6] And Olivia attributes much of her enthusiasm for life to the Young Women's Christian Association (YWCA) and to the people whom she met through the church.

Olivia has known both the richness of life and the strains of oppression and hardship. She attended the prestigious educational institution Hunter College High School (an academy for gifted young people), and she faced the necessity of preparing for a secretarial career at Wadleigh High School, where she transferred after the death of her stepfather and a shift in family finances.[7] She attended City College, New York University (B.A. in education in 1947; M.A. in religious education in 1948), and Columbia University Teachers College (Ed.D. in religious education in 1952) and was employed during her college years by the Baptist Educational Center, the New York State Christian Youth Council, and the United Christian Youth

Movement.[8] With each of these work experiences she was learning, and she was earning the honor of being the first black woman in the United States to receive a doctorate in religious education.

Olivia's life was enriched by education and work but also by the experience of growing up in Harlem during the 1920s and early 1930s.[9] Her pastor was Dr. Adam Clayton Powell, Sr., and she met Benjamin Mays, Mary McCloud Bethune, W.E.B. DuBois, Nannie Burroughs, and many renowned African Americans who were guests in her church, as well as in her home. In fact, an experience with Dr. Mays points to some of the assurance and gusto that were part of this little girl's life. She described a grade school experience:

> And one day Dr. Mays said, after Dr. Powell, Sr., died, that it was an interesting experience that as guest speaker he was not invited to dinner, because this hospitality was a normal church pattern. I said to him, "There are hundreds of people in this church that would be honored to have you for dinner. Come and go home with us." And so he became a regular guest in our house. . . . But you see, in the black community, the average person had always been fearful of approaching great leaders. But we were taught as children that we were as great as anybody.[10]

Olivia always focused more on the passion to give than on the experience of oppression. This is a familiar refrain in her speaking and writing, expressed recently in these words:

> I'm an ordained ABC minister. I know what it is to be discriminated against as a woman minister. But the pulpit is not the only place where it's at. The streets are full of people who need love, of people who want a bright future but will never get there by themselves.[11]

This is the spirit that motivated Olivia Stokes in her most recent work as founder and executive director of the Greater Harlem Comprehensive Guidance Center. She founded this institution in 1976 "to guide and counsel Central Harlem youth across the turbulent preteen and adolescent years to responsible adulthood."[12] Until the institution closed, Olivia continued to serve as a volunteer and member of the board of directors.

Olivia's early life also contributed to her fascination with, and knowledge of, Africa. Her mother had supported an African-American missionary to Africa from the time she was ten, so her mother had been learning about Africa long before Olivia was even born. This dialogue with Africa continued in the Abyssinian Baptist Church, through letters and visits with missionaries.[13] Thus began a relationship with Africa that was later to inspire Olivia to travel with seminar groups to the continent and to write books of African stories and poetry for young people.

One further incident from Olivia's roots is particularly significant. When one interviewer asked her if she wanted to add anything about what she had called her "marvelous romance life," she replied, "No, I think it's more important to talk about the people that keep helping young people's minds"; we need an "environment which motivates and feeds" young minds, so that youth can be contributing citizens.[14] Olivia connected these concerns to a memory of her first day at Abyssinian Baptist Church, August 8, 1925: "We'll never forget that date. We went in, put our hands in the hands of Dr. Hill, the educator. My mother said, 'These are my children. Educate them.'"[15] Such was the introduction of Olivia Stokes to the world of religious education and to the potential in education to nourish the faith and dignity of young people! Today she lives in retirement in New York City, and she still sparkles and dreams when she speaks of youth.

Historical and Social Context

What is the character of the world in which Olivia Pearl Stokes has lived? The answer is an important prelude to the discussion of her scholarship and teaching. Olivia's work was clearly influenced by her world, and it was also addressed to that world, where she always hoped to make a difference. Olivia Pearl Stokes was born an African-American girl-child into a family that knew emotional solidarity, a deep Christian faith, a sense of proud history, a vision for the future, and the value of education and social action in empowering people to influence the world. She was always eager to embody the same values in her own work.

What may be easy to forget is that the United States went through enormous change during her lifetime. African Americans lost the right to vote in some states through Jim Crow laws in the early 1900s, and the Civil Rights movement in the 1950s and 1960s finally led to the right of African Americans to vote in all states. The Civil Rights movement also generated a spirit of urgency to guarantee human rights and dignity for all people, a spirit of anger against injustice, a radical hope for building a more just society, and a sense of the power of people to change history. Olivia's world was one in which the spirit of the Civil Rights movement was present in every gathering of the Abyssinian Baptist Church and in many of the denominational and ecumenical organizations in which she worked. She met the leaders of the movement as a child, and she came to know many of them very well as she gave leadership in her adult years.

Further, Olivia personally experienced much of the drama of U.S. history. She grew up in Harlem when it was the social and artistic center of African-American culture and when that culture was bursting with creativity. She studied religious education during a period when it was one of the most dynamic and generative fields in the theological curriculum, and she studied at Columbia University's Teachers College and Union Theological Seminary when these institutions, working together, formed the center of religious education theory building. Further, by living in New York City and in the particular university and church institutions that influenced her the most, she daily encountered people who were making history, and these people were making marks on her life as they made marks on a nation. We should not be surprised, therefore, at the inspiration, confidence, and enthusiasm that Olivia brought to her scholarship and teaching.

Scholarship and Teaching

Olivia Pearl Stokes contributed a great deal to the field of religious education through her scholarship and teaching. She wrote numerous journal articles, chapters in books, curriculum guides, course outlines, and resource materials, including two children's books featuring African culture and art. Beginning in 1952, she was also teaching in higher education, the church, and ecumenical agencies.

Scholarship

Although her scholarship covers a wide range of topics and interests, four dominant themes emerge throughout Olivia's work: (1) leadership training and development, (2) the role of education in the black church, (3) the experiences and contributions of black women, and (4) the educational implications of black theology in the African-American church.

Leadership Training and Development

Leadership was a major theme for Olivia from the time of her youth. Reflecting on her extended family, she recognizes that they were "the leadership group" in their North Carolina church:

> My grandfather gave the ground for the church. . . . My grandmother led the choir, my uncles were the preachers, the members of the family were the deacons and deaconesses. . . . We were the leaders of the church, and that went on for eighty, ninety years.[16]

Olivia was also influenced by the strong emphasis on leadership training through the Leadership Development School at the Abyssinian Baptist Church in New York. Through the church and the YWCA, she gained a personal, ecumenical, communal, and global perspective on leadership. She writes:

> [Abyssinian Baptist Church] was the first black church in America with a master's degree educator who developed all kinds of programs, created after-school programs for us in Bible study, in music and art, in drama, in education—everything we wanted was at that church. Right around the corner was the YWCA. So we had the combination of the Y, the church, and then those two organizations were linked to the world.[17]

As a child and a youth, she took numerous courses through the Leadership Development School at Abyssinian Baptist Church, which prepared her to take on various leadership roles within the educational ministry of the church, the community, and other Christian organizations.

Olivia's interest in leadership training and development inspired her to write her doctoral dissertation on leadership, titled "An Evaluation of the Leadership Training Program Offered by the Baptist Educational Center, Harlem, New York, with Recommendations for Its Improvement." In it she analyzed the effectiveness of the Baptist Educational Center, which was sponsored by American Baptist Churches to provide in-service training for church leaders. She offered suggestions for strengthening the training program to meet the growing needs of church leaders in various areas of education, including curriculum, the teaching and learning process, faculty, and administration. She herself served as associate director of this center from 1941 to 1952.[18]

In her writings on leadership training and development, Olivia was concerned about the need for religious educators to reflect on the relationships between methodology, theology, and issues of life. Her primary concerns were to identify the major problems of human existence, to relate scripture to these problems, and to determine the best methods to address the problems and to communicate the gospel effectively so that people can build a strong Christian community, life, and philosophy. For Olivia, "leadership is key to the development of concepts," and new concepts facilitate education. They stimulate dialogue, encourage growth, and challenge us to work toward a better community.[19]

The Role of Education in the Black Church

Another prominent theme in Olivia Stokes's scholarship is the role of education in the black church.[20] In addressing this theme, she reflects on three particular areas: the historical legacy of the black church; the educational ministry of the black church; and a proposal for a Saturday Ethnic School, designed to affirm and celebrate African culture, contributions, and art.

From its inception, the black church has played a significant role in the education and uplift of African-American people. Olivia was well aware of this fact and often reflected on the *historical legacy* that is unique to the African-American church. She was proud of the fact that the black church was the source of hope and inspiration that compelled black people to strive for freedom and liberation. She observes:

> Historically, beginning with slavery and continuing into the 1980's the black church has been the most powerful force of the black people's struggle for justice, equality, liberation and freedom. The black church has been the communities' protest center, the spiritual powerhouse, and the fellowship community center for radical unity, talent launching, and fund raising for survival causes.[21]

The black church has also been a sanctuary for healing and wholeness, particularly in worship. This was the place suffering people could come, release their emotions, and renew their "hopes, faith and courage."[22] This unique experience inspired black people to continue in the struggle for liberation.

Rehearsing the history of the African-American church is vital to the educational process, because it reflects the early efforts of the church to educate a race of people who had been systematically denied their right to freedom and education. As Dr. Stokes observes:

> The Sunday school was a necessary appendage of the church because the public school did not admit Black children in those pre-emancipation days before the Civil War. In the black church, the church school was the center of literacy training for children, youth, and adults. In the church school in those early days, the textbooks were the speller and the reader (public school instruments for general education) for small children and the Bible for the older Blacks.[23]

Olivia recognizes that black history challenges the church to continue the educational efforts that have not only empowered black people to overcome adverse oppression but also inspired them to deepen their relationship with God and to strive for unity with all of humanity.

Although Olivia celebrates the contributions that the black church has made in educating black people, she is not afraid to critique the *educational ministry* in an effort to strengthen the quality of religious education provided through the church. One of her strongest criticisms is that the black church is not addressing the practical needs of the African-American community and has lost sight of African-American traditional values. She maintains that one reason for an increase in the suicide rate in the black community (which was not a problem in the past) is that "parents lost two things: faith and hope." These elements, she argues, were foundational for African-American foreparents and unfortunately are "fading like a Christmas tree."[24]

To address this problem, she offers several suggestions: (1) examine the church's ministry to determine why it is failing to meet the needs of the congregation; (2) draw upon concrete ideas in order to regain African-American traditional values; (3) develop practical ministries, such as daycare centers, that encourage community involvement in nurturing children and supporting parents; and (4) develop values and standards within the community.[25] In short, Olivia advocates a "problem-centered" and "this-worldly" approach to religious education. She maintains that "instead of expecting the world to come to the Church, Christian education in Black Churches must address the problems of the real world faced by Black people. For the Black Church, education must be concerned with living this life, to the fullest."[26]

Olivia has argued that, with the growing emphasis on black consciousness, self-understanding, and cultural appreciation, the educational ministry of the African-American church must be equipped to teach the Christian faith in relation to African heritage and African-American experience. To facilitate this process, she proposed a *Saturday Ethnic School* that would offer a curriculum centered on "Black history, Black church history and contemporary issues viewed from the Black perspective."[27] The school's major thrust would be to "celebrate the genius of the Black experience, as expressed in the life of the individual, the Black family and the Black Christian community. It would aim to develop creativity within its members, to express their religious insights through drama, music, dance, painting, poetry and creative writing."[28] Through her innovative ideas, Olivia revealed her passion for improving the quality of religious education in the African-American church.

When asked for words of wisdom for religious educators and for the African-American church, she responded:

> The African-American church is special because it has come through so much trouble, and it has always been a church of deep faith. I hope the church will help African-American children know the Word and be saved. The church needs to continue to introduce children to the church and to God, and to help children learn how to live a good life. I hope that the African-American church will remain a deeply religious church rather than a secular church.[29]

Experiences and Contributions of Black Women

Olivia Stokes has also been deeply concerned in her scholarship about the experiences and contributions of black women. In her writings, she addresses the role of women and women's movements, both in Africa and in the United States. In an effort to relate the untold story of African and African-American women, Dr. Stokes has given much attention not only to the plight of black women but also to the contributions that black women have made to society. In a three-part series on Women of Africa and African Descent, she highlights the lives and contributions of three African-American women and three African women. This effort was intended to celebrate the life of black women, to give insight into the African and African-American cultures, and to dispel misleading stereotypes that often hinder our appreciation and understanding of black women.

Olivia Pearl Stokes worked to create a positive image of Africa not only through her writings on African women but also through the publication in 1971 of two books for children and youth that highlight various aspects of African culture and art.[30] She said that she wrote these books

> because I became tired of blacks being considered a problem. . . . It just made me angry. I grew up and I wanted the white churchmen to consider me a person, not always a problem, but they just looked at every black as a problem. So I wrote two books, and I involved Africans in the writing of them.[31]

The first was a children's book titled *Why the Spider Lives in Corners: African Facts and Fun*. It provided background information on several African countries, introducing children to basic facts about the countries' history, economics, and leadership; to everyday people who lived in these countries; and to popular African stories, songs, folklore, and art. The second book, *The Beauty of Being Black: Folktales, Poems, and Art from Africa,* was designed to give youth an appreciation of the rich artistic expressions of African people.

Olivia was not concerned with changing African culture or imposing stereotypes on the people of Africa. Explaining her choice to write these two books in the same year, she maintained, "I was interested in what Africans were, and so I took their poetry, and their sculpture, and their folk stories, and their customs, and put them in a second book."[32]

Educational Implications of Black Theology in the African-American Church

Black theology in the African-American church is another theme in Olivia Stokes's scholarship. In "Black Theology: A Challenge to Religious Education" (1982), she critiqued religious education in the black church through the lens of black theology. She charged that the popular forms of religious education in the black church were outdated and irrelevant for contemporary society.[33] She placed these popular forms of religious education into two basic categories: liberal Christianity, with its lack of in-depth Bible study and its emphasis on progressive educational methods, and ultra-conservative or fundamentalist religious education, with its primary focus on the Bible and its lack of sensitivity to contemporary social concerns.[34] According to Stokes, the traditional emphasis on a "banking" form of education, whereby educators are expected to pour information into receptive students, further led to a lack of critical thinking, indoctrination, and an acceptance of oppressive ideologies and structures.[35]

Black theology, Olivia wrote, "is relevant to the problems of a people oppressed in the American and African societies."[36] It enables persons to reflect on their Christian faith, as well as on their human condition in society, from an African-American perspective. Christian education in the African-American church (as well as in other churches) can benefit from black theology because it encourages critical thinking, appreciation of blackness, and action toward liberation and social change. According to Dr. Stokes, the critical task for all Christian educators is "translation of black theology and its underlying concepts and implied theoretical assumptions into goals, objectives, curricula designs, educational materials, and teaching methodologies."[37]

Functioning in a world that is often seen in black and white terms, Olivia has chosen not to make a sharp distinction between "white theology" and

A Living Testimony of Faith

"black theology." Instead, she has always been more concerned with one's character and behavior. Out of this conviction she asks persistently, "What kind of person are you?"[38]

Teaching

Olivia enjoyed success not only through her scholarship but also through a career as a renowned teacher and educator, earning critical acclaim both nationally and internationally. Her educational work spans more than forty years. It has included numerous positions: director of the Baptist Educational Center in New York City (1941–1952); director of religious education for the Massachusetts Council of Churches (1953–1964); educational consultant in urban education for the National Council of Churches (1966–1973); associate professor of education and chairperson for the development of a multiethnic, multicultural teacher education program at the Herbert H. Lehman College of the City University of New York (1973–1976); associate professor at New York University (part time, beginning in 1978); executive director of the Greater Harlem Comprehensive Guidance Center, Inc. (beginning in 1979); and educational consultant at Drew, Princeton, Colgate-Rochester and Andover Newton theological schools. When asked what kind of work gave her the most joy, she referred to her work with people and her teaching in schools, community centers, churches, the Baptist Educational Center, and the Massachusetts Council of Churches.[39]

Olivia was a gifted teacher and educator, who wanted to make a difference in the lives she touched. "I enjoyed religious education; I gave all I had. It enriched my life, and I hope I enriched the lives of others too."[40] Teaching was not just her career; as she states, "Teaching is my calling—teaching Christian faith as God has revealed it to us."[41] This passion for teaching inspired her to explore a variety of teaching methods and techniques that would help persons to build relationships with others while increasing their knowledge. Her most practiced approaches to religious education are (1) discussion, (2) experience, and (3) travel.

Discussion

Dr. Stokes advocates discussion because it encourages open dialogue: "You learn a lot about the other people and you can respond to them."[42] This method of teaching was instrumental in 1967, during a meeting of the World Council of Christian Education in Nairobi, Kenya. Amid cultural conflicts and divisions, her emphasis on dialogue and her use of games and ice-breakers helped people get to know one another and break down barriers that impeded communication at the conference.[43]

Experience

Experience has also been central to Olivia's teaching. She believes that religious education should provide a variety of experiences and include a global focus. In her view, people from all walks of life need "to come together and have an experience."[44] During the turbulent 1960s, she took a group of white, middle-class Christians to a Black Panther meeting in order to show them that people were hungry in New York City. This revelation was shocking to the white Christian community, because they were under the assumption that "everyone was eating." For Stokes, experiencing other cultures and communities is a practical way to raise cultural awareness, to encourage appreciation of other people and their way of life, and to challenge biased assumptions that promote separation and misunderstanding rather than harmony and acceptance.[45]

Travel

As one who has traveled extensively throughout Africa and in other parts of the world, Olivia also promotes travel as an effective mode of education. She led twenty graduate student seminars to West, Central, and East Africa from 1958 to 1981. During her frequent trips to Africa, Olivia developed graduate teacher education programs in five Nigerian universities (1973–1976), researched African family life and women's roles in twenty African countries (1973–1976), and studied Yoruba civilization at the University of Ife, Nigeria, as a Fulbright fellow (1976).[46] She considers teaching by way of travel a wonderful way to learn about cultures and people.[47] When asked about her most challenging experience, she noted that it was discovering how God works when you go around the world—rejoicing in getting to know the people, to work with them, to teach them, to love them.[48] Olivia Stokes's life and work have exemplified learning by way of travel, for she has gained wisdom, insight, and a deeper appreciation for others through this mode of education.

Impact on the Field of
Religious Education: Faith, Courage, Change

Descriptions that others have used of Olivia Pearl Stokes include "civic leader," "educator," "author," "devoted Christian educator," "distinguished leader of the church," "ordained minister," "ecumenical leader," "administrator," "missionary," "bridge," "gifted," "exceptional," "extremely articulate," and "versatile." While these accolades describe a woman whose life and work have advanced the field of religious education, she would simply say, "People speak about me with great gratitude."[49]

A Woman of Faith

What can one say about the contributions that Olivia Stokes has made to the field of religious education? First of all, she is a woman of deep faith. Nurtured from her childhood in the teachings of Jesus Christ, she carried with her a strong faith and sense of God's presence in her life. She notes that everything she has accomplished was in response to a "faith pull."[50]

Stokes continued to believe in God's divine providence and trusted that God would open doors for her to minister in areas that were not always open to African-American women. When in 1953, she became the director of religious education for the Massachusetts Council of Churches, she was responsible for directing and planning "with thirteen denominational executives and their staffs the educational program for a million and a half Protestants."[51] This position was commonly held by a white male, and she recalls that many church leaders "couldn't believe that a black woman could have a doctorate and thirteen years' professional experience."[52]

Olivia Stokes identifies two major contributions to the Massachusetts Council of Churches. First, after realizing that many people in Massachusetts gave up their religious activities in the summer in order to work at the beaches, she implemented educational programs at the resort center churches. These programs were scheduled at various untraditional times, such as midnight or seven or eight o'clock in the morning, as needed to accommodate the workers.[53] A new concept at the time, the program was successful.

The second contribution that she identifies is her pioneering effort to model, particularly for white people, quality black leadership. She believes that her efforts "proved to a lot of white people that black leadership could be equal or superior."[54] In her position with the Massachusetts Council of Churches, opportunities opened for her in the 1960s, such as for her to pray at the opening of the Massachusetts senate. This was the first time that these "legislators had ever seen a woman, and a black woman, lead them in prayer."[55] Other opportunities included teaching, lecturing, and consulting with numerous prominent universities and educational institutions, which allowed people to see a competent black woman with a doctorate. In short, she maintains that her second contribution "was just being a capable educator [and] administrator."[56]

As a woman of faith, Dr. Stokes's contributions influence the field of religious education in ways that parallel her self-evaluation. First, she challenges religious educators to design programs that meet the needs of communities and congregations. This may involve offering courses at staggered hours, to accommodate working people. It may also require the church to offer courses that address everyday concerns and issues, such as divorce, parenting, marriage enrichment, financial planning, college preparation, and job training,

OLIVIA PEARL STOKES

along with biblical studies. In addition, Olivia believes that the church must meet the needs of communities such opportunities as mentoring programs, day-care centers, and computer training. In sum, religious education should emphasize people, not buildings or programs.

Second, Olivia Stokes challenges religious educators to acquire the training they need to give quality service to the churches or institutions they serve. This is particularly important for African-American churches, which traditionally have focused primarily on preaching and worship rather than education. A competent and well-trained religious educator can help these churches to see the importance of religious education and to invest more time and energy into providing well-rounded, comprehensive religious education ministries.

A Woman of Courage

Olivia Stokes is not only a woman of faith but also a woman of courage. As a woman and as an African American, she has faced both sexism and racism. Throughout her life she has encountered people who have tried to deny her opportunities because of her gender, her race, or both. Despite these obstacles she stood up for her rights, maintained her dignity, and participated in the struggle for freedom and liberation.

Olivia recalls a time in 1952 when Union Theological Seminary sought to fill a position requiring someone under the age of thirty-seven with thirteen years of "professional teaching experience" and a doctorate in education. Out of all of the candidates, she was the only person qualified. When she responded to the search, she remembers:

> The personnel director, in shock, took one look at me and said "*And you are Negro!* Don't worry, I'll get you a Fulbright fellowship, teaching abroad." My response was a resounding "NO!" Columbia had educated me, as one who had received the highest evaluation in defense of my dissertation on leadership, and no lower standard in any position did I seek.[57]

Stokes left the interview with anger, determination, and a decision to focus her work in the church, where the need and calling were clear.

In another incident, Olivia delivered an address in Boston that focused on racial, educational, economic, and social issues. In this presentation, she voiced her concern about the song they had sung at the gathering, referring to black people as "darkies." After several complaints from participants, the executive director of the Massachusetts Council of Churches told her that, as director of religious education, she was not to speak on race relations; that was the task of the social action director. After listening patiently, she responded to the executive director:

> I am three things, *Black,* a Black *educated woman,* and a holder of a Columbia/Union Theological Doctorate, and none of these can I now change

nor do I desire to. Therefore, you have the option of requesting my resignation, or experiencing the gift of double insights, coming from the Black Christian's experience and the best training in Higher Education.[58]

Olivia did continue in her role, and also in her insistence on being herself in that role, thus inviting other moments of creative tension.

A woman of courage, Olivia Pearl Stokes has brought at least two things to the field of religious education. First, she challenges religious educators to be concerned about social structures that are destructive of human personality. Educators must be willing to identify issues, to enter dialogue with appropriate people to determine a course of action, and to work together to develop programs that will empower people to bring about positive change in their individual lives and communities.

Second, Stokes challenges religious educators to value the gifts that others bring to the field. She believes that everyone, whether educator or student, brings something unique to the learning experience. This awareness challenges religious educators to embrace an ecumenical, multicultural, and global vision, focusing on "one God, one faith, one baptism into the Spirit of God."[59] Religious education must be a bridge that unites people of various ages, races, cultures, and countries.

A Woman of Change

A woman of faith and of courage, Olivia Stokes is also a woman of change. Throughout her life she has striven to bring about positive change in the lives of individuals, the church, the community, and the world. Whenever she entered a hostile situation, she tried to model the love of Christ in order to help individuals change racist and sexist attitudes. She reflects:

> When I went to Massachusetts, I had to pray hard to be kind to people who were not kind to *my* people. I learned from my mother to be kind to everyone. Black and white didn't matter; what mattered was that you love people and help them serve God. I kept praying that God's will be done; the most important thing is to keep loving people. I have seen plenty of people change—black, white, Indian, African, and people everywhere.[60]

She was also concerned to change ineffective educational programs within the church, particularly in the African-American church. This motivated her to propose a Saturday Ethnic School that would combine Bible training, African and African-American heritage, and social action. Her involvement in the Civil Rights movement during the 1960s is evidence of her desire to change unjust racist policies that denied blacks and women certain rights. She also worked diligently to change negative images and stereotypes of Africa and of African and African-American women through her books and journal articles celebrating the cultures and the contributions of these women. These efforts affected curriculum materials, textbooks, classroom procedures, and individual attitudes toward people of color.

As a woman of change, Olivia Pearl Stokes challenges religious educators to provide education that empowers people as agents of change. First, educators should promote dignity and human rights, respecting the personhood of all people. Second, religious educators should continually evaluate programs to ensure they are effective. Stokes argues that an action-reflection approach to education will help leaders provide quality educational programs. Finally, religious educators should continue to critique books, resources, songs, and other practices to determine if they promote negative images and stereotypes of people of color and women. Educators must strive to replace these negative images and stereotypes with positive ones.

Threads of Feminist
Approaches to Education

Three questions emerge as we reflect on Olivia Pearl Stokes's life and work in relation to other approaches to education, especially in relation to the feminist threads identified in the Introduction. The term *feminist approaches* is used throughout this book as a framework for comparison, although the women examined herein actually use diverse words to describe themselves. What threads does Olivia Pearl Stokes share with the "feminist approaches" of other women educators? What threads does she give a distinctive twist? What threads does she not share? Although she has not identified herself as a feminist or womanist, she shares many concerns with other women in the field, and her understandings of religious education provide insights to womanist and feminist educators today.

Threads Shared with
Other Feminist Approaches

The feminist approaches to education that Olivia Stokes shares with other women educators include, first, the *integration of life and experience with the educational process*. Education for Dr. Stokes is a "holistic process," involving the entire person. Her own family life helped her integrate a variety of life-shaping experiences with her educational approach. She came to believe that experience was essential to the learning process, and she encouraged people to share with one another and to experience others' worlds. In her view, people need to experience the world because education is more than an intellectual exercise. Further, she has expressed a deep concern that study should lead to "action which brings about social change, from the perspective of the Christian faith."[61] Thus education should draw from life experiences and bring about change for individuals and society.

Another feminist thread that Stokes shares is her understanding that *religious education happens in community*. One of the primary modes of teaching for her is discussion, which can take place only in relationship to others. One of the reasons she prefers this approach is that it provides opportunities to learn about other people, to appreciate other cultures, and to hear the joys and pains of people all over the world. She is fond of using art and stories to facilitate discussion about other people and their way of life. One of the gifts that Olivia brings to religious education is her ability to build bridges. These bridges have helped connect communities: black and white, young and old, rich and poor, at home and abroad.

Olivia also shares an awareness of the *contextuality of religious education*. This requires awareness of one's history, socioeconomic status, community involvement, family background, and culture. She has embodied contextuality by being aware of her own context and by leading herself and others into diverse contexts, seeking to expand the boundaries of learning to include the totality of human experience. This is evident in her efforts with local churches, ecumenical bodies, and community organizations; in her ministry with people of all races; and in her interaction with people in North Carolina, Massachusetts, New York, and Africa. Stokes wants people to know their own contexts and to expand their understandings of others.

The last thread that Olivia shares directly with other women educators is the *integration of theory and practice*. She is deeply concerned about helping people take what they have learned and put it into action. She believes that one's behavior is the most important evidence of one's learning. Throughout her career, she held many positions that forced her to integrate theory and practice. One way she did this was to embrace her childhood experiences of love, acceptance, and dignity and to model these virtues for other people. She says:

> People with the Massachusetts Council of Churches were amazed that I didn't have any prejudice; I worked with whites more than with blacks. I worked with people—bishops, pastors, lay people—all colors, all economic levels. I tried to help people discover that what is really important is to love God, and to help oneself and one's fellow man. Everything I have done is concerned with behavior and with love. My mother taught me not to have prejudice against anyone. Behavior first is-must be-a manifestation of love—concern for others and prayer.[62]

Threads Given a Distinctive Twist

Olivia Stokes manifests some feminist threads in a distinctive way. First, she recognizes that *religious education is grounded in partnering;* but while Olivia encourages mutuality and respect in the learning process, she goes beyond the immediate learning community to invite people who are not present in the room to be partners in learning. She shares information and communicates values from people across the world, often drawing on their arts. From Stokes's perspective, the teacher and learner share equally in the teaching-learning process. Hence everyone's experience is important. Further, "the search for solidarity requires dialogue, community-building, and interaction for the discovery of meaning."[63]

Another thread that Stokes shares, but with a distinctive twist, is a commitment to *education that leads to liberation*. She believes that Christian education should be involved in teaching liberation, and she maintains that through "this process people are helped to decide what are the important issues in the American society in the achievement of justice and liberation: economic, financial, spiritual, and educational."[64] Stokes broadens this perspective, however, by emphasizing the importance of God's influence on liberation. She affirms, "Only God can make you free."[65] Liberation thus is both a human and a divine process, and God's activity leads to individual and social liberation.

The last feminist thread that Olivia Stokes shares with a distinctive twist is *attention to power within the church and emphasis on the collegiality of laity and clergy*. This thread is more implicit than explicit. Although she discusses the ministry of laity, she does not use "power" language. She focuses instead on recognizing the gifts and potential in others, thereby encouraging persons to strive for their hopes and dreams. For example, she nurtured the gifts of youth through the Greater Harlem Comprehensive Guidance Center, helping them identify their gifts, develop practical skills for living, and prepare themselves for educational programs of their choice. For Dr. Stokes, cooperative efforts of laity and clergy are important for equipping others to identify, develop, and use their gifts in Christian service.

Threads Not Shared

The thread least represented in Olivia Stokes's educational philosophy is the understanding that *language shapes religious knowing*. Although she has spoken out against language that promotes negative images and stereotypes of black people, she does not emphasize inclusive language, particularly as it relates to male/female language and pronouns for God. In most of her writing and speaking, Stokes identifies God in the male gender. She is probably influenced here by her experience in the African-American church, where God is described primarily in male language. Although she does not dwell on inclusive language, she *has* been concerned about inclusivity, having fought herself to be included in all arenas of life and having spent her life fighting for the same rights for others.

Olivia Pearl Stokes can be seen as a unique thinker and leader, as well as someone who contributed to the common legacy of women in religious education. To her unique legacy we now turn.

A Living Testimony of Faith

Feminist or Womanist Legacy

Olivia Pearl Stokes defies categorization. Most of her writing and church leadership activity predate the contemporary womanist movement, but she may well have resisted the category "womanist" just as she has consistently resisted identification as a feminist or black theologian and educator. While affirming the primary values of the feminist movement and black theology, she has never chosen to identify herself with such labels. Even so, she prefigured many accents in recent womanist work, particularly with her emphasis on dignity, on the distinctiveness of black women's experience, on the power of reclaiming African and African-American traditions, and on the urgency of struggling for justice and liberation.

Olivia Pearl Stokes's primary contribution is probably her life as a strong woman of faith, who envisioned a more just and loving world and who gave her life to make it so. In her being, she was more than a person; she was a symbol. As the first African-American woman to earn a doctorate in education, she symbolized what could be, and would be, done by many others after her. As an ecumenical leader, she symbolized the vision of bringing people together across denominations, races, and countries. As a religious educator, she symbolized the possibility of engaging in education that was concerned with whole persons and whole communities; hence she had no patience with education that did not hold together both mind and body, church and community, beliefs and values. She demonstrated these complementary values in her writing and also in her unique combination of teaching, church service, and community initiative (as with the Greater Harlem Comprehensive Guidance Center).

A less obvious contribution by Olivia Stokes is her ability to bridge opposites or oppositions. She is a woman who has combined tradition and conventionality with subversion and unconventionality. For example, she devoted herself to serving in and through the traditional church, but she often engaged in nontraditional approaches to ministry, such as her persistent focus on building ecumenical and interracial relationships. She evoked controversy from the very beginning of her ordained ministry with her ordination paper "Ecumenical Leadership: Nurturing and Preaching"—a paper focused on the ecumenical church rather than on one particular denomination. Likewise, she frequently described the values of black theology, and just as frequently, she urged that people avoid distinctions between black and white theology. With this propensity to bring diverse people, cultures, denominations, and approaches together and to find her own way amid opposing views, she saw herself as a bridge,[66] and she gave much of her life to helping people bridge different races, religious traditions, regions of the United States, even continents.

OLIVIA PEARL STOKES

The legacy of Olivia Pearl Stokes can be found in the distinctive emphases of her work, many of which move beyond the feminist themes identified in this book. Some of the themes that Stokes adds to other approaches include:

> the importance of relying on the Holy Spirit, who is the source of all accomplishments;
>
> an emphasis on Christian behavior and action, as demonstrated both by individual persons and by communities in the larger social arena;
>
> an emphasis on the church as a community through which to serve the world;
>
> an emphasis on valuing one's heritage, including what she calls "Judeo-Christian" heritage and one's own ethnic heritage;
>
> the recognition of the distinctiveness of black traditions, represented in a black theology that "is rooted in neither American liberalism nor conservatism, but in black spirituality and black struggle";[67]
>
> a recognition of God's revelation in and through African traditional religions;
>
> an ecumenical vision, including a vision of ecumenism within the black church;
>
> an encouragement of people to struggle for justice, liberation, and freedom;
>
> a commitment to excellence, freedom, and community in the education of the black church;
>
> a critique of Christian education that is more concerned with programs, buildings, and individual salvation than with Bible study, exploration of Christian values and hopes, Christian behavior, and social transformation;
>
> a recognition of the power of story to allow people to enter the experiences of others and to appreciate and accept other people.

What is important in this representative list of distinctive themes is the fullness of Stokes's concerns.

Olivia Pearl Stokes, now in retirement, is a woman who loves God and loves life. Throughout her years she has sought to find God in all people and places, to proclaim good news as she understands it, to affirm the dignity of people near and far, and, most exuberantly, to enjoy life. That is a legacy to celebrate!

NOTES

1. Olivia Pearl Stokes, "Faith, Freedom and Fulfillment" (lecture presented at conference on "Feminism, Spirituality and Wholeness: Naming Our Songs," Claremont School of Theology, Claremont, California, 20 April 1985), 3.
2. Ibid.
3. Olivia Pearl Stokes, telephone interview with Yolanda Smith and Mary Elizabeth Moore, 25 September 1996.
4. "Olivia Pearl Stokes," *ABC People* (Valley Forge, Pa.: The Ministers and Missionaries Benefit Board, 1992), 11.
5. Stokes telephone interview.
6. Ruth Edmonds Hill, ed., *Black Women Oral History Project*, 10 vols. (Westport: Meckler, 1991), 9:124. We refer frequently to this oral history because it is rich in detail; corroborated by other, more sketchy sources; and not broadly available to the public.
7. Ibid., 140, 124–25. Olivia made this change of schools without telling her mother.
8. Ibid., 140–41, 125.
9. Ibid., 124.
10. Ibid., 129.
11. "Stokes," *ABC People,* 11.
12. Ibid.
13. Hill, *Black Women Oral History Project,* 128.
14. Ibid., 141.
15. Ibid., 142.
16. Ibid., 134.
17. Ibid., 138.
18. Olivia Pearl Stokes, "An Evaluation of the Leadership Training Program Offered by the Baptist Educational Center, Harlem, New York, with Recommendations for Its Improvement" (Ph.D. diss., Teachers College, Columbia University, 1952), 5; cf. American Baptist News Service, "Olivia Pearl Stokes" (press release, 15 July 1994).
19. Allen J. Moore (interviewer), "Oral History Project: Dr. Olivia Pearl Stokes," videocassette 1 (Claremont, Calif.: Claremont School of Theology, 1985).
20. Olivia Pearl Stokes, "Blacks, Engagement, and Action," *Religious Education* 67, 1 (1972): 22–25; idem "Education in the Black Church: Design for Change," *Religious Education* 69, 4 (1974): 433–45; idem, *The Educational Role of Black Churches in the 70s and 80s* (Philadelphia: United Church Press, Joint Educational Development, 1973), 3–26. The last work was one of three monographs in the packet *New Roads to Faith.*
21. Olivia Pearl Stokes, "Black Theology: A Challenge to Religious Education," in *Religious Education and Theology,* ed. Norma H. Thompson (Birmingham, Ala.: Religious Education Press, 1982), 84–85.
22. Ibid., 85.
23. Stokes, *Educational Role of Black Churches,* 4.
24. Allen J. Moore, "Oral History Project."
25. Ibid.
26. Stokes, "Education in the Black Church," 438.
27. Ibid., 440.
28. Ibid.
29. Stokes telephone interview.
30. Olivia Pearl Stokes, *Emerging Role of African Women* (New York: Friendship Press, 1971); idem, *Why the Spider Lives in Corners: African Facts and Fun*

(New York: Friendship Press, 1971); idem, *The Beauty of Being Black: Folktales, Poems and Art from Africa* (New York: Friendship Press, 1971).

31. Hill, *Black Women Oral History Project*, 164.
32. Ibid.
33. Stokes, "Black Theology," 86.
34. Ibid., 85.
35. Ibid., 86, citing Paulo Freire, *Pedagogy of the Oppressed* (New York: Herder & Herder, 1971), 58.
36. Stokes, "Black Theology," 94.
37. Ibid., 97.
38. Stokes telephone interview.
39. Ibid.
40. Ibid.
41. Ibid.
42. Ibid.
43. Mary Elizabeth Moore (interviewer), "Oral History Project: Dr. Olivia Pearl Stokes," videocassette 2 (Claremont, Calif.: Claremont School of Theology, 1985).
44. Allen J. Moore, "Oral History Project."
45. Ibid.
46. Olivia Pearl Stokes, résumé (n.d.); American Baptist News Service, "Olivia Pearl Stokes"; Hill, *Black Women Oral History Project*, 126.
47. Mary Elizabeth Moore, "Oral History Project."
48. Stokes telephone interview.
49. Ibid.
50. Mary Elizabeth Moore, "Oral History Project."
51. Hill, *Black Women Oral History Project*, 146.
52. Ibid.
53. Ibid., 147.
54. Ibid., 148.
55. Ibid.
56. Ibid., 149.
57. Stokes, "Faith, Freedom and Fulfillment," 9.
58. Ibid., 10; cf. Hill, *Black Women Oral History Project*, 150.
59. Mary Elizabeth Moore, "Oral History Project."
60. Stokes telephone interview.
61. Stokes, "Blacks, Engagement, and Action," 23.
62. Stokes telephone interview.
63. Stokes, "Education in the Black Church," 442.
64. Stokes, "Blacks, Engagement, and Action," 22.
65. Stokes telephone interview.
66. Mary Elizabeth Moore, "Oral History Project."
67. Stokes, "Black Theology," 74.

Sara Little

~

EMBRACING THE CALL
TO TEACH

Laura Brooking Lewis

"Let not many of you become teachers."[1] Who would begin a book about teaching with these unsettling words from the biblical letter of James, which continues, "For you know that we who teach shall be judged with greater strictness"? Only one who honors and loves the ministry of teaching as much as Sara Little.

These challenging words of scripture, quoted at the beginning of Little's book *To Set One's Heart: Belief and Teaching in the Church,* never fail both to sober me and to make me smile. How like Sara to underscore the faithfulness required of those who teach by offering this text as a starting point, thereby transforming it into an invitation to consider teaching that warns and beckons simultaneously. Cognizant of the great responsibility involved, Sara has taken the ministry of teaching seriously enough to devote her life to this calling and, through her own teaching, has supported and encouraged many to embrace the call to teach.

Appropriately, I first met Sara Little in a class. I had gone to the Presbyterian School of Christian Education because I believed I was called to be a Christian educator and teacher, but I had not yet read the text from James. As she has done for so many, Sara helped me discern my calling and to prepare for it. Later, when I moved from congregation to seminary, Sara, a friend and colleague, was also model and exemplar as a woman in theological education, and for her presence in that teaching role, too, I continue to give thanks.

SARA LITTLE

To place Sara Little in her historical and social context as a Christian educator, I use a version of the schema Sara developed to describe three major shifts in Protestant religious education in the United States during this century.[2] Because her own continual "becoming" as a Christian educator spans much of this century, I connect significant moments in her biography and scholarship with events in the larger context of religious education. This is followed by discussion of some of Sara's contributions to the field of religious education and by reflections on ways in which Sara's work may address the common threads in emerging feminist approaches identified in the Introduction.

The Context of
Becoming a Christian Educator

A new century ushered in the first shift in religious education, which Sara calls "the birth of religious education." With the founding of the Religious Education Association in 1903, religious education became closely allied with the progressive education movement. This shift, characterized by the resolve of religious educators and churches "to do as professional a job in church education as the one expected in education generally," extended through the 1940s.[3] The influences of progressive education and liberal theology, coupled with a growing interest in educational experimentation, can be seen in the practice of denominational leaders and religious education professors of the time, particularly that of George Albert Coe, with his emphasis on the social implications of religious education. Also during this period, denominational activity in publications, curricula, youth work, and leadership education expanded, and the Sunday school, which began outside denominational structures, became a more regularized part of denominational religious education.

Meanwhile, in Charlotte, North Carolina, in the late 1930s, Sara Little was experiencing a "Southern" version of this shift in religious education as a young person. Family and church were formative early influences in Sara's life. Sunday school, catechism, Bible study, and an environment at home and at church where thinking and questions were encouraged were significant elements of Sara's Christian nurture and education. She was very active in the youth fellowship in the small Presbyterian church where she was a member. She also was a leader on presbytery and synod youth planning councils and participated in Christian Endeavor, a nondenominational youth society. Looking back she observes, "It is very hard for me to know when I moved from being religiously educated to being a religious educator."[4]

These experiences of Christian community expanded Sara's understanding of the nature of the church and also introduced ethical and social issues, through denominational curricula and published programs for the young people to read and discuss. "That was a very significant part of, not only my going into religious education, but of my whole perspective. I remember using the *Program Builder* and then the Presbyterian Youth Fellowship bulletin which Nelle Morton edited. I think I was probably on a program every other Sunday night, and I remember making speeches about race relations. . . . I believed it because I said it."[5]

Church involvement continued to be a significant factor in Sara's formation as a young adult. After receiving her baccalaureate degree in English and mathematics from Queens College in Charlotte, North Carolina, she taught English and advanced math in public high school. At the same time, she was an adult youth adviser and worked in summer church camps and conferences.

After three years of teaching, Sara began graduate studies in 1942 at the General Assembly Training School for Lay Workers (renamed the Presbyterian School of Christian Education [PSCE] in 1959) in Richmond, Virginia. In 1944 she completed a master's degree in religious education. Her thesis, "Projects and Principles of Social Action among Young People," was supervised by Nelle Morton, of whom Sara has said, "She was the first person to invite me to write, first a manual on youth and social action, then curriculum materials that led to other invitations. Needless to say, she has been a powerful influence on me, not only in youth ministry, but elsewhere as well."[6]

Sara returned to her home state after graduation to become assistant to the regional director of the Synod of North Carolina, a position she held for six years. Her responsibilities included starting new Sunday schools in communities without churches, coordinating campus and youth ministries in the synod, and planning programs for leader development. She helped organize the first interracial synod conference for college students and the first interracial work camp in North Carolina. She recalls this time as among "the most exhilarating in my whole life, in terms of religious education. . . . I would go home at night with so many things I wanted to do."[7]

She was also reading "voraciously" during this period—particularly such authors as George Coe, Harrison Elliot, Paul Vieth, and others she had not read in graduate school but now found on her own. "I would always be raising questions about 'why' and I was always active in the teaching or training of leaders . . . a sort of back-and-forthness between the Bible and theology and what we were doing, but the focus was on the activity in the forties."[8]

Religious education was changing in the 1940s, however, as a second shift in religious education loomed on the horizon. The progressive vision was giving way to a new emphasis on biblical and theological foundations, urged by educators influenced by Karl Barth and neo-orthodoxy. The publication in 1947 of Paul Vieth's *The Church and Christian Education* underscored the continuing transition. Protestant religious education was becoming Christian education, reclaiming its theological and biblical heritage as well as its ecclesial context. By 1950, when Randolph Crump Miller declared in his *Clue to Christian Education* that the "clue" was theology, the second shift, which Sara names "a call to reform," was underway.[9] The "reform" called for theology to be a significant dialogue partner with Christian education along with the social sciences, which previously had been the dominant partner discipline.

In 1950, Sara began the Ph.D. program in the graduate school of Yale University after accepting the invitation to teach Christian education at PSCE. "I said, 'If I do it, I have to go study some' so that's when I had a year to go to Yale, with a commitment to come back in the fall of '51."[10] Her first year at Yale was "sheer intellectual excitement" and Sara wanted to stay, but she returned to Richmond and began her work as a professor. She also began another period of "back-and-forthness" between teaching and studying, which lasted until she received her doctorate from Yale in 1958. Among her significant dialogue partners at Yale during this time were H. Richard Niebuhr, Paul Vieth, and Randolph Crump Miller. Niebuhr's book *The Meaning of Revelation* proved especially influential, leading to dissertation research on the meaning of revelation and the Bible's role in Christian education.

Sara's early years of teaching were busy ones. Her doctoral studies and her previous work in Christian education influenced the structure and content of the courses she developed. She changed the name of the basic course to "The Church and Christian Education," beginning from the doctrine of the church, like her teacher Paul Vieth. The course in teaching was shaped from her synod experiences of teaching in churches, camps, conferences, and workshop settings. Sara also had ample freedom to experiment. She involved local Christian educators, for example, in creating a "teaching church" program where students could observe in congregations and work with educators in small groups.[11]

Sara also was writing, working in denominational curriculum development, and participating as a leader in academic and professional organizations. *Learning Together in the Christian Fellowship,* her guide for adult study groups, was published in 1956; *The Role of the Bible in Contemporary Christian Education,* based on her dissertation, appeared in 1961; and *Youth, World, and Church,* her book on youth ministry and mission, came out in 1968. Sara was part of the development committee for the Presbyterian Covenant Life Curriculum, which embodied much of the renewed emphasis on Bible, theology, and church heritage that characterized this period. Her book for high school juniors and seniors, *The Language of the Christian Community,* was published in 1965 as part of this curriculum series.

During these years, Sara also taught courses at Union Theological Seminary in Virginia as an adjunct professor and served on the editorial board of *Religious Education,* and the Faculty Fellowship Commission of the Association of Theological Schools. In 1966 she was the first woman to be elected president of the Professors' Section of the National Council of Churches Division of Christian Education, which became the Association of Professors and Researchers in Religious Education in 1970.

The stability and focus of Christian education achieved during the 1950s was short-lived, however, and a decade later, theology was not the unifying "clue." As religious education moved into the 1970s, it was once again in transition. Leaders in the field began to explore a variety of models and approaches. For example, with the publication of his *Where Faith Begins* in 1967, C. Ellis Nelson introduced a socialization model of religious education with an emphasis on congregations; during this period of transition John Westerhoff was examining the relationship between liturgy and religious education, and James Fowler focused on a theory of faith development. By 1982, Jack Seymour and Donald Miller were able to offer an edited volume, *Contemporary Approaches to Christian Education,* that characterized the state of religious education in terms of five major approaches: (1) religious instruction, (2) socialization in faith communities, (3) stage theories of human growth and faith development, (4) liberation and transformative education, and (5) interpretation.

Sara characterizes this third shift, which began around 1975 and continues to the present, as a period of "critical reflection" with "no one clue, no dominant theory."[12] Instead, religious educators have pursued many different approaches to religious education, reflecting in part "the struggle to know how to deal with pluralism of religions, of culture, of points of view" so prevalent today.[13]

For Sara, these years brought honors, changes, and new opportunities. In 1975 she was one of six women recognized as outstanding religious educators by the Department of Education of the U.S. Catholic Conference. She and Iris Cully were the two Protestant educators so honored. Other honors followed: Educator of the Year by the Association of Presbyterian Church Educators (1979); Woman of the Year in Religion in Richmond (1981); and citation by the Presbyterian Women at the General Assembly, for leadership in securing the equality of women (1986), to name only a few.

Other changes were in store, as Sara made her transition from PSCE to Union Theological Seminary in Virginia—beginning, in 1973, with a joint appointment to both schools and then followed by full appointment to Union in 1977, where she became the first woman to teach full time on the faculty. In 1980 she became the Robert and Lucy Reynolds Critz Professor of Christian Education at Union. Sara continued to serve as an adjunct professor at PSCE until her retirement from both schools in 1989. During this period she met other challenges as well: curriculum revision for Union's master of divinity degree program, development of a required seminar for Ph.D. students at Union to prepare them for teaching, and development of a new doctoral degree program at PSCE. All of these called for Sara's insight and skills. Further, with the publication of *To Set One's Heart,* Sara added her own research and reflection on the relationship of teaching to belief formation to the variety of approaches to religious education being developed during this third period of change.

Throughout her career as a teacher and educator, Sara has also been deeply involved with Christian education in congregations and communities of faith. Theory and practice are constantly woven together in her participation in and service to the church. As an ordained elder in the Presbyterian Church (U.S.A.), she serves as a church leader locally and in the church at large. On the national level, for example, her work as a consultant, along with Lawrence Jones, Robert Lynn, and Ellis Nelson, to study the educational mission of the eleven Presbyterian theological institutions in 1989–1990 was an important contribution, helping the denomination examine the nature of the theological education offered to those preparing for ministry. In addition to leading workshops and seminars, speaking at church conferences, and consulting with church organizations, however, Sara has always been an active church member —teaching Sunday school classes, serving on Christian education committees, working with long-range planning groups, and assisting teachers and other leaders in the local congregation.

In her very active retirement, Sara continues to do the things she has always done—teaching, writing, speaking, consulting—and takes on new challenges. She has been a visiting professor of Christian education at several seminaries, and for two years she was the interim dean and vice-president of academic affairs at the Pacific School of Religion in Berkeley, California.

Where religious education goes next is uncertain. Some of the hopes Sara has for religious education in the future are that, as a discipline, it will learn from its history, honor its diversity, value interdisciplinary collaboration and interreligious dialogue, and renew its long-standing concern for the common good.[14]

Contributions to Religious Education

Among the many contributions Sara continues to make to religious education, are the four briefly considered here: (1) her focus on the teaching-learning process and its contribution to belief formation, (2) her continuing dialogue with theology, (3) her advocacy of youth ministry, and (4) her leadership in theological education.

A Heart for Teaching
That Contributes to Belief

Throughout her career, Sara has focused on the nature of the teaching-learning process in religious education. It has been a "continuing center of change and reflection" for her.[15] Her approach to teaching about teaching is a laboratory experience wherein students are challenged to choose or design a teaching process appropriate to the subject matter to be taught. Such a participatory, experiential, and reflective experience is both memorable and effective. Sara's emphasis on the way in which both subject matter and the teaching-learning process bear content and meaning highlights how important it is that teachers be intentional in making decisions about what approaches to teaching are most appropriate for what is to be taught.[16]

In *To Set One's Heart: Belief and Teaching in the Church,* Sara moves beyond her previous work with the teaching-learning process to explore the relationship between teaching and the formation of belief. Her work in this volume is a major contribution to our understanding of the role of teaching in the Christian community and its relationship to faith and belief. Further, her careful attention to the nature of the teaching-learning process with respect to different teaching approaches makes clear the theological dimension of teaching as a pastoral ministry.

As she explores the relationship between teaching and belief formation, Sara asks "whether and how teaching, as a ministry, could serve a more intentional function" in the way in which a faith community "transmits its values and beliefs."[17] To answer this, she takes on three complex tasks and brings them together in a remarkable manner. First, she offers a lucid analysis of the nature and function of belief systems in the Christian community. Second, she defines the nature and function of teaching in the church and develops a set of teaching approaches to serve as a "basic frame of reference for thinking about teaching, as well as a way of focusing teaching on belief formation." Little's teaching approaches are (1) information-processing, (2) group interaction, (3) indirect communication, (4) personal development, and (5) action/reflection.[18] Third, she discusses what each of the five approaches identified by Seymour and Miller in 1982 may contribute to the process of forming and reforming belief.

Sara makes no elaborate claims for teaching as a pastoral ministry. Teaching is never to be the whole of Christian education; instead, she believes, it is a more focused aspect, requiring intentionality on the part of both student and learner. Also, the ministry of teaching is always, for Sara, set within a faith community and is not to be understood apart from this context. Yet teaching as a pastoral ministry is essential —perhaps especially so in a postmodern world. Sara's disciplined and rigorous theoretical and practical focus on the teaching-learning process in the Christian community is a substantial contribution to the discipline.

A Dialogue Partner with Theology

Another important contribution that Sara continues to makes to religious education is her ongoing dialogue with theology. She probes the theological implications of educational decisions and assesses the educational implications of theological conclusions with equal skill and interest. Through the years, she also has written insightful reviews of the interaction between these two disciplines.

Several experiences have shaped Sara's theological perspective and deepened her interest in theology as it relates to education. Her master's program at PSCE, where Christian education was taught in the context of biblical studies, theology, and mission, and her doctoral studies at Yale, where she did work in history of doctrine, contemporary theology, and ethics, have shaped her interdisciplinary approach. Another influence has been Sara's concept of Christian education as a "mediating"[19] discipline, inviting "frequent, purposeful interchange of thought among many disciplines."[20] Her analysis of different ways in which theology may be related to education demonstrates the multiple relationships possible. She identifies five different relationships: (1) theology as source, (2) theology as resource, (3) theology as norm, (4) "doing theology" as educating, and (5) theology and education as interactive dialogue.[21]

When theology serves as *source,* it offers the content to be taught—often doctrine, creeds and confessions, as well as theological language and heritage—while education determines appropriate teaching forms and practices. When theology is consulted as *resource,* education is the discipline that determines the structure and content—often in terms of learners' questions or life experiences—and then seeks answers from the Bible and theology. Theology serves as *norm* when subject matter, programs and processes are "reflected on theologically to ascertain their appropriateness, for religious education."[22]

When teacher and learner "do theology" by engaging in critical theological reflection on "the meaning of life situations in the light of generally accepted theological understandings," theology functions as *educating.*[23] Finally, Sara envisions a fifth alternative, in which education and theology as "separate, but related," disciplines engage in an "interactive, dialogical process" to develop "plans for educational ministry."[24]

In a recent essay on Reformed theology and religious education, Sara expressed her concern for more collaboration between the two disciplines: "Whether the move is from theology to education or from education to theology, the conversation is needed." She concludes, "We in the Reformed tradition must so reconceptualize the understanding we bring to educational ministry that we will take an interdisciplinary approach to our task."[25] If and when educators and theologians develop such a stance on matters of educational ministry, it will be in large part because of Sara Little and others like her, who not only envision the connectedness of education and theology but also live it.

An Advocate for Youth Ministry

Recently Sara wrote that "youth ministry has never disappeared for more than a few months from my agenda."[26] Throughout her career she has been an advocate of young people and the distinctive ministries they offer as church members. Her own active involvement in youth ministry, her years as adviser to student groups, her high school teaching experience, her extensive work with adult leaders of youth in workshops and seminars, and her ongoing reflection on youth issues in published articles and lectures all continue to yield keen insights for youth ministry today.

Her two books related to youth ministry also deserve special attention as "classics" in this field. *The Language of the Christian Community,* part of the Presbyterian Covenant Life Curriculum, was written to introduce high school juniors and seniors to theological language and concepts in the Bible, church history, and the creeds and confessions of the church.[27] Using an inductive approach to teaching and learning, the student book and leader's manual stimulate conversation and reflection by relating theological language to students' experiences in school and in the world. Both manuals engage youth and adults together in theological discussion.

In *Youth, World, and Church,* Sara developed a rationale for the church's ministry "to, in behalf of, with and by youth."[28] Almost three decades later, its thesis still deserves consideration: "Youth who are members of the church are called to Christian discipleship *now,* as people of God placed in the world for ministry; they are a part of the ministering Body of Christ, within which they are supported and equipped for the fulfilling of their common calling."[29]

Exploration of at least two aspects of Sara's thesis seems timely for youth ministry today. First, because "young laity" are church members who engage in mission now, Sara suggests that the main focus of "ministry *to* youth" should be supporting and equipping these younger members for their particular service as Christians. Second, by affirming that youth are "placed in the world for ministry," Sara asks where young people are best able to fulfill their "common calling," suggesting that one important context to be considered is the school. Not unlike Christian adults who deal with questions of how they are the "scattered church" in the marketplace, young people may ask similar questions about their role as Christians in the world of school. Given the various pluralisms in high school life, to say nothing of the increased violence in many schools, conversations about youth in mission in these settings are perhaps most urgently needed today. How are young laity being equipped and supported to be God's people called to minister in their particular contexts?

SARA LITTLE

A Leader in Theological Education

To do justice to Sara's contribution as a leader in theological education, we could consider the number of major lectures she has delivered at theological institutions, nationally and internationally, or detail the many courses, seminars, and consultations she has led. Instead, our focus here is on two areas of significant service: Sara's recent work with the Youth Ministry and Theological Schools project and her contribution to the Association of Theological Schools.

Prior to her 1989 retirement from Union Seminary in Virginia, Sara directed the Youth Ministry and Theological Schools project, funded by the Lilly Endowment. This five-year study on leadership development for youth ministry involved forty-three theological schools, five additional educational institutions, fifty-one faculty members, twenty-two graduate students, and eight pastors. It has yielded a wealth of well-documented research studies that give promise for youth ministry in the future. But even more important is the promise of this project for reforming theological education and the way in which seminaries and theological schools prepare pastors and church educators for leadership in youth ministry.[30]

Sara also has contributed to theological education through her long service to the Association of Theological Schools (ATS), the major accrediting body for theological schools and seminaries in the United States and Canada. For three decades she has exercised perceptive and skillful leadership as a teaching professor and one of the few women in an organization largely composed of male administrators, deans, and presidents.

As a member and chair of various ATS commissions, Sara was responsible for awarding sabbatical fellowships and grants, ensuring full participation of underrepresented constituencies, conducting accreditation visits, and revising accreditation standards. She served on the executive committee and was elected vice-president of the association. Her work with ATS also offered opportunities to address issues related to women in theological education. For example, in 1980, Sara and Barbara Wheeler, president of Auburn Theological Seminary in New York, addressed seminary presidents and deans at an ATS biennial meeting on "ways seminaries must augment their efforts to be responsible to women."[31] Their presentations, based on consultations with women in seminary settings, identified four significant areas for improvement or change related to women students, women faculty, women's studies, and the intellectual perspective of feminism.

At the end of her term on the executive committee, Sara was asked to share some reflections on her work with ATS. She characterized it as a "broadening experience" that had taught her how much administrative functions were related to theological education. She also pointed out, however, the importance of including more teaching professors in the association's work: "I said I would really like to leave the message that teachers

. . . did have something to offer to theological education, and that to let it be turned over to administrators was shortsighted."[32]

In 1994, Sara was awarded the Distinguished Service Medal of the Association of Theological Schools—the first woman to receive that honor. The medal citation reads in part, "This act is public testimony to the extraordinary contributions that Sara P. Little has made to the advancement of theological education and to the fulfillment of its central purpose."

Threads Held in Common with Feminist Approaches

Woven throughout Sara Little's practice of religious education and her published works are threads similar to those Barbara Anne Keely identifies in the Introduction as significant in a feminist approach to religious education. Some similarities are stronger than others, but most important, all threads held in common with a feminist approach are given Sara's distinctive twist.

The emphasis feminist religious education places on *integrating life and experience* with the educational process may be linked to Sara's concept of religious education as a mediating discipline that "has to do with everything that affects the life of the people of God . . . helping people understand, making connections among the events of their lives."[33] The importance she places on belief formation also supports this integration. Beliefs, which incorporate affective, volitional, behavioral, and cognitive dimensions,[34] "can be an important factor in bringing integration and integrity to life."[35]

Learning *in community*, where mutual listening and "hearing into speech" (Nelle Morton) are sources of connectedness, seems compatible with two of Sara's teaching models. The group interaction approach to teaching, rooted as it is in the doctrine of the priesthood of all believers, "has the potential for becoming a fellowship where there is a mutuality of support as persons relate belief to faith."[36] Further, the personal development approach takes seriously those persons who long to be able to say "I" in the community of faith,[37] which is a special kind of hearing into speech.

For another perspective on the contextuality of religious education, consider, as Sara does, the relationship of context to the formation of belief. Because beliefs must be held in some context to be meaningful, religious educators must be aware of the many contexts or frameworks that support belief formation. In addition to intentional teaching, other contexts include the community of faith, the developing self, and the "shaping influence of action," where beliefs, attitudes, and commitments are formed and nurtured through faithful deeds and behavior.[38]

The concern for how *language shapes religious knowing* and communicates beliefs is a significant shared thread in Sara's work. She, like many, has reshaped her own language to speak of human beings and of God in ways that say more clearly and explicitly what she believes. Another fiber in this thread is her commitment to communicate the language of the Christian community, as in the book and study guide she wrote "to provide help to young people as they formulate for themselves what they believe and why."[39] She believes that such communication is crucial because "we are not only nourished in community, but we have within it the instruments for reflecting together about our own calling—in our language, our beliefs, always to be viewed as dynamic, not static."[40]

The *partnering of teacher and learner* is at the heart of Sara's conception of the teaching-learning process. In *The Language of the Christian Community,* she models this learning partnership in print: the heading in large letters and bold type at the beginning of the book reads, "A Word to the Student," but the line in parentheses beneath reads, "Both Teacher-Student and Pupil-Student."[41] In *To Set One's Heart* she describes teaching as "a form of ministry intentionally directed toward helping persons seek and respond to truth,"[42] where teacher and learner, in this image of mutuality, are "companion pilgrims" who "stand before Truth together."[43] As Sara wrote in a manual for adult leaders of youth in 1952, "Do remember that the basic approach of the leader is 'we,' and the basic method, that of 'working with'."[44]

Sara has described the interdependence of *theory and practice* as "theory tested and clarified as it is actualized in practice; practice opening up new questions and new meanings and thus helping to determine ongoing theory, contributing to it and even to theological formation."[45] In teaching-learning seminars, she models integration of theory and practice by asking students to teach using methods appropriate to what is to be learned.[46] She notes, "When a person seeks to embody or translate a particular kind of knowledge into a methodology, the interdependence of theory and practice is obvious. More important, one learns to think about the theory in any teaching situation."[47]

To clarify the relationship between *religious education and liberation,* Sara likely would say that God revealed in Jesus Christ liberates, and that we as disciples are freed to embody God's liberating activity in the world. We see aspects of this in her discussion of action-reflection as a teaching model for believing and doing.[48] It also appears in her recent reflection on the nature of responsible membership, which Christians exercise as disciples and citizens: "In most of its early history, the Protestant Church in the United States had built into the fabric of its congregational life, in preaching and education, concern for the public good. How have we lost that concern? . . . Because truth must be 'done' as well as 'understood,' we are calling for an education for faithfulness, for obedience, one that draws on heritage as the source for the value we place on care for the common good."[49]

Finally, Sara addresses *mutuality of power* in the church by extending it to a variety of relationships. Teaching, for example, is to be done in a relationship of mutuality between teacher and learner. For teachers, this is a "matter of respecting the learner's uniqueness and independence, a refusal to use techniques of persuasion or influence that infringe upon the learner's right to choose, to decide."[50] She also points to the necessity of sharing power and responsibility among the laity, emphasizing the full membership of youth as "young laity."[51]

A Living Legacy

Sara continues to fashion the legacy she leaves; yet some of her many gifts as a religious educator are already clear. She is a woman of intellectual rigor who continues to bring religious education and theology together in ways that reform and reshape both disciplines. She is a leader in theological education who is able to discern the educational implications of processes and structures and to give guidance in both administrative and curricular concerns. She is a theological religious educator who grounds theory in practice and practice in theory by being an active member of her denomination and in her local congregation.

Above all else, she leaves a legacy of lifelong attention to the teaching-learning process. Conversations with those whom Sara has taught point to the importance of her understanding religious education as an integrating discipline, inviting different dialogue partners to sponsor connectedness in people's lives. Many emphasize her insight that religious education is connected to every aspect of the Christian life—to mission and worship and fellowship as well as to formal study. Others point to her definition of teaching and learning, especially to the teacher as mutual learner. Still others comment on the way in which she helped them understand that a teaching method is much more than a neutral process and helped them become intentional teachers.

Sara's legacy also includes the numbers of students with whom she has taught and learned, who now teach around the world in schools and pulpits; in seminaries and offices; in households and hospitals; in churches, camps, and conferences; and in many other contexts. They are the living legacy of this gifted woman whom God, in all wisdom, called to teach.

NOTES

1. James 3:1 R.S.V.
2. Sara Little, "The 'Clue' to Religious Education," *Union Seminary Quarterly Review* 47, 3–4 (1993): 7–21.
3. Sara Little, "What We Should Not Forget," *PACE: Professional Approaches for Christian Educators* 24 (February 1995): 10.

4. Sara P. Little, interview by William Bean Kennedy, tape recording, 24 January 1994, Religious Educators Oral History Project, Oral History Collection, Burke Library, Union Theological Seminary, New York (transcript, 6–7).
5. Little, interview by Kennedy (transcript, 5).
6. Little, "What We Should Not Forget," 8.
7. Little, interview by Kennedy (transcript, 11–12).
8. Ibid., (29).
9. Little, "'Clue' to Religious Education," 15.
10. Little, interview by Kennedy (transcript, 23).
11. Ibid. (36–37).
12. Little, "'Clue' to Religious Education," 20.
13. Ibid., 18.
14. Little, "What We Should Not Forget," 11–12.
15. Little, interview by Kennedy (transcript, 113).
16. Sara Little, "An Approach to Teaching about Teaching," in *Process and Relationship,* ed. Iris V. Cully and Kendig Brubaker Cully (Birmingham, Ala.: Religious Education Press, 1978), 15–21.
17. Sara Little, *To Set One's Heart: Belief and Teaching in the Church,* (Atlanta: John Knox Press, 1983), 86.
18. Ibid., 39.
19. Sara Little, *The Role of the Bible in Contemporary Christian Education,* (Richmond: John Knox Press, 1961), 163.
20. Ibid., 7.
21. Sara Little, "Theology and Religious Education," in *Harper's Encyclopedia of Religious Education,* ed. Iris V. Cully and Kendig Brubaker Cully (San Francisco: HarperCollins, 1990), 649–51. See also Sara Little, "Theology and Religious Education," in *Foundations for Christian Education in an Era of Change,* ed. Marvin J. Taylor (Nashville: Abingdon Press, 1976), 30–40.
22. *Harper's Encyclopedia,* 650.
23. Ibid.
24. Ibid., 650–51.
25. Sara Little, "Reformed Theology and Religious Education," in *Theologies of Religious Education,* ed. Randolph Crump Miller (Birmingham, Ala.: Religious Education Press, 1995), 34.
26. Little, "What We Should Not Forget," 8.
27. Sara Little, *The Language of the Christian Community* (Richmond: CLC Press, 1965).
28. Sara Little, *Youth, World, and Church* (Richmond: John Knox Press, 1968), 17.
29. Ibid., 11.
30. Sara P. Little, "Introduction," *Affirmation,* 2, 1 (1981) : v–x. Little was also the editor of this issue of *Affirmation.*
31. Four specific areas for improvement or change are discussed in the issue of *Religious Education* on "Women and Religious Education," edited by Sara Little. See Barbara Wheeler, "Accountability to Women in Theological Education," *Religious Education* 76, 4 (1981) : 382–90.
32. Little, interview by Kennedy (transcripts 78).
33. Little, "What We Should Not Forget," 9.
34. Little, *To Set One's Heart,* 7.
35. Ibid., 9.
36. Ibid., 40.
37. Ibid., 74–75.
38. Ibid., 22–31.

39. Little, *Language of the Christian Community,* 9.
40. Little, *To Set One's Heart,* 21.
41. Little, *Language of the Christian Community,* 5.
42. Little, *To Set One's Heart,* 41.
43. Ibid., 9.
44. Sara Little, "The Adult Leaders of Youth," in *Handbook: Senior High Fellowship, Presbyterian Church, U.S.,* ed. Bettie Currie (Richmond: John Knox Press, 1952), 33.
45. Sara Little, "Paul Herman Vieth: Symbol of a Field in Transition," *Religious Education* 59, 3 (1964) : 204.
46. Little, "An Approach to Teaching about Teaching," 16.
47. Ibid., 20.
48. Little, *To Set One's Heart,* 76–85.
49. Sara Little, "'Experiments with Truth': Education for Leadership," in *Caring for the Commonweal,* ed. Parker Palmer, Barbara Wheeler, and James Fowler. (Macon, Ga: Mercer University Press, 1990), 174.
50. Little, *To Set One's Heart,* 62.
51. Little, *Youth, World, and Church,* 29.

Dorothy Jean Furnish

CLAIMING TEACHABLE MOMENTS

Linda J. Vogel

D orothy Jean Furnish was a "preacher's kid" who claimed her vocation as a laywoman, Christian educator, workshop leader, supporter of local church Sunday school teachers, and seminary professor—roles that were not always viewed as compatible. She is best known as "D.J.," the nickname she acquired while teaching part time in the 1950s at Nebraska Wesleyan University in Lincoln.

In 1988, Furnish preached a sermon at Garrett-Evangelical Theological Seminary in Evanston, Illinois, on a text from Amos—one that she embodies in her life: "But let justice roll down like waters, and righteousness like an ever-flowing stream" (Amos 5:24 RSV). In that sermon, she offered a glimpse into her roots:

It was 1929. I was eight years old, sitting on the front porch of my parsonage home in Earlville, Illinois, helping my mother and a member of the parsonage committee choose wallpaper for my room in our new home. And although we lived in that parsonage for four years, my room was never repapered, because onto that porch was thrown the afternoon paper with the headline: Stock Market Crashes!! The national economic scene had finally touched my eight-year-old existence! And I, along with my family and the farmers in our church, learned to watch grain prices with one eye, and the weather with the other. For it was the right combination of those two factors that might make my new wallpaper possible.

It was 1945. I was in my first job as a director of Christian edu-

136

cation in Kansas. Although more than a decade after the Great Depression and the Great Drought of the dust-bowl days, the people of Kansas still felt their impact. "We must be extremely cautious about future plans," some would say. "The next disaster may be just around the corner. We never know when, once more, no rain will fall."

It was several hundred years before Christ. A farm boy in Tekoa watched the weather, and experienced the life-giving qualities of water. And these farm days impacted his life, so that many years later, after he had left the farm and gone to the city, one of his most powerful utterances reflected his understanding of the essential nature of water: "Let justice roll down like waters, and righteousness like an everflowing stream."

As that eight-year-old girl on the parsonage porch, I knew this verse! I had memorized it in Sunday School. I had even drawn pictures of it for display along the classroom wall. I wasn't sure what "justice and righteousness" meant, but I knew that God could do it! Just as God sends the rain, so will God someday roll down a mighty stream of Justice water![1]

Dorothy Jean brought her childhood parsonage experiences and her twenty years of experience as a local church educator with her into seminary classrooms and into her local congregation. Later, it was her passion for doing justice that led her to become a part of the Wheaton United Methodist Church family in Evanston, Illinois. There she joined with other persons who combined deep faith with a passion for doing justice. Wheaton was a small congregation that embodied a mutual model for ministry, where laity and clergy shared power and leadership for the total life of the congregation and for justice ministries in the world.

I first met D.J. at a consultation for professors of Christian education, sponsored by the Board of Education and the Section on Curriculum Resources of the United Methodist Church, which was held at Estes Park, Colorado, in the summer of 1974. I was a part-time college teacher of Christian education. Relationships between seminary and college teachers of religious education tended to be nonexistent at best and suspicious, if not antagonistic, at worst.

This consultation eventually gave birth to UMAPCE (United Methodist Association of Professors of Christian Education), which is now UMASCE (United Methodist Association of Scholars of Christian Education).[2] It was during the five-day UMAPCE and UMASCE consultations, which have been held biennially since 1974, that D.J. and I became friends.

Her love of children and the Bible, her love and care for both professionals and laity who sought to take educational ministry to heart, and her love for nature and the Rocky Mountains were shared with passion at these meetings. An ability to listen with care, to ask hard questions, and to confront with a vigor that left no easy ways out characterizes the woman I gradually came to know.

DOROTHY JEAN FURNISH

D.J.'s Scholarship

Dorothy Jean Furnish's scholarship has had two foci throughout her life, which began to be woven together in her earliest books. Her first focus was children, particularly engaging them in learning. In 1975 she published her first book, *Exploring the Bible with Children*.[3] D.J.'s passion for approaching the Bible and children in holistic ways has been central to her work. That passion has continued into her retirement; in 1995 she published *Adventures with the Bible: A Sourcebook for Teachers of Children*.[4]

As a liberal laywoman who takes historical-critical biblical scholarship seriously and who taught her students and colleagues much about child development, D.J. advocated holistic ways of teaching and learning the Bible with children. She created a profoundly simple model for encouraging children to experience the Bible, one that not only works well with children but that can be used effectively and in age-appropriate ways across a person's life span.

This model invites teachers to design a plan that engages children in (1) *feeling into* the text, (2) *meeting with* the text, and (3) *responding out of* the text.[5] D.J. insists that being attentive to children, to their local and global contexts, and to the Bible as a "confronting event" with "unlimited meanings" can lead to creative, growth-filled and life-enhancing experiences that are also engaging and fun.[6] She recently agreed to publish a workbook that offers laity and church professionals who teach children at the congregational level five of her tried-and-true workshop plans, used in more than thirty states and in Canada over many years.[7]

The second focus of D.J.'s work is her scholarship, which she has woven into and throughout her work. Her concern has been for the profession of Christian education. Her second book, published in 1976, was *DRE/DCE: The History of a Profession,* examining the positions of director of religious education (DRE) and director of Christian education (DCE).[8] In this work, too, we see the "staying power" that D.J. has exhibited throughout her vocation as a religious educator. Her careful scholarship and her tenacity in holding the history of this emerging profession ever before Christian religious educators became evident with her 1976 book and continue today with an essay titled "A New Profession for the United Methodist Church in the Twentieth Century: The Director of Christian Education."[9]

D.J. proposes in this essay that "as long as the Christian Church survives as an institution of our society which ministers to persons, there will be a need for the skills, insights, and visions embodied at the present time in the persons who are members of the profession known as 'Directors (or Ministers) of Christian Education." [10] D.J. explores many possible scenarios, but of one thing she is sure: as long as faith communities exist, the need for teachers-learners who have skills to share the story, encounter the Word, and support, challenge, and empower others will continue. This is the profession to which she believes persons will continue to be called—some lay and some ordained, but all committed to holistic approaches to encountering the Bible and discovering how it connects to the life issues and questions with which people struggle as they seek to grow toward wholeness.

The fabric that D.J. continues to weave thus is made by engaging children and the living faith found through exploring the Bible and by knowing who and whose we are as Christian religious educators, by knowing and claiming the history and legacy that are ours. This might be described as a *praxis* that insists on holding theory and practice in creative and re-forming tension. This deep commitment to having theory inform practice and practice re-form theory can be seen in Furnish's essay "Rethinking Children's Ministry."[11]

In this essay, D.J. points out that a great danger exists when "the church insists upon exposing children only to 'right answers'." Her plea is that religious educators instill an appreciation for diversity and openness in children. She advocates helping children to build on their innate sense of justice and to "develop a sense of justice that is the right of all people." Those who teach and learn with children need to foster compassion, to "encourage discomfort—even anger"—at the injustices in our world. At the same time, she believes Christian educators must challenge and empower the entire faith community to advocate for all children, in a world where we are sacrificing our future by refusing to deal effectively with difficult societal and personal issues.[12]

D.J.'s Embodied Teaching-Learning

In 1985, I got a call from D.J., asking me if I would apply for a teaching position at Garrett-Evangelical Theological Seminary in Evanston, Illinois. I had just taken a position with a local church and felt I could not apply. In 1986 she called again. In her gentle but persistent way, she urged me to be open to the possibilities that teaching at a seminary would bring. And in the fall of 1987, Dorothy Jean Furnish and I became colleagues in teaching Christian education; thus I experienced her as both colleague and friend for one year before her retirement in 1988.

In D.J.'s educational model, which she exemplified, teachers are collegial and share what they know and the resources they have with those who can benefit from that sharing. She showed how being present with students and walking with them into their questions is much more helpful than having the answers and giving them away. Being a resource person is one of the vitally important tasks of a teacher.

At Garrett, D.J. was responsible for supervising students in the Religious Education Curriculum Library. Many students chose to work there throughout their seminary years. Her careful planning, attention to details, and recognition that creating hospitable space was a key to fostering independent learning became more lessons learned by the students working with her.

When she retired, I inherited the task of supervising the curriculum library, a job made manageable by the manual that D.J. had carefully created, revised, and put on a computer disk so that we could continue to perfect this part of the library. When I was asked by our head librarian to colead a preconference workshop, for the American Theological Library Association (ATLA), on designing, cataloging, and managing a religious education curriculum library, I learned that Dorothy Jean's method was ground-breaking. Her legacy includes a curriculum library that provides a model for others that are in development.

But her contributions to curriculum resources go far beyond the pioneering work she did with the Garrett-Evangelical curriculum library. D.J. began writing curricula for the United Methodist Church in 1960, with an article on working with junior high school students, and her most recent contribution is the leader's guide *Romans, 1 and 2 Corinthians, Galatians, Ephesians, Philippians* for the United Methodist adult study series Journey through the Bible (1995). She has written ten other curriculum resources for teachers, children, youth, and adults.

At the national level, Dorothy Jean served as a member of the Curriculum Resources Committee (CRC) of the United Methodist Church (1976–1984) and as chairperson of the CRC's long-range planning committee. Her insights and contributions, especially in the area of resources for children, were pivotal and far-reaching.

Dorothy Jean Furnish was also instrumental in developing educational opportunities for those already engaged in the educational ministry of the church. Mary Alice Donovan Gran, a single mother who was supporting her family by serving as a Christian educator in Iowa, recalls:

The time came for me to explore my options. I wrote to three seminaries asking for information on a master's in Christian education program in which I could continue to work full time. Results were a mixed bag. One seminary did not reply. Another seminary responded with a curt, formal letter stating no such program existed. Doug Wingeier, a professor at the third seminary—Garrett-Evangelical—responded, saying no current program like that existed but he would forward the letter to D.J. Furnish. Soon I also heard from D.J.—a telephone call, I think. Anyway, she said, "Come to summer school; we'll discuss the possibilities."

At a later time, I remember receiving a telephone call from D.J. She was coming through Iowa and could she stop and talk about what such a program might look like. What were the needs? What would the parameters be that would draw persons like me, yet fit into the expectations set by the seminary? We sat on my back screened-in deck and talked. To make a long story shorter, D.J. put together a plan for a master's degree program for persons working full time in Christian education.[13]

One of D.J.'s greatest contributions to the religious education profession was the envisioning and creation of this "in-ministry" track of the master of Christian education (M.C.E.) degree, designed for persons working in local congregations who wanted to complete a graduate degree and develop new understandings of Christian education and greater skills but who could not leave their jobs and relocate to attend seminary. It was D.J.'s task, together with her colleagues in Christian education, to convince those colleagues at Garrett-Evangelical that this pioneering vision was doable and that theirs was the school that could and should do it.

The genius of this program is that local church practitioners and others working in curriculum development or church agencies are able to come to campus for two-week intensive courses,[14] which also include full-time M.Div. and M.C.E. students. The in-ministry students are able to participate in chapel and in other formational events and activities and to use all the seminary's resources, which is not possible in most distance-learning options.

These in-ministry students bring real-life questions and are quick to spot something that sounds good but would not "play in Peoria" (or Lakeland, Houston, Des Moines, Detroit, or the cluster of five rural churches from which one student came). They, in turn, are enriched by students who are engaged in full-time study. Each group learns to know and appreciate the other, and thus when they find themselves or others like them on a church staff together, there is bound to be a sense of mutuality from having shared in the same classes and achieved at the same level in their seminary experiences.

The excitement and possibilities of this degree program were crucial to my decision to teach at Garrett-Evangelical and were also important factors for my colleague, Jack Seymour, who joined the faculty in the fall of 1988. At graduation in the spring of 1996, Dorothy Jean returned to help us celebrate the tenth anniversary of the M.C.E. in-ministry track. We have had twenty graduates who are serving across the United States in local congregations and in national church agencies. These graduates have published resources that are being widely used throughout the church,[15] and together they and we know this program is making a significant contribution to the educational ministry in the United Methodist Church and beyond.

Dorothy Jean modeled team teaching with her colleagues in Bible and theology. They acknowledge that they learned as much as the students about what it means to teach in ways that are as attentive to the process as to the content. Her former New Testament colleague Ernest W. Saunders says, "For D.J. the study of the Bible is not to be a recital of texts but a sharing of experiences which open up new possibilities for existence in ancient times and in contemporary times. That would be truly living the Bible."[16]

DOROTHY JEAN FURNISH

D.J.'s Feminist Threads

Feminist threads are at the very heart of D.J.'s identity and of the weaving she continues to create in her retirement. *Holistic* ways of understanding all persons, no matter their age, are central to her understanding of what it means to teach and learn in communities of faith. It is the *community* that nurtures, teaches, and challenges persons "to do justice, and to love kindness, and to walk humbly with [our] God" (Micah 6:8b RSV).

D.J. realized early that *religious language shapes the ways in which we know God and ourselves.* Pastor Susanne Burwell recalls:

> When I first began seminary in 1981, I was not at all sensitive to inclusive language. There would be times when I sat with D.J. in chapel that she either just made changes in the words of the hymn as she went along, to make it more inclusive, or she muttered that something really needed to be done about this. I thought it was fine that she wanted to make those changes, but I went ahead and sang the hymns with the exclusive words. I guess I hadn't yet had enough personal experiences of sexism, of which I was aware, to know that I too needed to be out there working for a more inclusive church. Now, when I'm singing a hymn, and making numerous changes wherever the human language or God language seems too limiting, I can't help but think of D.J., who was outspoken about her beliefs, yet patient enough to help bring me along.[17]

Partnership, mutuality, and a commitment to praxis, in which practice informs theory and theory re-forms practice, are key to Dorothy Jean's teaching-learning ministry. That is how she worked in the local church; that is how she leads workshops; that is how she taught and learned with her seminary students; and that is how she lives her life in her own community of faith.

One of her former students observed that D.J. seemed to have a kind of "lovers' quarrel" around the issue of roles relating to ordained versus lay ministries. Always clear that her own calling was as a baptized laywoman, she worked to help students claim a positive identity as Christian educators—whether lay, professionally certified or consecrated, or ordained. She listened and talked with many students as they sought to clarify their calls. Whatever the call, she remained loud and clear that to be an intentional and effective teacher-learner of the gospel of Jesus Christ was certainly a part of what it meant to be faithful in whatever calling one had.

D.J.'s Gift to the Profession

D.J. knows who she is—from that young child hoping for new wallpaper, who could not define "justice and righteousness" but was sure "God could do it!" to the mature and wise woman who addresses the issues of power and ageism in a 1995 article "Coming Out Old: Issues of Ageism and Privilege." She now asserts that she is "growing older in Colorado."[18] In a prefatory note to a paper she prepared for the History Task Force of the Association of Professors and Researchers in Religious Education, which met in Denver in 1989, she claims to have "rediscovered that I am an unrepentant liberal."[19]

D.J.'s perspective is that of one who knows herself to be liberal even though she sees both herself and the world through the eyes of history and in the context she occupies. She believes the Bible is a confronting event that is ever new and takes us places we did not expect to go. She is open and eager to learn from those whose perspectives differ from her own, valuing diversity and pluralism. For D.J., there are always many different teaching strategies from which to choose; there are many different viewpoints, and there are often missing voices that one must seek to discover and recover as one encounters scripture and the world.

New beginnings are integrally woven into the pattern of Dorothy Jean's life. She set out to be the most faithful and effective local church educator she could be, and she was. Wherever I go, people ask me if I know D.J.— "She was the director of Christian education when I was a youth (or Sunday school teacher) in Lincoln (or Hutchinson)!" And as often as not, they are still in touch with her and know that she has retired and is living in Colorado.

D.J. left her position as director of Christian education at First (United) Methodist Church, Lincoln, Nebraska, in 1965, after serving twenty years as a local church educator, to enter the joint Garrett Theological Seminary/Northwestern University Ph.D. program in Evanston, Illinois. She worked part time as a field education supervisor and graduated in 1968 with her Ph.D. in religion, with a major in Christian education. Upon her graduation, she was invited to join the Garrett faculty.[20]

The transition from student to faculty colleague at the same institution is never easy, but it is a transition Dorothy Jean made with grace and integrity. She found herself for a time the only woman faculty member, and she became the hospitable presence and the mentor for an increasing number of women who were trying to make it in a male-dominated world— and who were often angry. Becoming the only woman professor at a theological seminary in 1968, when blacks and women were militantly working to find a place at the theological table, was not easy.

Bishop Sharon Z. Rader says of D.J., "Many of us women students were confrontational, angry, dissatisfied with 'the way things were' in the seminary, church, and society. D.J. found some of our rabble-rousing to be confusing and uncomfortable, but she stayed with us: supporting, building bridges, encouraging, *teaching* us how to work in and with the system. She said she was learning from us; we certainly were taught by her." Dorothy Jean often found herself called to be in places that were not comfortable, but she went and stayed the course. Sharon Rader recalled such a time:

I remember one time when a delegation of women students demanded a meeting with the president. We took D.J. into the meeting with us. At one point, our badgering of the president got so painful he began to cry. "What do the women want?" he asked. Brazenly, I began to tell him. Later when the meeting was over D.J. said to me, "I would never have presumed to speak for all the women, Sharon. What you said was probably right, but how could you speak for all the women?" It was a gentle question, but a strong reminder to acknowledge my own shortcomings and fallibilities.[21]

D.J.'s *intention* seems to be to grow toward wholeness herself, and to teach and learn with others so that they, too, might come closer to wholeness. She believes one does this, in part, by recognizing and naming "teachable moments"—those times and situations when persons recognize that they need some new information, insight, or skill to fulfill their task or calling. For example, she was so excited during the Jurisdictional Conferences of the United Methodist Church, whose primary function is to elect bishops for the church, that she called our home to tell us that M.C.E. graduate and curriculum library staff worker Charlene Payne Kammerer had been elected the first woman bishop in the Southeast Jurisdiction (July 1996).

Charlene remembers D.J.: "It has been 24 years since I completed the M.C.E. degree at Garrett-Evangelical. Dorothy Jean Furnish has remained, in all of that time, my professor, teacher/learner with me in the life of the church, my teacher, mentor, my friend. Her strong character, love of the church, and gentle presence, helped me see many 'teachable moments' in my own life of faith and now in the practice of ministry."[22]

D.J. often helped people by offering them an opportunity to "role-play" an upcoming situation with her, so that they might find their own voice and clarify their own sense of who they were and what they wanted and could do. Her intention was always to empower persons to name and claim for themselves their own call and vocation.

D.J.'s worldview is centered in her deep desire for and commitment to God's justice. That she embodied this worldview is reflected in comments made by Bishop Edsel Ammons, a colleague on the Garrett-Evangelical Theological School faculty during those tumultuous years of the late 1960s. He describes her as "not only friend but mentor, . . . a very excellent teacher . . . [whose] demeanor during those days was one of quiet confidence and a kind of gracious insightfulness." As an African American, Edsel found himself at the center of the civil rights struggle on the seminary campus, and "Dorothy Jean belonged to the small cadre of faculty persons who helped, in fact, in the design of the Church and the Black Experience. Especially helpful was her voice relative to the fact that [Church and the Black Experience] was not to be a 'special study' program, but was intended to impact the totality of the life of the institution for the sake of the training of students of all colors and cultural histories, and the faculty and institution."[23]

D.J.'s worldview sees children as full and current members of the body of Christ. Children minister to us even as we teach and model faith for them. Her perspective includes the Bible as that "confronting event" that is always full of surprises, if we will engage it with our whole being. It shows us who and whose we are and challenges us to act on this good news in concrete and justice-making ways in the world.

Dorothy Jean Furnish embodies in her voice—which is gently gracious and truth-speaking, question-asking, and vision-challenging, hospitality-sharing, and justice-pursuing—her own "perspective, conceptual horizon, intention and worldview," which contributes much to the profession of Christian religious education and to the churches and lives she has touched as laywoman, religious educator, feminist, professor, mentor, and friend.

NOTES

1. Dorothy Jean Furnish, sermon preached in the Garrett-Evangelical Theological Seminary chapel, Chicago, July 1988. Dorothy Jean says this is her "first 'creative writing'" after her retirement.
2. "Scholars" replaced "Professors" in 1994, in an effort to be more inclusive of researchers and national staff who are full members.
3. Dorothy Jean Furnish, *Exploring the Bible with Children* (Nashville: Abingdon Press, 1975).
4. Dorothy Jean Furnish, *Adventures with the Bible: A Sourcebook for Teachers of Children* (Nashville: Abingdon Press, 1995). Other of her books dealing with the Bible and children include *Living the Bible with Children* (Nashville: Abingdon Press, 1979) and *Experiencing the Bible with Children,* (Nashville: Abingdon Press, 1990), which brings together in an updated format her previous two books on this topic.
5. Furnish, *Experiencing the Bible with Children,* 83–121.
6. Ibid., 17–37.
7. Furnish, *Adventures with the Bible.*
8. Dorothy Jean Furnish, *DRE/DCE: The History of a Profession* (Nashville: Christian Education Fellowship, 1976).
9. Dorothy Jean Furnish, "A New Profession for the United Methodist Church in the Twentieth Century: the Director of Christian Education," to appear in a book by "seasoned" Christian educators of the United Methodist Church, compiled and edited by UMASCE (forthcoming). Other works by Furnish that reflect this commitment to hold history before the profession include "Women in Religious Education: Pioneers for Women in Professional Ministry," in *Women and Religion in America,* vol. 3: *20th Century,* ed. Rosemary Radford Ruether and Rosemary Skinner Keller (San Francisco: Harper & Row, 1986); "The Director or Minister of Christian Education in Protestant Churches," in *Changing Patterns of Christian Education,* ed. Marvin Taylor (Nashville: Abingdon Press, 1984) "The Future of the Profession (Director of Religious Education) in the Protestant Church," in *Local Church Parish Education,* ed. Maria Harris (New York: Paulist Press, 1978); and "Henry F. Cope," in a festschrift in honor of Herman E. Worman, "Pioneers of Religious Education

in the 20th Century," ed. Boardman W. Kathan (published as a special issue, *Religious Education* [1978]).

10. Furnish, "A New Profession," 28 (MS).

11. Dorothy Jean Furnish, "Rethinking Children's Ministry," in *Rethinking Christian Education: Explorations in Theory and Practice,* ed. David S. Schuller (St. Louis: Chalice Press, 1993). This text reflects on the findings of a major Search Institute research project into the educational ministries of five mainline Protestant denominations and the Southern Baptists.

12. Ibid.

13. Mary Alice Donovan Gran is a diaconal minister from the Iowa Annual Conference of the United Methodist Church who currently works for the Board of Discipleship of the United Methodist Church in Nashville, Tennessee. She shared these reflections in a telephone interview on July 14, 1996.

14. These two-week intensives, offered in January and in two summer sessions, require reading before the coursework and a paper afterward and are regular courses in Garrett-Evangelical's master's degree curricula.

15. For instance, Charlotte T. Brent wrote two chapters, "Helping Others When a Child Dies" and "When a Young Child Dies,"in *The First Three Years,* ed. Mary Alice Donovan Gran (Nashville: Disc Resources, 1995), 83–84, 170–71. Joanne Chase was a contributing author to *The Inviting Word* curriculum resource and *Children's Teacher* (Nashville: Cokesbury Press, 1995), "Snacks in the Classroom." Mary Alice Donovan Gran edited *The First Three Years,* to which Judith Mayo contributed a chapter titled "Nurturing the Young Child's Spiritual Needs" as well as one she coauthored with Kim Giana, titled "The Church's Challenge: Families and Young Children." Barbara Mittman has contributed to the TREK Senior High Curriculum Resource (Nashville: Cokesbury Press, 1995). Shirley L. Ramsey and Edie G. Harris wrote *Sprouts: Nurturing Children through Covenant Discipleship* (Nashville: Disc Resources, 1995). Ellen Shepard assisted with *Teaching the Bible to Elementary School Children* by Dick Murray, with assistance of Ruth Alexander (Nashville: Abingdon Press, 1990) and wrote *Who Dared? Joshua Dared* (Nashville: Abingdon Press, 1996); *Mission Education beneath the Story-Telling Tree,* VBS Director Ed. by James H. Ritchie, Jr. (Nashville: Cokesbury, 1994); *Children's Fund for Christian Mission* (Nashville: GBOD, 1989–1994); "Dealing with Children's Hard Questions," in *Children's Teacher* (Nashville: GBOD, Church School Publications, 1994); *New Invitation* (Nashville: GBOD, Church School Publications, 1996), for ages five to six. Judy Newman St. John edits curriculum resources for Cokesbury Press. Kathryn L. Wadsley has devised Advent-Christmas and Lenten calendars based on the three-year common lectionary (Cedar Falls, Iowa: Wolverton Printing Company, 1987–1996) and "Benedictions I, II, III" (1987, 1989). Janet Porfilio Westlake has written "Special Friendships with Older Adults," in *Children's Teacher* (winter 1995–96) and "Eliminating Substitute Nightmares," *Children's Teacher* (fall 1996).

16. Ernest W. Saunders, New Testament professor emeritus, Garrett-Evangelical Theological Seminary, Evanston, Illinois, letter to the author, 5 July 1996.

17. Pastor Susanne Burwell, Christ United Methodist Church, Greenfield, Wisconsin, letter to the author, 14 July 1996.

18. Dorothy Jean Furnish, "Coming Out Old: Issues of Ageism and Privilege," *Open Hands* 11 (fall 1995): 12–13.

19. This paper was subsequently published in an edited version; see Dorothy Jean Furnish, *Liberal Religious Education,* (fall 1990).

20. Garrett merged with Evangelical Theological Seminary of the Evangelical United Brethren Church in 1974 and became Garrett-Evangelical Theological Seminary.
21. Bishop Sharon Zimmerman Rader, letter to the author, (Wisconsin Area) 17 June 1996.
22. Bishop Charlene Kammerer (North Carolina Area), previously senior pastor at Saint Paul's United Methodist Church, Tallahassee, Florida, letter to the author, 25 June 1996.
23. Bishop Edsel A. Ammons, retired and bishop in residence, Garrett-Evangelical Theological Seminary, Evanston, Illinois, letter to the author, 11 July 1996.

Freda A. Gardner

MASTER TEACHER
WHOSE FAITH
HELPS US UNDERSTAND

Carol Lakey Hess

In the address she gave on the day that the renovated Tennent Hall, the Center for Christian Education at Princeton Theological Seminary in New Jersey, was dedicated, Freda Gardner shared several of her favorite stories about children. In the first, Freda related that a small child was put to bed one night and later woke her parents when she fell out with a thump. After picking up and soothing the child, one parent asked how the child happened to fall out. The child replied, "I guess I fell asleep too close to where I got in." Freda then brought the story home: "Some Christian people do that too—fall asleep soon after they reach older childhood or adolescence and try to live their whole lives on what they might have learned as a child in Sunday School."[1] She went on to emphasize the lifelong learning that God calls each one of us to, "that God's Kingdom might, more and more, take shape in the world."

This story provides a helpful frame for introducing the teaching of Freda Gardner. In telling and interpreting this brief and powerful story, Freda underscored the organizing principle in her view of teaching. Teaching is "a response to faith in search of understanding," and it plays a central role in the quest for understanding. The understanding that faith seeks is not an arrived state of being, an "at-restness." Rather, the understanding that faith seeks "is the recognition that the quest *is* the life of faith."

The story also indicates some of the essential elements Freda has pointed us to in teaching: the value of learning from "the least of

148

these"; the importance of sustaining a lifelong adventure; the need along the way for folks who can pick us up and soothe us when we need it, as well as folks who can challenge and prod us to move beyond our present ways of being; and the future that is God's kingdom, which draws us toward its present realization.

I come back to these specific themes later in this chapter. First, we consider more fully Freda's organizing principle of faith as a journey in search of understanding. Then we look at Freda's journey as a teacher. Finally, we return to the essentials of her theory of teaching, framing them in light of the threads of feminism.

Freda's Pilgrimage of Faith

Freda's own faith development provided her with a wonderful image for the journey of faith. In a sermon she preached on images of God, she painted a striking picture of how her own faith journey seemed mirrored in a floor-to-ceiling stained-glass window depicting Jesus the Good Shepherd: "As a very young child, I identified with the lamb carried so tenderly in Jesus' arms. As a young adolescent, I was drawn to the rocky, thorny path under Jesus' bare feet. It wasn't until I was a young adult that I realized that the path seemed not to end at the base of the window but to extend across the floor, into our midst and beyond."[2]

The journey that is the life of faith begins in childhood, and it is the task of all members in a community of faith to recognize and support the questing child. "The child is on the threshold of a long quest for his or her own faith and needs encouragement for the search."[3] To help adults remember what it was like to be a child (and thus better attend to children) and to help them recover the sense of journey, Freda regularly prompts them to reflect on their own childhood experiences: "Go back to your own childhood or adolescence and identify something you once thought or felt to be true that you no longer see that way. What do you think determined the change in perception?"[4]

Freda considers adolescence to be a critical time in one's faith journey. Her work on youth ministry enables leaders to understand the connection between the "rocky, thorny path under Jesus' bare feet" and the rocky, thorny issues in the lives of young people. Adolescents "engage in a search for values, beliefs, and commitments that they may call their own." The "church's opportunity for ministry is found in the realization that the teenage years are very appropriate times for persons to be on a faith pilgrimage," and thus it is the work of the church with teenagers to encourage them to "ask questions, to doubt previously given answers, and ultimately to arrive at their own conclusions about life, values, and faith."[5]

Supporting youth, however, is not simply a matter of getting them through the brambles in their lives. It is also to enlist their help in locating and clearing the rocky, thorny, unfaithful places in the life of the church.

The quest continues into adulthood, until the end of life. Freda is gifted in giving people permission to struggle with faith issues in their adult lives, and she works to counteract the kind of "triumphalism" in the church that prevents people from honestly and openly grappling together. "A searching faith is not consistently, if ever, upward and onward with Jesus, bumper stickers and cute tag lines on church bulletins notwithstanding, if by that sentiment we mean to say that the path is clearly marked and straight from Go to Goal," she stresses.[6] Furthermore, "in a real search, even the most unflappable among us appear strangely 'flapped.'" Because the pilgrimage is lifelong, we are called to be open to renewal at every stage in that journey. Standing under faith is a stance "of equal helplessness and equal strength—common recognition that no matter how old or how far along or how long in their search, the person of faith is vulnerable to new insights, upsetting awareness, blinding implications, overwhelming glory."[7]

Although the life of faith is a never-ending quest, the wisdom and experience of older people are not to be devalued. Freda humorously yet poignantly refers to older people as being "chronologically gifted." In addition to history, wisdom, and experience, older people bring a kind of freedom to community life. Having moved through both the conforming and the climbing stages of life, older people can be signs of liberation from convention. In her courses on the education of adults, as well as in her later courses on ministry with the aging, Freda exposed students to the whimsically prophetic poem "Warning"[8] and to the directly prophetic message of Gray Panthers activist Maggie Kuhn.

Although Freda believes that it is the Christian church's responsibility to seek to "discern the mind of Christ" and to act according to its discernment, she also insists that it is an "illusion" to "say with finality what we are about."[9] Freda resonated with Carol Christ's approach to quest in *Diving Deep and Surfacing,* in which Christ introduces the reader to women writers who "celebrate the quest [for life's meaning] and do not expect that a solution will or should be found for the puzzlement that is life."[10]

Freda's Life Journey

In her work on children, Freda names the impact of early experiences on children's capacity for trust and security. The impact of her own family life on her development as a person and as a teacher is evident. "My parents were *for* me, and they let me know that I *was something* to them," she states. "I wanted the kids I taught to know that same feeling."[11]

Freda Gardner was born in Albany, New York, in 1929. She grew up in a household where "education had a positive glow around it." She loved elementary school, and she played school often with her brother and sister. Her father was a school principal, and he enjoyed his work and took it very seriously. Living in a small town, he was highly honored and one of the leading figures in the town's life. This left young Freda with the feeling that teaching was an important and dignified profession. Her grandmother, Adelaide Wood Gardner, who started teaching at the age of sixteen, was one of the first superintendents of schools in upstate Michigan. Freda remembers her grandmother as a "small, stern, and loving woman," who often told stories about her teaching experiences.

It was not, however, simply the glow of teaching that moved Freda Gardner into the profession. She had some "bad teachers" in high school, who diminished the self-esteem of students. She particularly remembers a math class where she "didn't learn a thing about math, but I learned a lot about what you don't do as a teacher." These negative experiences sensitized her to the dignity of all people and the respect that is owed each learner. "To be privileged to enter students' lives is to walk on holy ground," she believes. Her lifelong experiences with education have made her very aware of the privilege and responsibility of teaching—not simply to subject matter but also to persons. Her "prayer" was "Don't let me hurt anyone." Gardner feels that it is a gift of God to be sensitized to the value of each learner.

In addition to learning the value of each person from her parents, Freda also learned to appreciate differences between persons. Each of the Gardner family members had a different learning style, which impressed upon Freda the importance of variety in teaching approaches. Her family members were a rich blend of thinkers, doers, public speakers, and quiet supporters. "Everyone in my immediate family taught me something about teaching," she reports. Their differences helped her avoid the temptation, common for teachers, to teach exclusively to those who mirrored her own preferred learning style.

Although the tug toward teaching began early and was persistent, it competed with a draw toward nursing. "In those days," says Freda, four basic options were open to women: teaching, nursing, secretarial work, or marriage. Her own mother's love for and dedication to nursing made that profession a compelling option for Freda. Gardner remembers how her mother, Kay, worked nights as a nurse and managed their home during the day. Though invariably tired from her work, Kay was happy and very satisfied. As a high-school student, Freda worked in a ward as a nurse's assistant. She enjoyed everything about it, except she "couldn't imagine puncturing anyone with a needle"; thus she opted for teaching.

Though not through nursing, Freda continued her mother's legacy in another way. Kay Gardner regularly sought out works of ministry. In particular, during the evenings Kay used to call on women whose husbands had died. Knowing the evenings would be a difficult time for them, she wanted to help fill the void created by loneliness. Many of Kay's friends would remark that she had a natural gift for ministry, but she always demurred from taking any credit for her gifts. Though rather shy in public, she was "full of life" in private, and she knew how to affirm and support people in quiet, unremarkable ways. Kay Gardner's important lay ministry was not lost on daughter Freda, who would make lay ministry one of the central themes in her teaching later on.

By her college years, Freda was focused on a teaching career. Having worked a number of summers as a camp counselor, she was prepared to enter Teachers College at the State University of New York, New York City. "One of those rare people who liked education courses," she flourished in the environment. Freda valued the laboratory style of her training at Teacher's. She was·one of those proverbial people who learned to swim by being thrown into the water at the beginning. Assigned to be a student teacher in a fourth-grade class, she and her partner ended up teaching the class themselves, due to the teacher's resignation. Though anxious about teaching in the beginning, her sense of calling as a teacher was fully confirmed through this experience. She left SUNY with a conviction of how special teaching really was. It "calls for the best you have to offer," she mused. After her graduation in 1951, Freda taught sixth grade for several years, and she embraced her lifelong love of the classroom and students.

Her calling to teaching was clear, but Freda completed her work at SUNY with the feeling that a dimension of teaching was missing from her training—the spiritual. Although she wasn't then sure where it would lead her, she continued her education at the Presbyterian School of Christian Education (PSCE) in Richmond, Virginia, which trains Christian educators for the church. She was drawn there for many reasons, including her interest in studying the Bible and theology. She was also impressed by the participatory style of education that PSCE trained its students to bring to the church. It was during her fieldwork at PSCE that Freda had her first opportunity to shape a church educational program.

Freda seriously considered the ordained ministry during this time—and at other times in her life. She decided not to pursue ordination, however, because it was important to her that there be leaders in the church who were not ordained and who could reinforce the value of lay ministries. She says, "I never felt bereft because I couldn't officiate at the sacraments," and she feels that she has participated in the fullness of ministry. Thus, when the issue of ordination recurred for her at retirement, she felt that she could already serve the church in a number of important ways. "I believe in Christian education, and I know it's a profoundly significant activity," she concluded, reaffirming the value of the educational ministry in the church. Freda also considers it important to remain in solidarity with non-ordained educators, particularly given the "hierarchical ordering of the church and of ministry," which has scandalously marginalized lay professionals in the church.[12] She remains a strong proponent for the collegiality of laity and clergy and an advocate for church educators in particular.

After finishing at PSCE in 1957, Gardner was called to be a director of Christian education (DCE) in Plainfield, New Jersey. She "absolutely loved it," and people were very receptive to her leadership. The programs were vital, the children and youth were legion, and the adults were active in education. Although Freda modestly qualifies her obvious success with the disclaimer "This was at the height of the boom in the church; the ground was absolutely fertile," many noticed her gifts for administering and teaching. The president of Princeton Theological Seminary was quick to identify her success; he invited her join the faculty of the seminary as assistant professor of Christian education.

Although she was reluctant to give up the richness of teaching children, youth, and adults in the congregation, Freda agreed to go to Princeton for an interview. "I had not set my face to come [to Princeton] or to go anywhere else. I loved what I was doing," she recalled later.[13] There was, however, a draw and a sense of purpose to seminary teaching: having known what was possible for education in the church, she wanted to share that enthusiasm with others. Thus, after four years as DCE, she went to teach at Princeton in 1961. Eventually she became the first full-time female professor who was tenured. However, she initially insisted on a one-year contract, with option for renewal; she was not ready to make a permanent commitment to seminary teaching.

Freda did, in fact, stay at Princeton for thirty-one years, and over the years she was promoted to associate and then full professor, retiring as the Thomas W. Synnott Professor of Christian Education in 1992. But she never lost touch with the pulse of education—public or religious. In addition to maintaining a full schedule of leading workshops and consulting with congregations, Freda spent two sabbaticals traveling across the country to observe programs in public and religious educational institutions. During the span of her career, the gender demographics of the faculty shifted. She came in as the only full-time female professor; she retired one of twelve.

Freda became the director of the School of Christian Education at Princeton Theological Seminary in the late 1970s, and she was an influential force in shaping the master of Christian education degree program there. The program is known for its sophisticated yet grounded integration of theology and practice. Educational leaders were prepared to recognize biblical and theological themes in the practice of ministry and to train others to "think theologically" in their life experience.[14] Freda was also quite instrumental in developing the Reigner Reading Room, "one of the really loved places in Tennent," which "houses the printed, audio, and visual resources for the educational ministry of the church."[15] The reading room not only provides resources for students but also draws church educators, who regularly use its offerings.

Freda's greatest legacy at Princeton, however, has been her philosophy and style of teaching. I develop this later, but it can be said here that Freda was a "master teacher," who made it her life's work to help people understand the faith to which she herself witnessed. She was a teacher who confidently and boldly offered herself but who also pointed beyond herself to others and to the God by whom she was empowered. When she was selected by the Association of Presbyterian Christian Educators as the Christian Educator of the Year in 1981, the honor was fitting.

While teaching at Princeton, Freda began doctoral work in educational administration. Although she loved the courses, and she ended up taking a good number of them, she didn't like the time it took away from her teaching. Along with a few other professors at the time, Freda made the decision not to complete a doctorate. As with ordination, once again she was certain that she could do what she was called to do without an elevated status. She was, however, awarded an honorary doctorate from Bloomfield College in New Jersey in 1979.

At Princeton Seminary, the board members of the Women's Center regularly invite female faculty members to share their stories with students. The power and meaning of Freda's story have become legendary. Freda tells how she has lived on a number of boundaries at the seminary: at first, as the only woman in a man's world; then as a non-ordained person in an environment where the majority of persons are training for ordination; and as a master teacher who chose not to become one of the highly prized "doctors of the church." This boundary existence has, however, strengthened rather than weakened her sense of herself as a woman, church leader, and professor. Freda has also been single all her life, and this provides another dimension to her experience and wisdom. Her choices have given Freda a sense of unique calling as a model for other women. She feels responsible to show that she is comfortable with who she is, and she wants to affirm for others that choices on the boundaries can be good alternatives. These choices are thus deeply connected to her understanding of discipleship.

Freda is a longtime elder at Nassau Presbyterian Church in Princeton, and her service to the Presbyterian Church at all levels—congregation, presbytery, synod, General Assembly—has been enormous. Busier than ever in retirement, she continues to teach courses, offer workshops, and provide consulting services across the country. Her most recent book, jointly written with Herb Anderson, is titled *Living Alone*.[16] The book is a theological look at what it means to live alone, addressed to people who live alone, their families, and those who minister to them. It explores the topic from the perspectives of living alone after living with someone, living alone temporarily, and, as an adult, always having lived alone.

Central Threads:
Teaching and the Journey of Faith

One easily finds the common threads of feminism that are discussed in the Introduction in Freda's theory and practice of teaching. Most of these threads were evident before Freda self-consciously identified herself as a feminist, but her reading of feminist writers and her increasing passion for justice for women deepened the color and strengthened the fiber of these threads. As the metaphor implies, one cannot pull out the individual threads of a rich tapestry in order to inspect the particular detail and beauty of a single strand. One can focus for a while on a particular thread, but the richness of the weaving stands out by the way in which the threads cross and complement one another. The thread gains its beauty in the larger weaving. So, too, when considering the detail and beauty of the feminist threads in Freda's teaching, we find that the threads intertwine richly. Though we tarry on one thread at a time, we necessarily glimpse the others as well.

The Partnership of Teacher and Learner

"There is content to the process of teaching,"[17] Freda contends, and part of that content conveys whether or not we deem the learner a valuable human being. Freda consistently aimed to teach others the worth of each learner. For the teacher, "the primary subject matter is the life of the student."[18] Freda's perceptive article on the school-age child remains one of the best introductions for those who wish to understand and respond to children. She has clearly done what she believes parenting and teaching call for: caring and attentive listening to children.[19]

A teacher who understands learners will also be able to draw upon a variety of teaching methods that help elicit the learner's interest in new ideas and experiences. "We know that learning involves trust, risk, vulnerability, as well as a shift in perspective and a capacity and willingness to live with ambiguities and to tolerate more than one answer. These conditions for learning must be matched by a need to learn: a recognition of one's own relationship to the subject or concern or experience which constitutes the 'stuff of the educational event.'"[20] Freda thus uses methods that make the link between the content we hope to share and the life of the learner.

Freda's lifelong commitment to the value of the learner is joined with a deep awareness of the importance of the teacher. "Good research, good visioning, good listening inevitably leads to the teacher as the single most significant factor in learning and education," she contends.[21] Good teaching requires disciplined attention to the learner and sufficient awareness of the nature of the task. "Those who are called out to be teachers often succumb to a vision of teaching that is too narrow both for the community of learners and for the nature and significance of the search [that is intrinsic to the life of faith]."[22]

Freda was so well able to communicate her respect for the learner that students frequently came back, again and again, for her courses—even students whose theological viewpoints and life commitments were strikingly different from her own. She was also able to nudge students to stretch beyond their comfort zones. One of her former students, Choon-Leong Seow, now a distinguished scholar and professor of Old Testament at Princeton Theological Seminary, took as many courses as he could from Freda. He recalls a course on teaching he took with her. Because it was the style with which he had the most experience, he chose to lecture for his first assignment. Freda affirmed the qualities of his lecturing but then suggested that he take a risk and try another method of teaching for his next assignment. She assured him that the class was a safe place to take such a risk. He accepted her challenge, explored creative teaching styles, and is now known as a teacher who blends rigor and creativity. For example, rather than simply lecture on the theme of theodicy, he carefully orchestrates a "trial" (replete with real-life judges) in which God is the defendant. "Freda was the most influential teacher I had," he recently stated.

Good teaching, as Freda sees it, requires solidarity with, and not simply knowledge of, the learner. "Teachers ought always to be putting themselves in the position of the neophyte and learn something new so they know what it's like not to know."[23] In addition to seeking out new topics and adventures, one of the ways in which Freda puts herself in the position of a learner is through reading literature that exposes her to experiences of the human situation that are not her own. "Because I have read so consistently, I understand a lot of things I've never experienced. Literature takes me where my life has never taken me."[24] She particularly reads gay literature, fiction dealing with loss and grief (including losses she herself has experienced, as well as those she has not), and the stories of people outside the church in whose lives God is at work. One of the marks of her teaching, as well, has been her use of story, literature, and film for exposing students to the lives of others.

Good teaching, however, requires more than attention to and solidarity with the learner. The teacher's affirmation of the learner is, for Freda, inextricably tied to the empowering of learners to interact with one another. Freda does not promote a "bicycle spoke" approach to teaching, which keeps the teacher as the only point of access to a conversation. She fosters community and interaction among learners. By nurturing in learners the dual capacities to "name" themselves and to "hear others into being," she provides a safe atmosphere both for coming to voice and for learning from others. Both confidence and humility are inspired. Furthermore, wonder and not knowing are affirmed by Freda.[25] "The meeting place of searchers for understanding has space for 'I wonder,' 'I don't know,' 'let's think about that.'

It has space for 'I do not know' and for 'I need to know more.'" [26] Learners are thus joined together in a common search for truth, and part of that truth is the capacity to remain on the search together. This is where process and content most fully join in faith's search for understanding. "Giving credibility to another's experience and way of being does not rob me of my own, nor is it so seductive that I cannot interact with it without great fear that I will get lost. Interactive teaching strategies and collaborative learning seem so much more compatible with faith's search for understanding."[27]

The rich thread of the teacher-learner partnership is thus, for Freda, intertwined with the strand of the community context for education.

Education Happens in Community

This is where Freda's second favorite story about children comes in. A small child cries out with fear in the middle of the night, and the groggy parent calls back that there is nothing to be afraid of. The child is unconsoled: "I don't care. I'm still scared and I don't like to be alone." The parent calls back, "It's O.K., God is with you and will take care of you." "There is a pause and then the child calls back, 'but I'd rather be taken care of by someone with skin on.'"[28]

Faith is a palpable, incarnate journey with others who are real. Because the journey of faith frequently leads down paths that are difficult, having others along is critical:

> The path from the manger to cross (and beyond) is the path of Jesus' own direct facing of sins and agonies in a tortured world; it is, sadly, in one sense, a path wide enough to allow each of us and all of Christ's disciples to follow . . . some with hands ready to lift up and support the fallen, some with arms outstretched to take in the refugees of life's power to wound, some with minds planning for the tearing down of systems which treat people as things, some with voices articulating the unspoken terrors of the voiceless, some with food for the hungry or work for the unemployed, some absorbing the violence of the weak as a strong witness to peace.[29]

In fact, for Gardner, as the kingdom of God is more fully realized in our lives, we will seek and be joined not only by those who have skin but by those who represent the array of skin tones. Gardner, too, would "rather" be joined by those "with skin on": white, black, brown, yellow, and red skin. The community that follows Christ is a community of diversity.

Freda's sense of the need for diversity within community has its roots in her early childhood. As her small, largely Christian and Caucasian, town began to diversify, her father, the school principal, impressed on her the importance of hospitality and justice toward "outsiders." When a black family moved in, he talked to the class about the new family's coming and prepared them to welcome the children; he asked his daughter to sit next to the new girl and to befriend her.

Her parents also modeled an openness to other kinds of diversity, and they helped shape her ecumenical spirit. Though her family was Presbyterian, there was no Presbyterian church in their town. Her parents, committed to the local community, thought being part of the local church was more important than finding the right denomination. Hence the family attended a Dutch Reformed church during her early years. They also nurtured her appreciation for other religious traditions. When a Jewish family moved to their town, Freda's father made it a point to adjust the Christmas pageant so the son could take part. Freda built on these early teachings and developed a broad sense of community that stretched the local bounds of religious and community life:

> We are called to witness to God's activities by affirming and supporting those outside the church who call themselves by other names but who work at attending to and tending the world. This responsibility belongs to us who confess that we have not captured God in our belief system or in our church structures, but, rather, worship and serve a God who establishes a kingdom by any means consistent with the characteristics of that kingdom, using works and their efforts for peace and justice wherever they may be found.[30]

Even as community is, for Freda, primarily a place for face-to-face interaction, it is also a place that implicitly reminds us that there are those who are among us who cannot be in our daily midst. She remembers listening, as a child, to mission speakers and being afraid that God would send her someplace she didn't want to go. She wasn't particularly interested in hearing these speakers, until one day "it dawned on me that they were out there on my behalf." Her sense of community expanded that day, and she began to feel a greater connection to these people who represented her in faraway places. When letters and reports came to the church, she took greater care to hear them. This created in Freda an ever-present awareness that the boundaries of a community are fluid.

Community is not simply that place where education takes place. Community life itself educates.

The Expansive Context of Education: Community Life as Teacher

I have noted Gardner's insight into the way in which process is content. She further elaborates on this in relation to the life of the church. *The life of the church is a teaching process.* "The truth of the content-in-process must extend to what is being taught by whatever the Church is or does, especially those parts of the life of the church that are rarely if ever labeled educational ministry."

Master Teacher Whose Faith Helps Us Understand

"To put it more bluntly and as a question, what teaches, and what teaches more effectively: the budget or the best efforts of a truly skilled teacher whose content would be approved by any ten of you theologians in the room?" she challenged at a seminar on teaching. "Illustrate it any way you will and even argue about the answers—one only needs to listen to people talk, to observe how we live, to watch how we respond to crises, to share their/our guilts and fears to know what most have learned. . . . People have learned in the Church what none of us have ever taught but which the Church has taught very well by the way it lives." She challenges her listeners to probe where it might be the case that "the life of the Church is a teaching process with content that is not always congruent with what the Church sets out to teach."[31]

Freda's understanding of community life as educator anticipates the next theme: the importance of holistic education. As we lead into that theme, it should be noted here that Freda regularly argued for the fullness of practice in community life. In her review of the book *The Mustard Seed Process,* she expressed enthusiasm for the book's emphasis on social justice, an issue dear to her heart. Yet Freda nudged readers of the book to enrich and extend its offering "with more attention to other disciplines of the Christian life which confront and sustain pilgrims on the way." Community life best educates when it sustains the full range of Christian practices. Thus Freda urges:

> Meditation, sharing the Eucharist, participation in the liturgy, corporate confession, the music of the church come to mind as resources of the church which would add to the purposes of the Mustard Seed Process, a helpful experience of growth for people who know that the God they worship asks for our participation in the establishment of justice which is an essential in God's purposes for creation.[32]

In addition to the range of practices, Freda frequently stresses the importance of the range of voices in community life. Just as the varieties of practices shape and renew us in different ways, so, too, the varieties of voices shape and renew our life together with greater richness.

The Holistic Nature of Education and Faith

Freda tells the story of a time when she was asked to lead a workshop on teaching for a large group whom she did not know well. She consulted the man who had invited her about the group's interests and styles of learning. The man dismissed her concerns, and he advised, "Speak about anything, but speak over their heads, and then they'll be impressed." "That goes against everything I believe about teaching and I've been doing my whole life," she responded. She ignored his advice and did it her way.

Freda is deeply committed to holistic education, which involves all the senses in learning and integrates the theories about faith and life with the actualities and particularities of faith and life. She is also attuned to the contextual nature of education: even if one decides to give a "good, long lecture," one needs to be aware of the particularity of the people to whom one is lecturing. Before elaborating further on her holistic style, it is crucial to understand the practical and theological undergirding of that style.

The holism of Freda's style is rooted in her understanding of Christian vocation. She believes that the calling of the Christian, so easily narrowed to profession, is a calling to discipleship in all areas of life. Freda took pains to describe teaching as "an expression of our vocation, one of the ways we lives as disciples of Jesus Christ," rather than as a vocation itself. Indebted to Karl Barth's theology of vocation, she understands it to be an inclusive rather than a narrow concept.[33] "I find it more useful to reserve the word vocation for our calling to be Christ's disciples and to see teaching, parenting, being neighborly, preaching, keeping order, tilling the earth, and the like as expressions of that calling, that vocation." She goes on to name a widespread temptation: "To equate vocation with occupation seems to me to let us off an important hook; it gives license to busy people to ignore family or community, to be Christ's woman or man on the job and something else at home or on vacation or in the midst of other powers and principalities."[34]

In her writings on parenting, she instills a strong sense of responsibility in parents and communities of faith. While taking pains to overcome sexist views that equate parenting with female nurturing, Freda has stressed the importance of caring and attentive adults in the development of children. I vividly remember the charge Freda gave my husband and me at our joint ordination service. She affirmed the strong commitment to parenting she had observed, and she challenged us to retain that commitment as a central part of our Christian vocation.

The call to caring for the next generation is not a particular calling. Although Freda viewed parenting per se as a particular responsibility for some, she emphasized that caring for children was part of every Christian's vocation: "In baptism the whole people of God accept the responsibility of supporting parents in their discipleship activities and supporting children as they grow in discipleship themselves."[35]

Thus, for Freda, education is about life, not just about ideas. Freda has a huge repertoire of teaching methods, and she always employs a number of them in any teaching event. Her style is to weave together the presentation of ideas with exercises that require learners to think about the complexities of the issue before them, the connection with their particular situations, and their own relationships to the tradition as it speaks to the given issue. In an essay on case studies, Freda argued for the value of interactive methods in the life of the church:

Scripture, creeds, encyclicals, and tradition speak volumes to the church and sometimes ancient words penetrate to the core of contemporary problems in a way that continues to surprise many of us. But sometimes these words do not help the parish or the parishioner to consider the multiple, critical factors or the hidden nuances which change an issue into a lived dilemma. The dynamics generated by persons interacting with each other, with institutions, or with the culture cannot always be dealt with or dismissed with an affirmation, simple or complex as it may be.[36]

The holism of education and its interactive nature contribute to human liberation; it is to this theme that we now turn.

Religious Education and Liberation: Renunciation and Resistance

The theme of Christian renunciation runs through many of Gardner's writings. Christians, she contends, need to have a "readiness to set aside our private goals and take up Christ's goals and to seek and accept the resources of the Christian community for our tasks."[37] Setting aside our private goals and taking up Christ's goals includes looking beyond the marks of status conferred by the world. In a Holy Week sermon preached on Jesus' footwashing, Freda charged her hearers to lay aside their accolades for the sake of service to God. Jesus knelt and washed his disciples' feet, she retells:

> But before he did that, Jesus laid aside his garments. Before He took up the towel . . . the symbol of servanthood, the embarrassing evidence that this savior is indeed the suffering servant . . . before He took up the towel, Jesus laid aside His garments. When Jesus said you ought to wash one another's feet, that command included the washing, the towel and the laying aside of the garments. Lay aside your garments? Take off this robe? Forget the title? Commissioners, Stated Clerk, Reverend, General Secretary, Moderator, professor, elder, president, chairperson? Take off your garments? Education, degrees, schools, travel, selfmade success, sold the most, walked the farthest, gave the most, most articulate, never borrowed, always paid my own way. . . . Take off those protective garments?[38]

Freda ends the sermon with a powerful interpretation of Jesus' command in the upper room:

> You who will go in my name to wash feet and to carry crosses if they be laid on you, you who will serve and vote and decide . . . you must first come to me as I came to you, with garments laid aside, with all that keeps you from looking silly or unready or unsure laid aside, with all the stuff that you think big folks, real Christians should do for themselves right there . . . and let me wash your feet. Then . . . after that, freed from all else that you count on to see you through, naked and weak and kneeling, then you will be part of me.[39]

As noted earlier, Freda was troubled by the hierarchies in the church—hierarchies that rendered Christian educators, laypersons, and women second-class citizens.

For Freda, however, Christian renunciation is balanced with passion and resistance. Renunciation to Christ is an empowering act. Those who follow Christ recognize that there is great "wounding" in the world, and it is often "no longer good enough to be nice"; "grace" is "something other than polite listening and smiling."[40] Grace can be expressed through passionate teachings and through resistance to evil.

In her 1986 inaugural address, when Freda was installed as a full professor at Princeton, she addressed teaching and argued for the importance of passion for one's discipline. Good teaching involves being "free to be so passionate that one may get called a history freak or a language loon or a pastoral pinko," even though such passion never should connotate "that is all that you are."[41]

Freda named the creative tension that exists between judgment and humility, refusing to collapse the Christian life into either side. Recognizing the way in which women must judge structures that exclude and demean them, she wasn't content to promote easy tolerance of viewpoints. In another context she posed the question: "Can we learn to speak judgment without casting stones or casting out? We shrink from judging while at the same time we live at ease in structures that judge, include and exclude."[42] Thus, when a prophetic word was needed on behalf of those excluded or oppressed, Gardner offered such. Her feisty review in 1975 of Emily Hunter's "Christian Charm Course"—a course designed for adolescent girls that offered "methods for improving the outer appearance along with spiritual instruction for developing the true beauty which comes from a heart surrendered to the Lord Jesus Christ"—culminated in her warning that the book's advice to girls was "an enslavement" and thus "heretical and sinful."[43] Similarly, in a review of the movie *Pretty Baby* that Freda wrote jointly with Hugh Kerr, the authors minced no words in judging the picture's failure to challenge the worldview and assumptions of the enterprise of female prostitution.[44]

The "resister" side of Freda was most fully expressed in her feminist commitments. Freda's self-understanding as a feminist, like her faith, was an ongoing journey. Her "first awareness of women's concerns" was early in her life. She was both moved and troubled by her mother's humility. Although a joyful person, her mother was consistently self-deprecating, never wanting to take credit for her gifts. "I remember quite early on thinking that's not right. Women like her are doing such important things."[45] She retained an acute awareness of the ways in which women were undervalued and underrecognized for their contributions to public and communal life.[46]

The next stage of Freda's feminism took shape "in the politics of education." She became aware of women's presence and absence in places, and she was attuned to ways in which women had and did not have voice in institutions. She explicitly named herself a feminist in the 1970s, and she was invited by Nelle Morton to work with Nelle in a course on feminist theology at Drew University's School of Theology in Madison, New Jersey. Freda and Katharine Doob Sakenfeld pioneered a course on "Teaching the Bible as Liberating Word" at Princeton, and they explicitly tackled issues pertaining to women and biblical interpretation. They exposed students to feminist interpretations of the Bible, and they provided a safe atmosphere for exploring methods of dealing with difficult texts. Ever the attentive educator, Freda tended very carefully to the importance of the teacher's sensitivity to those who struggle with change.

Freda readily acknowledges that her commitment to feminism was sometimes painful. She stresses the importance of discernment, noting that a prophet also needs compassion and wisdom in raising difficult issues. She is not afraid, however, to hold people accountable when she feels that is needed. She boldly stitched into her teaching the feminist thread that "language shapes religious knowing." In her classes, Freda explicitly named her passion for inclusive language. She helped learners recognize the ways in which language shapes reality. While sympathetic to slips of the tongue in speaking, she directly admonished students, "In your papers, you *will* use inclusive language."

The Giving and Receiving of Teaching

In grammar school Freda Gardner won a spelling bee, capped by her successful rendering of the word *precedent*. In many ways, she has set a precedent for teachers who come after her. Although embracing the boundaries, her work has impacted on the center of the life of church and seminary. Students who have taken her classes, educators who have been to her workshops, and colleagues who have taught with her are recognizable. By her witness to faith's journey, her deep respect for the learner, and her interactive style, Freda has served as midwife to the birthing of many a teacher.

Freda Gardner ended her inaugural address at Princeton with an excerpt given to her by a student, taken from John Steinbeck's *The Log of the Sea of Cortez:*

> Perhaps the most overrated virtue in our list of shoddy virtues is that of giving. Giving builds up the ego of the giver, makes [the giver] superior and higher and larger than the receiver. . . . It is so easy to give, so exquisitely rewarding. Receiving on the other hand, if it be well done, requires a fine balance of self-knowledge and kindness. It requires humility and tact and great understanding of relationships. . . . It requires a self-esteem to receive—not self-love but just a pleasant acquaintance and liking for oneself.[47]

FREDA A. GARDNER

Certainly, Freda has the humility, tact, and self-esteem to *receive*—evidenced in no small way by the fact that she ended her important address with a story that was *given* to her. Yet those of us who have been taught to receive by Gardner cannot help but acknowledge that which she has given. Her teaching, her story, and her person—given without an air of superiority but with a genuine and pleasant acquaintance with herself—make a splendid gift. She deserves to feel exquisitely rewarded.

NOTES

1. Freda A. Gardner, "Tennent as Center," *Princeton Seminary Bulletin* 4, 3 (1983): 185.
2. Freda A. Gardner, "Preaching and the Missing Parent," *Journal for Preachers* 15, 1 (1991): 18.
3. Andrew P. Lester, ed., "Faith Development and the School-Age Child," in *When Children Suffer: A Sourcebook for Ministry with Children in Crises* (Philadelphia: Westminster Press, 1987), 32–34.
4. Freda A. Gardner "Understanding Your Child," in *Active Parenting in the Faith Community: A Biblical and Theological Guide* (Louisville, Ky.: Presbyterian Publishing House for Family Ministries 1986), Session 2, 13.
5. Freda A. Gardner "Faith Values in Youth Ministry," in *Developing Leaders for Youth Ministry* (Valley Forge, Pa.: Judson Press, 1984), 37.
6. Freda A. Gardner "Teaching: A Response to Faith in Search of Understanding" (inaugural address), *Princeton Seminary Bulletin* 7, 2 (1986): 132.
7. Ibid., 134.
8. In Sandra Martz, *When I Am an Old Woman I Shall Wear Purple* (Watsonville, Ca.: Papier-Mache Press, 1991).
9. Freda A. Gardner, "Issues in Leadership," in *Always Being Reformed: The Future of Church Education,* ed. John C. Purdy (Philadelphia: Geneva Press, 1985), 69.
10. Freda A. Gardner, Review of Carol Christ's *Diving Deep and Surfacing* (Boston: Beacon Press, 1980), *Princeton Seminary Bulletin* 3, 1 (1980): 106.
11. Unless noted, the quotations in this part of the chapter are taken from interviews with Freda Gardner, done by the author, Princeton, N.J., fall 1996.
12. Gardner, "Issues in Leadership," 72.
13. Gardner, "Teaching," *Princeton Seminary Bulletin,* 137.
14. Gardner, *Active Parenting in the Faith Community,* 8.
15. Gardner, "Tennent as Center," 184.
16. Herb Anderson and Freda A. Gardner, *Living Alone* (Louisville, Ky.: Westminster John Knox Press, 1997).
17. Freda A. Gardner, "Teaching," *Journal of Presbyterian History* 61 (1983): 179. This is the printed text of a seminar.
18. Gardner, interview with the author, Princeton, N.J., fall 1996.
19. Gardner, "Faith Development and the School-Age Child," 34.
20. Freda A. Gardner, "A Case for the Use of Case Studies," *Living Light: An Interdisciplinary Review of Christian Education* 14, 1 (spring 1977): 56.
21. Gardner, "Teaching," *Princeton Seminary Bulletin,* 138.
22. Ibid., 131.
23. Gardner, interview with the author, Princeton, N.J., fall 1996.
24. Ibid.

25. Freda is influenced by the work of Parker Palmer, and she values his claim that "to teach is to create a space in which obedience to truth is practiced." See Parker Palmer, *To Know as We Are Known: A Spirituality of Education* (San Francisco: Harper & Row, 1983), 88.
26. Gardner, "Teaching," *Princeton Seminary Bulletin,* 141.
27. Ibid., 140.
28. Gardner, "Tennent as Center," 185.
29. Freda A. Gardner, "It's You I'm Calling," sermon, printed in *Princeton Seminary Bulletin* 4, 2 (1983): 113.
30. Gardner, "Issues in Leadership," 71.
31. Gardner, "Teaching," *Journal of Presbyterian History,* 180.
32. Freda A. Gardner, review of *The Mustard Seed Process,* by Helen Swift, S.N.D., and Frank Oppenheim (New York: Paulist Press, 1986), *Religious Education* 82 (1987): 159.
33. Karl Barth, *Church Dogmatics,* G.N. Bromily, T.F. Torrance, eds., Translated by Torrance (T & T Clark, Edinburgh, UK, 1961), vol. 4, part 3, second half.
34. Gardner, "Teaching," *Princeton Seminary Bulletin,* 138.
35. Gardner, *Active Parenting in the Faith Community,* 4.
36. Gardner, "Use of Case Studies," 56.
37. Freda A. Gardner, "Partners with Parents," *Association of Presbyterian Christian Educators Advocate* 13, 2 (May 1988): 9. See also Gardner, *Active Parenting in the Faith Community.*
38. Freda A. Gardner, "No Part of Me," sermon, printed in *Fellowship in Prayer* 38, 2 (April 1987): 9.
39. Ibid., 11.
40. Ibid., 7.
41. Gardner, "Teaching," *Princeton Seminary Bulletin,* 139.
42. Gardner, "Teaching," *Journal of Presbyterian History,* 181.
43. Freda A. Gardner, "Christian Charm," a commentary in Critics Corner, *Theology Today* 32 (April 1975–January 1976): 297.
44. Freda A. Gardner and Hugh T. Kerr, "Pretty Baby—A Film Critique," *Theology Today* 35, 3 (October 1978): 329–34.
45. Gardner, interview with the author, Princeton, N.J., fall 1996.
46. Professor Gardner encouraged students to call her Freda, and this helped overcome the hierarchical ordering of seminary life. When I began this chapter, I wanted to use "Dr. Gardner" and "Professor Gardner" rather than "Freda," even though such a move was, in a sense, unfaithful to her own practice and in conformity with the "master's tools" of hierarchy (Audre Lorde). Yet I also wanted to use language that fully honored the professor's contributions. When asked—for the sake of the overall consistency of the book—to change the monikers from the formal to the less formal I relented, but here I wish to register a sense of ambivalence.
47. Gardner, "Teaching," *Princeton Seminary Bulletin,* 145.

Letty M. Russell

EDUCATING FOR PARTNERSHIP

Barbara Anne Keely

Letty Russell is well known as a shaping voice in feminist theology. Since the 1950s, her work has influenced women and men who seek theological and biblical frameworks that liberate and empower. Although Letty is a professor of theology, she began her ministry and teaching as a church educator, and her reputation as a theologian has grown out of her ability to integrate feminist theology and education. Before there was a feminist language for theologians and educators, she was leading the way for students and scholars to come. She is included in this text both for her work as an educator and because she has been instrumental in shaping the work of women and men in religious education.

I began to explore Letty's work seriously as part of my doctoral studies. The more I explored, the more it both intrigued me and grounded my own thinking,[1] as she provides clues for those of us who wish to engage in diverse theological discussions while remaining in the church. Letty has remained grounded in the Bible and the Christian tradition even as she has challenged scriptural interpretations and traditions that have oppressed women and others on the margins of the church.

Letty Mandeville Russell was born in Westfield, New Jersey, in 1929, where she was a member of the Presbyterian Church of Westfield. She graduated from Wellesley College in Massachusetts in 1951. During her years in college, she was very active in the Student Volunteer Movement and the Student Christian Movement of New England. She taught third grade in Middletown, Connecticut, for one year after college while also directing the Christian education program of a small Methodist church in Higganum, Connecticut.

In 1952, Letty began her work with the East Harlem Protestant Parish, as director of religious education (DRE) at the Church of the Ascension and as a home missionary of the former United Presbyterian Church U.S.A. When asked how a white, well-educated young woman from an affluent area of New Jersey came to work in the East Harlem Protestant Parish, she reflected on her college-age involvement with the Student Christian Movement and her understanding of the Gospel as a source of transformation.[2]

Letty attended Harvard Divinity School and, upon graduation in 1958, was one of the first women ordained to the ministry of the Word and sacrament in The United Presbyterian Church in the U.S.A. She returned to the Church of the Ascension, where she served as pastor for ten years. Those were tumultuous years in Harlem, and Letty's feminist theology and educational theory were shaped by her ministry among the oppressed.

She earned her master of sacred theology degree (S.T.M.), in the area of Christian education and theology, from Union Theological Seminary in New York in 1967, and in 1968 she left the East Harlem Parish to continue her theological studies. Letty received her Th.D. in mission theology and ecumenics from Union Theological Seminary in 1969 and taught at Manhattan College thereafter, from 1969 to 1974. In 1974 she joined the faculty of Yale Divinity School, where she is presently professor of theology.

Letty's work is grounded in local contexts yet committed to worldwide ecumenics. Through her work with the World Council of Churches, she is known throughout the world. She has been on the forefront of theology and Christian education from liberation and feminist perspectives. She is nationally and internationally known as one who encourages theological dialogue that respects diversity and works for inclusivity. Through her writing, teaching, and leadership, she has proven to be both model and partner for many women and men.

Scholarship and Teaching

Letty has published over one hundred articles and books. In the introduction to *Christian Education in Mission,* she wrote that her work grew out of two directions, "that of my experience and that of my theology. My experience is that of life in a Christian community set in the midst of poverty, failure, and despair that has nevertheless learned to give thanks (Eph. 5:15–20). My theology is based on the conviction that the resurrection and victory of Christ is the starting and ending point of Christian life and nurture (I Cor. 15:51–58)."[3]

Her experience in ministry influenced her changing understanding of theology. Her experience of being in ministry with the poor and oppressed required her to rework both what "ministry with" looks like (partnership) and what a theology valid to that experience is (liberation).

Letty has described the team ministry that was developed in the 1960s in the East Harlem Protestant Parish. Central to her concept of team ministry was "the development of indigenous lay leadership . . . and the desire to include all the staff in a particular unit as part of a group or team ministry."[4] The team included the secretary/education assistant and the custodian. Over the years, the secretary did more and more educational work, and the custodian became a lay evangelist, preaching and teaching in Spanish. The church staff operated as partners, as the minister, education assistant, and custodian all shared in responsibilities that ranged from typing bulletins and sweeping floors to preaching and leading Bible studies.

Letty developed two resources during this time. The first is the *Daily Bible Readings,* written from 1960 to 1968 and published by the East Harlem Protestant Parish. The second is the *Christian Education Handbook* (1966), a "do-it-yourself guide" for developing indigenous curriculum resources in the parish.[5]

Part of the educational ministry of the East Harlem Protestant Parish was the opportunity to meet in weekly Bible study groups. Using the *Daily Bible Readings,* these groups would study the scripture passage that was to be the text for the following Sunday's sermon. For nine years Letty wrote the materials for these study groups.

But the material extended beyond the weekly group study; there were Bible readings for each day of the week. This was designed to encourage daily Bible study among the participants. The holistic structure designed by Letty followed this pattern: "The same text is studied by staff and Bible study leaders on Monday, by all the House Bible Study groups on Wednesday, by the children and youth on Sunday, and is the basis for the sermon."[6]

In 1966, Letty wrote the *Handbook* to enable churches to develop their own curriculum. It was designed as a supplement to the *Daily Bible Readings,* although the use of one with the other was not required. But the *Handbook* helped emphasize that "the dialogue of education takes place in the whole church family," and that "Christian education of children is not possible without being continually related to serious Bible study."[7] It is clear that even in these early days of her ministry, Letty was embodying a theory and theology of feminist work that would later be described as community-based, oriented toward liberation, and grounded in a feminist understanding of power.

When asked to review the development of her understanding of religious education, Letty wrote, "A constant factor in my understanding of religious education over the years is that it has *changed* as my life has changed." She goes on to acknowledge aspects that had been particularly influential:

> One is that my changing ideas in religious education reveal an emerging feminist consciousness and critique. The other is that, like other libera-

tion theologians, I would maintain that there are no objective descriptions of education. Each person's description is shaped by life experience and social location.

Another constant factor in education itself is that it is never completely described or defined. It is a *process* of actualizing and modifying the development of the total person through dialogical relationships. We never stand completely outside of this process for, in our own interaction, we are participants in naming what is going on in the learning-teaching situation. My own experience is that every time my learning-teaching situation changed, the way I named that process changed as well.[8]

From her early work, in which education was seen as ministry, to later writings that describe education as empowerment, each "description of Christian education has affirmed my continuing conviction that Christian education has to do with God's initiative and our partnership together with others in an ongoing process of growth."[9]

Letty also noted that one aspect "that has not changed is my use of the term Christian Education rather than Religious Education. This is simply because as a Christian theologian and educator from the Reformed tradition, my particular starting point is biblical and Christological. I have constantly returned to the biblical foundations of my faith to discover the way we learn as participants in God's saving and liberating action."[10]

Over the years, Letty has described Christian education in changing ways. In reviewing her own development, she categorized her educational emphases into biblical foundations (mission, tradition, and building up); liberating dimensions (liberation, partnership, and *diakonia*); and human community (exodus, nurture, and empowerment).[11] A review of her work reveals that she does not abandon any of these but integrates each into her thought.[12] She still talks about mission and tradition in educational ministry, but she does so now from a liberating understanding of partnership, lived in the context of an empowering community.[13]

Biblical Foundations

Letty began in the 1950s and 1960s with the idea of education as *mission*. In her first book, *Christian Education in Mission,* she wrote, "Christian education is participation in Christ's invitation to all people to join in God's mission of restoring men [and women] to their true humanity."[14] The role of Christian education is to equip persons for mission. For Russell, there is little difference between Christian education and mission, for Christian education is missionary education.

This influences her understanding of Christ, both as teacher and as the subject matter that is taught. "Influenced by my own seminary training in the 1950's, I wanted to make it clear that God in Christ is our teacher, and that we share with God in the process of learning through action."[15] The action we are learning is how to share the good news of God's work done for us in Christ.

The second of Letty's biblical foundations for Christian education is education as *tradition*. While in ministry in East Harlem, grappling with the upheaval of the Civil Rights movement, Letty wrote, "The question of reality and meaning in the light of the future brings to the fore the questionableness of traditions. The patterns of cultural heritage which make up the historical nature of [humanity] are crumbling in the face of unprecedented change."[16] In the midst of the social upheavals, she still asks critical questions of the Christian tradition: "Is it authentic? Does it have any meaning for me today? Does it bind my future by its existence?"[17] This approach is clear in Russell's "spiral of theological engagement," which is described later in the chapter.

In the 1970s, Letty moved to the image of *building up,* based on her interpretation of *oikos,* God's house, as a way to describe education. Moving from the parish ministry to teaching at Manhattan College and New York Theological Seminary, she sought "a word that would emphasize the congregation as the locus of educational growth."[18] As she tried to integrate her worldwide work with the YMCA with her commitment to congregational education, she chose *oikos,* for it was the root of both "world" (*oikoumene*) and "building up" (*oikodome*). "Education was participation in God's stewardship or housekeeping (*oikonomia,* I Cor. 9:17), in building up (*oikodome,* Eph. 4:11–16; I Cor. 3:10–11) the household (*oikos,* Gal. 3:27–28) of God for the whole inhabited world (*oikoumene,* Phil. 1:27)."[19] The image of household remains dominant in Russell's theology,[20] but "building up" is no longer an image she uses for education. She admits that it was an interesting academic exercise, "but it did not inspire any great 'aha's' among my students."[21]

Liberating Dimensions

As the language of liberation theologies and liberation movements took hold in the early and mid-1970s, Letty began to talk about education as *liberation*. Her focus moved to the gospel as liberation and God as liberator. Education was the process by which one came to understand one's liberation in Christ. This emphasis has remained foundational to her work in hermeneutics, theology, and education:

> Since the publication of *Human Liberation in a Feminist Perspective—A Theology,* I have constantly returned to a description of *education as liberation:* a process of action-reflection on " . . . the meaning of oppression in the light of our participation in God's creation of a fully human society." The perpetuation of structures of oppression such as racism, sexism, and classism became a key issue of critique, and the emphasis on participatory education as a process of action/reflection was a continuing theme.[22]

Educating for Partnership

Understanding education as liberation has influenced Russell's work as a theologian and seminary professor. In addition, her view of the complete inclusivity of the gospel has continued to shape her involvement in global conversations regarding the liberating gospel of Jesus Christ.

Throughout her writing in the areas of feminist hermeneutics, theology, and education, *partnership* has been a unifying theme. In 1979, Letty wrote, "Partnership is an idea whose fulfillment is long overdue." She went on to define partnership as "*a relationship of mutuality and trust* based on the gift of God's partnership with us in our lives. God has chosen to be partner with us as Immanuel so that we might become partners with ourselves, one another and with God."[23]

Although Letty began writing about participatory education early in her work, it was not until *The Future of Partnership* (1979), *Growth in Partnership* (1982), and numerous articles published from the late 1970s on that education as partnership began to emerge as a significant dimension in her liberating Christian educational approach:

> In seeking to describe both the process and goal of liberating education I began to make use of the concept of *koinonia* (community, participation, partnership; I Cor. 10:16–17). In writing *The Future of Partnership* I tried to explore the impossible-possibility that God's partnership with us might set us free to be partners with others. This was not a retreat from the analysis of oppression and liberation, but rather an attempt to ask eschatological questions about the struggle for freedom, responding to the question, "After equality—what?"[24]

This question points to the struggle of educating for partnership. Equality or liberation precedes partnership, so to educate for partnership is first (or also) to educate for liberation. Liberation and partnership are interwoven dimensions of Russell's understanding of educational ministry.

About the same time that Letty was giving form to her understanding of education as partnership, she was also including a description of education as servanthood (*diakonia*): "From this perspective all forms of Christian service are educational when the participants are intentional about the way that the service has as its goal their own self-development and that of others."[25] The three dimensions of liberation, partnership, and servanthood (*diakonia*) are still central to Russell's hermeneutics, theology, and ways of describing Christian education.

Human Community

The first dimension of the human community in Russell's thought is journey or *exodus*. Letty's movement from the 1970s to the 1980s was toward the understanding that "the process of learning is 'situation variable.' . . . In trying to describe the way in which we learn by joining in God's freedom movement, I returned to a biblical motif and began to describe education as *exodus:* going out together as part of God's freedom movement."[26] It appears that as she looked at the dimensions identified above and viewed them "from the other end" of new creation, her question became "How do we get there from here?" At this point, the exodus journey from bondage to liberation became important to her description of the educational process.

Continuing the imagery of moving forth in education, in the early 1980s, Letty also emphasized education as *nurture.* Nurture, she wrote, "explores how we can become what God intends us to become as full human beings. The stress here is on a process of becoming human by learning to help others as we are helped by God."[27] Because God has taken the initiative to be in partnership with us and to journey with us, we are called to journey together. This dimension gives a deepening sense of community to the educational process.

Letty's next emphasis is education as *empowerment.* "Moving away from paternalistic educational structures of dependency requires us to develop structures of community that empower persons of all ages for partnership, by inviting them to take part in their own educational journey."[28] This emphasis on empowerment through partnership, to free persons to move toward God's intended future, integrates important dimensions of Letty's educational thought.

When asked recently how she would currently describe her understanding of religious education, Letty chose the concept of *transformation:* "Not only does [theological education] seek to transform the lives of teachers and learners, but also on its agenda is the transformation of the communities of faith and struggle whose ministries they share. . . . Transformation implies that we share learning in the expectation that the person will be made new through the power of the Holy Spirit, and that the ministry of that person will be transformational in her or his context."[29]

Impact on Religious Education

Letty is unique in this collection of foremothers in that she understands her primary work to be that of a theologian. When being reviewed for tenure at Yale Divinity School, she made it clear that she would not accept a tenured position in the field of education.[30] Like other foremothers in this text, she knew she was called to the cutting edge; but she had to stand on the edge of theology. Aware of the power dynamics surrounding the theological enterprise, she understood that her impact on theological education could be much greater coming from the stance of one tenured in theology than from that of one tenured in religious education.

Although her scholarship and professional work over recent decades have been primarily in feminist theology and biblical interpretation, her impact on religious education is clear. Thomas Groome, a leader in religious education, has written, "I believe that Russell's entire corpus of writings is among the most significant literature available to religious educators today. Her current work on *partnership* has an urgent message that we need to hear."[31]

Letty's work, which is a powerful combination of feminist theory and practice of educational ministry, needs to be heard by those attending to feminist religious education. She brings extensive experience in parish ministry and academic teaching to her scholarship and embodies the development of a praxis of education that provides us with clues to transform the church.

Feminist Threads

According to Letty, "There is no one shape of Christian education,"[32] and so she describes it as emerging "out of the process of dialogue between our faith in Jesus Christ as Lord and our understanding of the world in which we live":[33]

> In searching for a verbal description of what we are about as Christian educators committed to partnership in learning, I have chosen to use the broader task description of *educational ministry*. Educational ministry is any form of serving in the name of Jesus Christ that involves us in mutual growth, and fuller self-actualization of God's intended humanity. Its goal is the development of critical and committed awareness among persons as they serve in Christ's name and seek to be a sign of God's New Creation. It is possible that educational ministry might have a style that brings people together in a *partnership of learning*.[34]

Letty describes this "possibility" through various clues, which I here discuss in relation to the threads of feminist education listed in the Introduction.

Integration of Life and Experience

When I met with Letty in April 1990, she gave me an illustration, titled "Theologizing in Mission," that she has used in courses over the past few years to help explain her spiral of theological engagement.[35] The spiral is an educational process, a way of doing theology that is committed "to the task of mending creation . . . with one particular group struggling for liberation."[36] For her, theological engagement begins with these commitments to God's work in the world and to a community of people who are marginal. With these as foundational, one can enter the spiral at any place.

The spiral has four movements of engagement: (1) sharing and understanding our experience, and our experience of struggle and commitment, within a worldview; (2) analyzing our reality as women and men; (3) raising questions about biblical and church tradition; and (4) creating alternatives for social transformation. The fourth movement spurs us on to a new sharing and understanding, for it is a process of "action/reflection and never reaches a conclusion. Instead it leads to some tentative clues and insights which in turn raise new questions."[37]

Consistent with her liberation/feminist methodology, Letty's process begins with one's own experiences and with the engagement of the community's experiences of struggle. In the process of sharing and understanding our experiences, we are driven to analyze our lives as women and men. As we consider those experiences, we begin to question biblical interpretations and church traditions, to see how they have influenced our reality. As we raise the questions, we begin to develop different ways of shaping reality, which leads to creating alternatives for social reality.

Education Takes Place in Community

Feminist education is done within the context of the life of a community of faith. For Letty, therefore, the educational ministry of the church should be part of the whole life of the church, and not compartmentalized apart from the rest of the life of the congregation.[38]

> My discussion of Christian education begins with this assumption that in fact education is involved in the whole of church life, and ceases to be education when it is taken out of the context of the witnessing community. Everything that happens in the witnessing community, be it faithful or unfaithful, is part of the educational process of Christian nurture of its members. . . . It is assumed that everything that happens in a Christian community should be viewed in an educational perspective if we are to understand how it is that Christ nurtures his people through their life together.[39]

Contextuality beyond Immediate Community

In this third thread, Letty is clear that education is contextual, with specific people in specific contexts. It is not generic. This has implications for educational resources that a congregation may chose to purchase and adapt to its context. It also suggests that liberating education is not "done to" people but "done within" people:

> The contextual style of liberation theologies is an important emphasis for education. There is no one way to teach and learn for we need content as well as experience to grow in the knowledge and actions of faith in Jesus Christ. Yet, if we are to begin where people are, we must seek to express the gospel message in their own context.[40]

But education must also go beyond the community of faith, especially if that community is white, middle-class, or otherwise a group of societal privilege. The struggle to include the insights of those oppressed and on the margins must also be part of the context of educating the oppressors for partnership.[41] Letty believes that "to be contexual one needs to enter deeply into solidarity with constituency groups. And in order to be committed to social change one must be willing to work collectively and to participate in communities of faith and struggle as they develop their theology."[42]

Language

Like other feminist educators, Letty recognizes that language shapes our understanding of persons and God. Her work has often addressed the power of naming humans in inclusive terms, as well as the importance of naming God in ways other than "Father."[43]

The Teacher-Learner partnership

In Letty's praxis of education, the teacher is not giver and the learner passive receiver. Instead, the teacher and the student "develop their power to perceive critically *the way they exist* in the world *with which* and *in which* they find themselves; they come to see the world not as a static reality, but as a reality in process, in transformation."[44] She describes her approach to this thread of liberating education:

> It would invite both teachers and students to take part in a collective style in which the community learns as it goes forward on the exodus journey together, learning from one another along the way. The experience of God's liberation would shape the commitment of those who have been through the waters of the baptism and themselves struggle to "not be conformed . . . but transformed" (Rom. 12:2). The learning would begin where people are in their own context and yet seek to include the insights of all those who know what it means to be marginalized and oppressed so that we can better understand the cost of slavery and the gift of freedom. In developing *critical* and committed awareness, education as exodus would encourage people to continue their journey of doubt and faith as people of God's covenant and promise.[45]

Feminist education recognizes that one person does not have the answers for another[46] but should be encouraged to ask the questions that will empower people to be on the journey toward new creation:[47]

> We are more able to deal with our own fears and inadequacies as teachers and learners if we recognize that questions themselves are important, whether or not we can answer them. . . . Freedom to ask questions is crucial for learning critical and committed awareness in a world of

change. Partnership in learning often makes it easier to ask without fear of appearing ignorant or of group rejection.[48]

To be partners on the journey is to share with others the questions we have and the answers we have found, but it is also to value others as unique, having both their own questions and their own way of searching for the answers.

The Integration of Theory and Practice

Letty has spend a lifetime integrating her experience with theology and theory of practice. As one of the first women ordained in the former United Presbyterian Church, U.S.A., she claimed a new place in ministry. But she claimed it in a context of ministry where she was surrounded by others who had known marginalization and oppression, and her years in Harlem shaped her theology and theory of education as profoundly as any life experience might. In recent years, she has focused on women who are struggling for both a place in their culture and a theology of liberation. Her work with women in third-world countries seems a natural, global extension for one who began her ministry in East Harlem.

Leads to Liberation

Liberating education carries the same emphases as liberation theologies, including being committed to the oppressed, the collective, the contextual, and the critical. Letty has written, "Just as God chose to be a partner with us, we must encourage others in the free choice of partnership through a process of mutual growth and service which sets us free for others."[49] This thread is essential for her. "*Educare* is understood to mean 'leading out,' and can also be seen as a journey. But education as a praxis of liberation is not just leading others out. It is going out together as part of God's freedom movement."[50]

Attending to Issues of Power

Letty points out clearly that within a community of faith is equality of every person but diversity of gifts. Liberating education includes differences in callings, responsibilities, maturity, knowledge, and experience, but none of these is permanent or static:

> The holistic perspective of educational ministry provides an opportunity to develop alternative styles of Christian community. One way to move beyond the separations of education and pastoral activity of children and adults, of clergy and laity, of women and men, is to structure the life of the church around the idea that educational ministry is the work of the

whole people of God. Such a structuring would involve the use of gifts and the sharing of power in such a way that needless hierarchy and structures of domination were eliminated.[51]

Her way of handling the unity in diversity is to suggest the functional understanding of "temporary inequality." This is manifest in one's willingness to empty oneself to serve another, yet doing it both within the context of freedom and with the understanding that the situation in temporary.[52]

Letty's Feminist Legacy

Letty Russell's legacy is as wide-ranging as her relationships and as deep as her scholarship. This chapter has focused primarily on her contributions to feminist approaches to religious education, which is only a segment of her teaching and scholarship. Her work is not yet completed. Letty continues to encourage feminist theologies and feminist approaches to religious education and to mentor those of us she has encouraged along the way.

My most vivid image of Letty as foremother and mentor comes from my trip to Connecticut in 1990 to interview her as part of the work on my dissertation. She invited me to stay in her home, visit her classes, and attend a conference with her. The first evening I was at Letty's, we were sitting and visiting in her study. I asked about her early years in ministry, those formative years in the parish before her work was being published. She disappeared into a storage closet and emerged with an old box. Sitting down on the floor, with the box beside her, she began to sort through unpublished speeches and manuscripts, reminiscing as she handed them to me. "Here, take anything that might help," she said.

Through a lifetime of ministry and teaching, Letty has not only led the way but freely given to anyone that which might help usher in God's new creation.

NOTES

1. My fascination with and appreciation of Letty's work led me to her understanding of partnership and its implications for Christian education, which became the topic of my doctoral dissertation.
2. Letty Russell, conversation with the author, Guilford, Connecticut, April 1990.
3. Letty M. Russell, *Christian Education in Mission* (Philadelphia: Westminster Press, 1967), 9.
4. Letty M. Russell, "Team Ministry in the East Harlem Protestant Parish: An Adventure in Lay Ministry" (speech, n.d.; late 1960s), 1. Photocopy provided by Dr. Russell.

5. Letty M. Russell, *Daily Bible Readings,* (New York: East Harlem Protestant Parish; 1960–68), published quarterly; Letty M. Russell, *Christian Education Handbook* (New York: East Harlem Protestant Parish, 1966).
6. Russell, *Christian Education Handbook,* 7.
7. Ibid., 4.
8. Letty M. Russell, "Changing My Mind about Religious Education," *Religious Education* 79 (winter 1984): 5.
9. Ibid., 10.
10. Ibid., 5–6.
11. Ibid.
12. The only possible exception is the dimension of building up. Although she does not find this a helpful image in educational ministry, the Greek root *oikos* nevertheless becomes central in her recent work, which focuses on the household (*oikonomia*) of God.
13. See especially Letty M. Russell, *The Church in the Round: Feminist Interpretation of the Church* (Louisville, Ky.: Westminster/John Knox Press, 1993).
14. Russell, *Christian Education in Mission,* 35. Although Russell changed to more inclusive language in the 1970s, her early writings sometimes use male-exclusive language. Where I have made changes in her writings to reflect what I understand to be her more inclusive intent, the changed words are noted in brackets.
15. Russell, "Changing My Mind" 6.
16. Letty M. Russell, "Tradition as Mission: Study of the New Current in Theology and Its Implications for Theological Education" (Th.D. diss., Union Theological Seminary, New York, 1969), 2.
17. Ibid.
18. Russell, "Changing My Mind," 6.
19. Ibid., 6–7.
20. See especially Letty M. Russell, *Household of Freedom: Authority in Feminist Theology* (Philadelphia: Westminster Press, 1987).
21. Russell, "Changing My Mind," 7.
22. Ibid. See also Letty M. Russell, *Human Liberation in a Feminist Perspective—A Theology* (Philadelphia: Westminster Press, 1974), 20.
23. Letty M. Russell, "Partnership in Educational Ministry," *Religious Education* 74 (March–April 1979): 143; see also Letty M. Russell, *Future of Partnership* (Philadelphia: Westminster Press, 1979).
24. Russell, "Changing My Mind" 7.
25. Ibid., 8. See also Letty M. Russell, "Handing on Traditions and Changing the World," in *Tradition and Transformation in Religious Education,* ed. Padraic O'Hare (Birmingham, Ala.: Religious Education Press, 1979), 73–86.
26. Russell, "Changing My Mind" 8. See also Letty M. Russell, *Growth in Partnership* (Philadelphia: Westminster Press, 1981), 72.
27. Russell, "Changing My Mind" 9.
28. Ibid.
29. Letty M. Russell, "Education as Transformation: Feminist Perspectives on the Viability of Ministerial Formation Today," *Ministerial Formation* 74 (July 1996): 23.
30. Russell, conversation with the author.
31. Thomas Groome, "Letty Russell: Keeping the Rumor Alive," *Religious Education* 77 (May–June 1982): 350.
32. Russell, *Christian Education Handbook,* 17; see also idem, "Changing My Mind" 5.

33. Russell, *Christian Education Handbook*, 5.
34. Ibid., 143–44.
35. Adapted from JoAnn DeQuattro, Rhonda Meister, Marjorie Yuite, and Judy Vaughn, comps. *HOW TO Skills with a Feminist Perspective,* (National Assembly of Religious Women, USA, 1988). Handout provided by Dr. Russell. The adaptation was revised by Dr. Russell in 1988.
36. Ibid.
37. Letty M. Russell, ed., *Changing Contexts of Our Faith* (Philadephia: Fortress Press, 1985), 103.
38. Russell, *Christian Education in Mission,* 21–22; idem, *Growth in Partnership,* 58.
39. Russell, *Christian Education in Mission,* 13.
40. Letty M. Russell, "Doing Liberation Theology with All Ages," *Church Educator* (February 1978): 4.
41. Russell, *Growth in Partnership,* 74.
42. Letty M. Russell, "How Do We Educate and for What? Reflections on U.S. Graduate Theological Education," *Journal of the Interdenominational Theological Center* 15 (fall 1987–spring 1988): 39–40.
43. See Letty M. Russell, "Power of Naming," Chapter 3, in *Household of Freedom,* 43–57.
44. Paulo Freire, *Pedagogy of the Oppressed,* trans. Myra Berman Ramos (New York: Continuum, 1984), 70–71.
45. Russell, *Growth in Partnership,* 73–74. See also idem, "Partnership in Educational Ministry," 144.
46. Letty M. Russell, "Education in Action," Manhattan College Magazine (December 1970): 3.
47. Letty M. Russell, "The Power of Partnership: Confronting Racism, Sexism and Classism in the Church" (speech given November 1982), 6–7.
48. Letty M. Russell, "Education as Exodus," *Mid-Stream* 19 (January 1980): 7.
49. Russell, "Partnership in Educational Ministry," 144.
50. Russell, "How Do We Educate?" 38.
51. Russell, "Partnership in Educational Ministry," 145. See also idem, *Christian Education in Mission,* 13; and idem, *Growth in Partnership,* 29.
52. Russell, *Growth in Partnership,* 79.

Maria Harris

AN AESTHETIC
AND EROTIC JUSTICE

Judith A. Dorney

It was her face I noticed first, and her trim cap of gray hair. Next I noted her vivid color: she was wearing a skirt, necklace, and earrings the shade of pink azaleas. Maria's petite frame seemed, paradoxically, to emphasize her presence in the midst of this towering city. As we embraced, I felt the power of our "coming together"[1] as women, as sisters, and as teacher and student. I was back in the company of my dear friend.

I had traveled that morning from New Paltz, New York, to have a conversation with Maria Harris about her life's work. Maria had been my teacher more than fifteen years earlier for two summer courses in religious education at Boston College. My last work with her, four years before this reunion in Manhattan, was as a colleague. We offered a weeklong workshop at Auburn Theological Seminary in New York City on "Women Teaching Girls," a subject we had both become absorbed in as our individual work progressed.

It was no accident that the location for this meeting was New York City. It is a place that has nourished and influenced Maria's sense of what religious education is, as well as how it can be done. Her apartment, the property of New York University, is on the edge of Washington Square, a crossroads for the people of the world. It is at this university where Maria is now a visiting professor of religious education and her beloved husband, Gabriel Moran, a full-time professor.

Place and Time: Maria and
the Field of Religious Education

Maria is Roman Catholic. "Like being short," she points out, she is "constitutionally Catholic."[2] Her understanding, her imagination, her spirit and heart are "essentially sacramental, essentially communal." This tradition is not, for her, a choice; Catholicism is in her bones and in her blood.

While these sacramental and communal dimensions of Maria's Catholicism are at the center of her writing and teaching, Catholicism has also played a significant part in locating Maria in a particular place and time in the larger field of religious education. Although the Religious Education Association was organized in 1903, Catholic Christians were not much a part of the religious education movement in this country until the 1950s.

Maria officially began her teaching in religious education in 1952, at about the same time that Catholics were becoming more involved in the Religious Education Association. When she started teaching elementary school students, Maria was also a member of a religious community, the Sisters of St. Joseph. She taught music, a lifelong passion and one that has also deeply informed her understanding of religious education. Her personal love of music and its centrality in Catholic worship enabled Maria to know early on that religious education is not the domain of schooling alone. Liturgy, community, preaching, and service are curricula for religious education as well.[3]

The radical liturgical and church-life reforms ushered in by the Second Vatican Council in the 1960s offered an exciting, reformed geography for Maria's doctoral studies in religious education at Union Theological Seminary and Columbia University Teachers College in New York City. Like New York University today, Union had a multidimensional, ecumenical student body and faculty population. This setting provided a medium in which to appreciate the religious understandings of others, particularly Protestants and Jews. Maria's doctoral work led her very consciously to reconceptualize the meaning of religious education. Her reformulation included insights, steeped in her own experience, about where religious education happens and how—for her, through the aesthetic. It also involved a deep understanding of the levels of curriculum that educate religiously, an appreciation for ecumenical dialogue, and a burgeoning clarity about how education for justice is a constitutive strand of all religious education.

These insights were extended during her twelve-year tenure at Andover Newton Theological School, in Newton Center, Massachusetts, (1975–1986) where she was one of three women and the only full-time faculty member who was Roman Catholic. Again, these essential factors of Maria's existence placed her as an outsider, albeit a welcomed and respected outsider, in the institutional seminary. And they may well have nurtured a critical consciousness of the dynamics of power in churches and a particular sensitivity to the marginal in the discourse and activity of religious education.

Her teaching experience overseas, in places such as Australia, Bermuda, New Zealand, and Korea, continues to deepen her perspective that religious education is what all people do to honor and extend religious presence in their midst. And her work in these countries reinforces the knowledge from her own life experience that learning about the religious traditions of others is necessary if we are truly to understand our own.

Maria finds that situating herself in the field of religious education is a complicated task: "We're still, in this twentieth century, trying to come to some understanding of what the field of religious education is." She has articulated three perspectives that currently contribute to defining the field, crediting Gabriel Moran for her own clarity in regard to the first two.

The first perspective is that religious education is the work of educating people to take part in a particular religious tradition. It is the task of passing on the story, the tradition, the ritual. Second, religious education is intended to cultivate religious understanding. This perspective actively values and draws on the variety of religious traditions' teachings about ethical perspectives, understandings of the Divine, sacred stories, and mystical elements, in order to deepen appreciation for diverse religions through understanding what they hold in common and what is unique to each one's story. In elaborating the third perspective, Maria referred to Alfred North Whitehead, who identified the essence of *all* education as religious.[4] That is, to honor and teach the dimension of depth present in all education is to educate religiously.

Maria is very much engaged in the work of realizing all three perspectives.

Maria's Teaching and Writing

Before discussing Maria's contributions as teacher and scholar, it seems appropriate to identify three essential themes or motifs in her work. The first is psychological insight. The second is a passionate commitment to justice. At the heart of Maria's work is the establishment of relationships that are just, compassionate, and loving. This offers the grounding for her emphasis on the interreligious and ecological nature of spiritual and religious growth, which challenges the field and calls for reflection on the definition of religious education.

The third theme is language. In *Fashion Me a People,* Maria writes, "My own educational work is a search to find new ways of speaking . . . since the language we use to describe our work has enormous power, either to support or to undermine what we are attempting to do."[5] Maria's language is a language of artistry that offers imaginative and organic openings into the work of religious education. Her poetic language links her other themes, thus articulating her psychological insight and her justice concerns.

Maria's Teaching

Maria is a teacher. While identifying herself as "constitutionally Catholic," she added that she was also "constitutionally a teacher." Maria began her career teaching elementary students but, since earning her doctorate, has taught at Fordham University in the Bronx and has held the Howard Chair in Religious Education at Andover Newton Theological School and the Tuohy Chair in Interreligious Studies at John Carroll University in Cleveland. She has also taught in summer or special programs at many schools, including Boston College; Fairfield (Connecticut), LaSalle and Villanova (Pennsylvania), Regis, University in Denver, and Santa Clara (California) Universities; Princeton, Union, and Immaculate Conception Seminaries in New York and New Jersey. Maria has also been scholar in residence at Loyola University in Chicago and delivered the Bradner Lectures at Episcopal Theological Seminary in Alexandria, Virginia; the Madeleva Lectures at St. Mary's College, Notre Dame, Indiana; and the Schaff Lectures at Pittsburgh Theological Seminary.

This record illustrates that teaching has been a significant part of Maria Harris's life's work. As she plainly says, however, it is even more than that. It is who she is.

I met Maria through her teaching, and it was a powerful introduction. I had been a high school teacher myself for close to a decade when I walked into her class on "The Aesthetic and Religious Education" at Boston College in the summer of 1979. While I think I already had good teaching instincts and really cared about my students, being in Maria's class made me *want* to be a teacher. My desire was inextricably connected to her energy, spirit, and passion, all of which took form in the way she shaped the course material. Audre Lorde connects this energy and passion within each of us to the deepest source of feeling, knowledge, and power at the center of our being. Lorde identifies it as the erotic, the union of the "spiritual and political."[6]

Maria has suggested that one of the central ingredients in her teaching is the connection between teacher and student. She writes, "In most circumstances we are asking of one another, 'Where does your life teach me about my life?'"[7] This is a quintessentially relational question. It recognizes that built into the teaching relationship is a desire, perhaps even a need, on the part of the student to find something in the person of the teacher that is authentic, that speaks truth, that reveals the depths of things. The person of the teacher, who, Maria claims, truly teaches. However, the teacher and student are brought together by the subject matter. Thus the relationship is extended to include connection to the material.

The teacher is also curriculum. Maria suggests as much when she asserts that "teaching is the incarnation of subject matter through various ways of fashioning, forming and embodying subject matter"[8] So the person of the teacher teaches, but the teacher has also been shaped by her or his love of the material that brings teacher and student together. The teacher gives personal and public form to the material and, in so doing, reveals what is of value. The educator Paulo Freire names this "consistency" between words and actions, one of his five elements of "bearing witness."[9] Teaching is an activity of giving flesh to word. It is part of what makes teaching a holy activity and, ultimately, political. This consistency is at the heart of Maria's teaching. It is also what gives authenticity to her writing.

Maria's Writing

Maria's written contributions to the field have been prolific.[10] Her work on the religious education and spiritual development of girls and women joins current developmental and educational research done by such groups as the American Association of University Women, the Harvard Project on Women's Psychology and Girls' Development, and the Wellesley Center for Research on Women.[11] In her work, she blurs the borders between religious education and psychological development, offering a holistic and healing educational perspective. This has enabled a much broader audience for Maria's work and, consequently, for her insights into religious and spiritual development.

For example, in *Women and Teaching,* Maria describes five themes essential in any pedagogy that takes seriously the education of girls and women: silence, remembering, ritual mourning, artistry, and birthing. I have used these themes as the basis of retreat work with groups of teachers and have found that participants are touched by the work in each theme: the work of identifying silences in curricula, of recalling one's dangerous memories of suffering and freedom, of naming what one knows and seeing how it serves as a tool for educational artistry. Exploring these themes, educators have changed their approaches to teaching and their relationships to students and colleagues. At the heart of the changes is an ability to integrate feelings such as anger, sadness, and tenderness with how people know. This process often reshapes the curriculum and the public space of the classroom in a way that encourages that all the knowledge of students be taken seriously and developed fully. Harris's five themes, from silence to birthing, provide the psychological framework for this transformational work.

In *Dance of the Spirit* and *Jubilee Time,* Maria extends her exploration of women's spiritual development, in the latter focusing on women in their "jubilee years," at age fifty or beyond. She again provides themes for reflection and growth, and as in *Women and Teaching,* these themes resonate with women's religious experiences as well as with their psyches. *In Dance of the Spirit*, for example, Maria begins with the theme of "wakening" and roots this experience in sensual, bodily awareness, as well as in both Western and Eastern spirituality. Beginning with the body is a potent way of helping women valorize their knowledge and use it as the ground for spiritual growth.

Maria offers a clue about her ability to link the spiritual with the psychological in a passage from *Teaching and Religious Imagination*. She suggests that the teacher who can provide experiences of profound learning for students has tapped into a truth of life and has found a way to make that truth live for students: "Every weaver of fairy tales, every psychologist, every shaman, rabbi and guru knows that if you pick up even one thread of reality and follow it to its end, it will take you to the heart of the universe."[12] Implicit here is that in order for the teacher to be able to grab hold of this thread, the teacher must be able to recognize it. Therefore the teacher's life experience is a critical, though often unconscious, tool in shaping the form and content of curriculum.

This passage offers a stunning wisdom very much connected to Maria's ideas about the importance of the teaching relationship as curriculum. I asked Maria what she felt her thread or threads might be: What was the truth she knew that connected to the heart of the universe? She responded by speaking about her father's death when she was eight and the devastating loss it brought to her family. Her own suffering made her aware of suffering as part of the human condition. She explained, "I don't have a limp. When I walk I look like I'm walking straight." Her voice softened: "But I do have a limp, and so does everyone else."

She added, "At the same time I have had such an extraordinary experience of being loved. . . . I know what it's like to be loved." In tracing the relationships that have sustained and graced her life, she spoke of family and friends, ending her list with Gabriel, with whom she experiences the love she names "sacrament."

Returning to my original question, Maria summed up her thoughts: "What we find at the heart of the universe, we find suffering and loss and sorrow . . . and love, if we're lucky." These are the threads at the heart of her work as a religious educator, and they are threads she finds in the heart of Catholic Christian experience. Maria noted this herself, adding, "Maybe it has fit for me to be a religious educator because the great mythos in my own tradition has been a myth of suffering and death and resurrection and that just resonates with my own experience."

In *Teaching and Religious Imagination* and *Fashion Me a People*, she challenges narrow definitions of the terms *religious* and *education* and offers a broad and bold educational vision. In the former book, Maria develops her theology of teaching. This theology is rooted in the imagination, which Maria asserts is linked to art, emotion, science, and the political. In pulling together these seemingly disparate elements of human experience, she offers a bridge across chasms of difference and provides a holistic educational vision.

Maria pries open the language of teaching in her discussion of the ways in which the religious and the imagination inform each other. She explores the presence and power of mystery, the numinous, the mystical, and the communal in the discipline. She therefore encourages a consideration of religious imagination as integral to the activity and relationship of teaching. She also advocates an understanding of teaching as itself sacred work and offers a conscious agenda for helping those who teach to know the prophetic potential and the "ontological tenderness" inherent in this vocation.

In his book *The Moral and Spiritual Crisis in Education,* educator David Purpel charges that the "crux of our [cultural] crisis . . . [is] the difficulty of creating a vital, authentic and energizing vision of meaning in a context of significant diversity, pluralism, division, skepticism, dogmatism, and even nihilism."[13] He adds that educators must work, both individually and communally, to help students interpret the messages from the larger culture and find or create meanings that will keep them from losing heart. Certainly, these capacities for critical interpretation and for making meaning are abilities we need to cultivate in teachers if we expect them to serve as guides for others. In light of the social need articulated by David Purpel and the awareness that teachers cannot teach what they do not know, Maria's plea for the stimulation of religious imagination in teachers charts a direction for teacher development.

In *Fashion Me a People,* a book intended for use with church communities, Maria explicates the meaning of curriculum, offering theological perspectives on different forms of curricula that educate religiously in the church and that, correspondingly, educate the church. These curricula include *koinonia* (community), *leiturgia* (prayer), *didache* (teaching), *kergyma* (proclamation), and *diakonia* (service). She articulates her commitment to justice as a central element of religious education in her final analysis of *diakonia,* curriculum of service. She begins with a critique of notions of service that are not born of genuine compassion for oneself as well as others and that are not about "troublemaking, empowerment," and public action for change. She goes on to articulate the essential forms of *diakonia:* social care, social ritual, social empowerment, and social legislation. Maria additionally argues that this service or justice-making activity must be personal as well as communal and must minister to human and nonhumans alike.

In *Proclaim Jubilee!* Maria offers a spirituality for the twenty-first century drawn from Leviticus 25:8–10a. The exhortation is to "observe a sabbath for the Lord" in which you shall count off seven weeks of years, seven times seven years, so that the period of seven weeks of years gives forty-nine years. Then you shall have the trumpet sounded loud; on the tenth day of the seventh month—on the day of atonement—you shall have the trumpet sounded throughout all your land. And you shall hallow the fiftieth year and you shall proclaim liberty throughout the land to all its inhabitants.

Maria sets out to examine what each of these commands involves and includes chapters on such themes as forgiveness, proclaiming liberty throughout the land, and jubilee justice. Her ecological and interreligious concerns are central to her encouragment to the reader to "let the land lie fallow." Maria points out that "the land" refers to two geographies: the first is the actual land, the earth, the planet; the second is the territory of the body, our bodies and the bodies of others.

In explicating the reverent relationship to the earth promoted by a jubilee spirit, Maria calls on the wisdom of diverse voices. Among them are Squamish Chief Seattle and Czech Republic president Václav Havel, as well as poet Gerard Manley Hopkins and *The Mustard Seed Garden Manual,* a seventeenth-century Chinese treatise on painting. In drawing these voices together she illuminates:

> The spiritual presupposition of this counsel . . . that humans stand in a relation of reciprocity with the world and that like them, all of the world is instinct with spirit and presence, the numinous and the sacred. As such, it must be treated with reverence and respect.[14]

As she underscores a consciousness about our nonhuman connections, Maria both subtly and emphatically emphasizes interreligious connections by her references to various religious traditions. In her chapter on forgiveness she refers to Christianity, Judaism, and Islam, identifying a God who forgives in each of these religions. She draws from the writing of Sister Helen Prejean, a Roman Catholic nun; Hannah Arendt, a contemporary Jewish philosopher; and Maimonides, a medieval Jewish philosopher, to help her uncover various interpretations of forgiveness. Ultimately, she recognizes what seems universal: the struggle, challenge, and yet necessity of forgiveness. A significant part of the richness of Maria's work is found in the colorful textures that emerge as she weaves these diverse traditions and interreligious understandings into one whole conversation.

Her efforts often result in interreligious consciousness raising. She recounted with delight the story of a woman who had attended one of her presentations and, commenting on Maria's many references to Jewish religious tradition, had asked if Maria was Jewish. Her work to promote interreligious understanding has been recognized by such educational organizations as Facing History and Ourselves, which infuses education for tolerance and understanding into traditional public school classrooms.

Feminist Themes and the
Legacy of Maria's Work

One of Maria's contributions to religious education, which resonates in a particular way with feminist perspectives, is her claim that community is the "starting point in educational ministry."[15] A strength of Maria's approach is to offer particular curricular tools to nurture the development of community in both parish and family, the forms she identifies as the basis of Christian community. In *Fashion Me a People* she describes inclusion, leadership, and outreach as the tasks of the parish, while presence, receptivity, and responsibility define the work of family. While Maria identifies the essential curricula of community, she shows how, as an educational form, community is responsible and accountable to its own people and, ultimately, to a larger global community.

Maria's poetic use of language provides for new ways of imagining religious education. For example, the themes framing her texts, such as the steps from silence to birthing in *Women and Teaching,* invoke metaphor in addition to naming actual, lived experience. Her work has evolved in an especially responsive way to women, because her words and her framing of the religious and spiritual dimensions speak back to the reality of women's lives. Maria's work with older women illustrates her sensitivity to the realities of life for older women as to well as the social injustices of ageism.

Maria addresses relationships of power, both explicitly and implicitly. She does this in her attention to issues of injustice and to those who are marginalized, a focus certainly evident in her ecumenical and ecological concerns. In recent writing she has shifted her own language, critiquing previous work that focused on the image, the visual, what can be seen or conjured in the mind's eye. In so doing, Maria provides a radical reformulation of relationship—one based on "thick listening." This attention to "sound or the absence of sound," to what is said and not said, to who speaks and who is silent, becomes her guide in assessing relationships and challenges hierarchical patterns and patriarchal forms of power. In teaching relationships (again, not limited to schooling), this kind of listening requires that we take seriously the knowledge of others and recognize that what each person brings to any educational encounter is the knowledge each will build on. Such an approach engenders mutuality, since it aims toward genuine respect for each person's starting point and each one's capacity for "birthing" sacred knowledge.

"Feminism," Maria noted, "has been the catalyst for . . . understanding" that we always speak from where we stand. Maria clarifies that today she speaks as a "white, old, upper-middle-class, well-educated, privileged person." She acknowledges that, given her social location, much of her work is "class-biased." The ability to make such identification and to recognize how social location is connected to power is central to her awareness as a religious educator. This consciousness enables a person to discern where her or his knowledge and comfort reside and work to challenge the taken-for-granted perspective. It correspondingly encourages the same kind of awareness of others. While there are many today who consider such distinctions a superficial bow to political correctness, in Maria's work this awareness becomes increasingly refined and a catalyst to greater responsiveness in relationships and in her continuing efforts to name and act on injustice.

In *Proclaim Jubilee!* Maria reveals the jubilee demand for justice: "Find out what belongs to whom and give it back."[16] Part of responding to this task involves recognizing who we are, where we stand, who is not with us, and what differences prevent us from standing together. This form of power analysis increases the possibilities for identifying what has been lost and by whom, thus enhancing the opportunities for building jubilee justice.

In "Sing a New Song: The Canticle of Jubilation," the final chapter in *Proclaim Jubilee!,* Maria notes that the Hebrew word *yobel* is often understood as the foundational word for *jubilee*. *Yobel* refers to the "ram's horn or trumpet sounded in the public arena."[17] Of course Maria would end this work with a word meaning, among other things, music! Music is an aesthetic form she cherishes in religious education, and it is part of my memory of her as teacher. In that first course I took with her, she sat one day at the piano leading a group of students with no voice training in a powerful rendering of sacred music.

The origin of her appreciation of and passion for music lies at the moment of her parents' marriage. Her father, Edward, gave her mother, Mary, a Steinway baby grand piano as a wedding gift. The gift of this piano enabled her mother "always" to play and sing, and Maria started as well at the age of five. "There was music in my mother's house," she said. "There was music in my mother. And then she had this grief."

While this story communicates the roots of Maria's connection to the aesthetic, it also joins her to the threads of suffering and love she identified earlier. This love and knowledge, wedded to the religious tradition of Roman Catholicism, continue to evolve in Maria's work. Maria's legacy to the field of religious education and its feminist dimensions, it seems particularly appropriate and poignant to note, began in her mother's house.

Several times during my conversation with Maria, she referred to herself as "old." I did not want to deny her self-definition; perhaps she was fighting to make it a word of power, a word both accepted and welcomed. So I turn to a scene in *The Small Room* by May Sarton, a writer Maria refers to often in *Jubilee Time*. It is the final conversation between the teachers Lucy and Carryl. As their time together ended and they prepared to part company, Carryl asserted that she was "very old." Lucy offered an alternative interpretation, suggesting that Carryl was "very complete."[18]

Maria Harris has shown how these two words, *old* and *complete,* can be joined.

NOTES

1. See Maria Harris, *Dance of the Spirit* (New York: Bantam Books, 1989), 189–92, for a discussion of women's bonding.
2. This quote and those not referenced in this chapter come from the transcription of my interview with Maria Harris, in New York City 7 June 1996.
3. See Maria Harris, *Fashion Me a People* (Louisville, Ky.: Westminster/John Knox Press, 1989), for a full exploration of these ideas.
4. Alfred North Whitehead, *The Aims of Education* (New York: Macmillan Co., 1929).
5. Harris, *Fashion Me a People,* 40.
6. Audre Lorde, "Uses of the Erotic," in *Sister Outsider* (New York: Crossing Press, 1984), 53–59.
7. Harris, *Fashion Me a People,* 119.
8. Ibid., 117.
9. See Paulo Freire, translator Myra Bergman Ramos, *Pedagogy of the Oppressed* (New York: Herder & Herder, 1971), 177, for an explanation of the elements of bearing witness.
10. During the three decades of her writing, Maria Harris's focus has shifted from an examination of parish religious education in such works as *The D.R.E. Book* (New York: Paulist Press, 1971) and *Parish Religious Education* (New York: Paulist Press, 1978) to a more comprehensive and ecumenical exploration of the meaning of religious education in such works as *Teaching and Religious Imagination* (San Francisco: Harper & Row, 1987) and *Proclaim Jubilee! A Spirituality for the Twenty-First Century* (Louisville, Ky.: Westminster John Knox Press, 1996). While the motifs I have identified in Maria's work are present in both her teaching and her writing, they are perhaps more easily charted in her texts.
11. See Maria Harris, *Women and Teaching: Themes for a Spirituality of Teaching* (Mahwah, N.J.: Paulist Press, 1988); idem, *Dance of the Spirit;* idem, *The Seven Steps of Women's Spirituality.* (New York: Bantam Books, 1989); idem, *Jubilee Time: Celebrating Women, Spirit and the Advent of Age* (New York: Bantam Books, 1995).
12. Harris, *Teaching and Religious Imagination,* 75.
13. David Purpel, *The Moral and Spiritual Crisis in Education,* (New York: Bergin & Garvey, 1989), 64.
14. Harris, *Proclaim Jubilee!,* 24.
15. Harris, *Fashion Me a People,* 75.
16. See Harris, *Proclaim Jubilee!,* 3. Harris notes this phrase was inspired by the work of Walter Brueggemann.
17. Ibid., 96.
18. May Sarton, *The Small Room* (New York: W. W. Norton & Co., 1961) 248–49.

CONCLUSION

Barbara Anne Keely

A deep legacy is brought together through and in these biographies. These women give shape and substance to religious education in many ways. They embody what it means to be mediators of the faith, through their lives and callings.

They live full and meaningful lives. Each has her own story, be it that of a woman committed to church and students or that of a life spent in relationship with another person whose calling dictated her own context. Some raise children; all mentor future generations of religious educators. Wihin her context, each faithfully cares for those in her charge.

They re-vision ways to teach. Sophia Fahs experimented with child-centered education and changed the approach to children's education in the church. D. J. Furnish and Iris Cully taught and wrote on teaching the Bible to children, in ways that bring the Bible alive and change children's lives. Committed to ministry with youth, Sara Little's legacy includes passing on that commitment to the next generation of religious educators and scholars. Freda Gardner believes that the journey of life is faith seeking understanding, and she teaches adults to engage the journey well.

Teaching is a way of faithfully living out a call, of engaging each learner with respect and value. These women understand that each human being, regardless of age, religious belief, race, or gender, is a gift; and teaching each person is a gift offered in return.

Out of their personal faith, some of these women become politically radical. Nelle Morton works for integration in the South, changing the face of churches and conferences. Later, she, like some of the other foremothers, reimagines the male image of God into an inclusive God who is life-giving for women and men alike. Letty Russell teaches that the personal is political and that education which is religious must also be radical. Religious education cannot be limited to passing on religious tradition; it must engage persons in ways that challenge them to work for justice and mercy throughout God's world.

CONCLUSION

These women understand religious education as religious imagination. Creativity is essential to educating people about a creative God. Hulda Niebuhr uses art, music, and the aesthetic to empower her students to be creative educators. Maria Harris teaches that, in the religious imagination, we are the subject matter and our curriculum is all that we do as church. We are challenged to move the boundaries of religious education to encompass all that we are and do in the name of God.

These women live faithfully to their call. Women often out of place in a male-dominated world and church, they are pioneers on many frontiers. Most are among the first women on graduate school faculties; all encounter professional barriers because of their gender. Still clear that her calling as an educator is strong, Rachel Henderlite steps into ordination to lead the way for other women in her denomination. Encountering racism, Olivia Pearl Stokes steps into contexts of ministry that challenge her right to be there. With quiet force and dignity, she goes about her calling.

These women remind us that religious education is not about separating people from one another but about bridging traditions and finding dialogue. Lest our religious education be too parochial, Norma Thompson encourages us to engage in interreligious conversations, so that religious education is not defined by only one faith tradition.

These women live their lives well. As I read their life stories, I am reminded time and time again that these women come up against as many walls as doors yet continue to seek ways to move through life and ministry with vision, intelligence, imagination, commitment, and grace. I suggest in the Introduction that these twelve women can be viewed as foremothers and mentors. They help us see ways to re-vision religious education. They mentor many women and men to do as they do, and to do more. They challenge all of us to take our calling seriously, to widen our view of the world, and to teach others to go and do likewise.